A Flannel Shirt and Liberty

edited by Susan Jackel

A Flannel Shirt
and Liberty

British Emigrant Gentlewomen
in the Canadian West,
1880-1914

UNIVERSITY OF BRITISH COLUMBIA PRESS
VANCOUVER AND LONDON

A FLANNEL SHIRT AND LIBERTY:
BRITISH EMIGRANT GENTLEWOMEN IN THE CANADIAN WEST,
1880-1914

© The University of British Columbia 1982

Reprinted 1982

This book has been published with the assistance of the Canada Council.

Canadian Cataloguing in Publication Data
Main entry under title:
A Flannel shirt and liberty

ISBN 0-7748-0149-2 Hardbound
ISBN 0-7748-0180-8 Paperback

1. Women — Canada, Western — History — Sources.
2. Women — Great Britain — Social conditions.
3. British — Canada, Western.
4. Canada — Emigration and immigration. I. Jackel, Susan, ed.
HQ1453.F59   305.4'88 21'0712   C82-091068-6

ISBN 0-7748-0149-2 Hardbound
ISBN 0-7748-0180-8 Paperback

Printed in Canada

CONTENTS

Illustrations   vii
Acknowledgements   ix
Introduction   xiii

I. THE BEGINNINGS: THE 1880's

1. From *A Lady's Life on a Farm in Manitoba*   3
                         Mary Hall
2. *What Women Say of the Canadian North-West*   31
3. "Women Wanted"   66
            Jessie M. Saxby

II. THE DOLDRUMS: THE 1890's

4. The 1890's   77
   "The English Ranchwoman"   79
            J.R.E.S.
   "A Lady's Life on a Ranche"   95
            Agnes Skrine
   "Women's Work in Western Canada"   111
            Elizabeth Lewthwaite

III. THE WHEAT-BOOM YEARS: 1905-1914

5. From *A Woman in Canada*   126
            Marion Cran
6. Land and the Woman in Canada   150
   "Hilaria's Adventures — A Night Out"   152
   "Are Educated Women Wanted in Canada"   162

"Conditions of Life for Women in Canada"   170
"Land and the Woman in Canada"   178
                        Georgina Binnie-Clark
7. From *A Home-Help in Canada*   189
                        Ella Sykes
8. "The Women of the West"   217
                        Elizabeth Mitchell
9. "The Woman Canada Needs"   222
                        Emily Weaver

ILLUSTRATIONS

following p. 28

Plate 1. Postcard urging female emigration
       2. Waiting for the train, C.P.R. station, Bassano, Alberta, 1910
       3. School at Rife, Alberta
       4. Washday
       5. Armstrong's Store, Nanton, Alberta
       6. Woman churning
       7. Telephone operator
       8. Log house at Content, Alberta
       9. Two women homesteaders

following p. 76

Plate 10. The Shaw Ranch, Midnapore, Alberta
      11. Interior of a log house
      12. Hugh Lorraine Robinson
      13. Margaret Hattam Robinson
      14. Women working in fields
      15. Louisa and George Blake and their ranch at Beaver Creek, Alberta
      16. Polo at Millarville, Alberta
      17. Winnipeg, 1876
      18. Calgary, 1912

following p. 156

Plate 19. Patriotic Tableau, Dawson
      20. Market fair, Cereal, Alberta
      21. Nurse carrying water
      22. Women operating graders
      23. Lady with plow and team
      24. Horseless carriage
      25. Marion Cran
      26. Elizabeth Mitchell
      27. Canadian Women's Press Club, 1913

PHOTOGRAPHIC CREDITS

Plates 2, 3, 5, 8, 10, 12, 13, 15, 16, 18, 19, 20, 21, 22, and 27 (NA-729-33, NA-2806-15, NA-3535-33, NA-2925-18, NA-2520-47, NA-3042-1, NA-3042-2, NA-3535-183 and 184, NA-2520-35, NA-644-11, NA-3128-1, NA-2116-3, NA-1500-2, NA-1758-15, and NA-1951-3) are reproduced with the permission of the Glenbow Archives, Calgary, Alberta. Plates 4, 6, 7, 9, 14, 23, 24 (442-14245, 44-14244, 271-08680, 163-05133, 173-05415, 348-11202, 449-14441) have been provided by the Western Canadian Pictorial Index, University of Winnipeg. Plates 11 and 25 are taken from Marion Cran's *A Woman in Canada;* plate 26 is reproduced from Elizabeth Mitchell's *The Plan That Pleased;* plate 17 is from the collection of W.E. and Jane C. Fredeman.

ACKNOWLEDGEMENTS

We are now sufficiently separated in time from the pre-War settlement years for Canadian scholars to approach the subject of British immigrant groups with some detachment — the home or Barnardo children, for example, or female domestic workers, or the public school men surveyed by Patrick Dunae in *Gentlemen Emigrants* (Vancouver, 1981). As the field of Canadian women's history matures, work already published, or in progress, by such authors as Joy Parr, Barbara Roberts, Suzann Buckley, Alison Prentice, and Marilyn Barber, among many others, will help to clarify our understanding of the complex cross-currents of nationality, class, and sex at work among British settlers here. Nowhere were those complexities more urgently combined, more finely tuned, than in the female middle-class Briton suddenly forced to re-examine her identity as a person of leisure and of privilege, but also as a dependent, an incompetent, and part of a mounting social problem. In Canada, the marriage and labour markets combined to offer such women opportunities denied them at home. When gentlewomen turned working women, and yet did so with such deeply felt expressions of personal and social reward, we are faced with evidence bearing on questions that Canadian social historians are only beginning to explore.

This book has been some six or seven years in the making, and during its preparation I have accumulated more debts, personal and intellectual, than simple notice of obligation can adequately convey or repay. Particular thanks must go to Jane Fredeman, Senior Editor of the University of British Columbia Press, who kept the project alive by her encouragement, and then gave the completed manuscript her usual careful, intelligent attention. My thanks also to the anonymous readers of earlier drafts who, by their criticisms and suggestions, aided materially in the book's improvement. Colleagues in the Department of History at the University of Alberta have also helped through their interest and informed comment, in particular Rod MacLeod, Pat Prestwich, Dave Hall, and Doug Owram. Needless to say, none of these people is to be held responsible for remaining oddities or inaccuracies in the editorial material.

My scholarly debts are many and wide ranging. A few are noted in the foot-notes, but others deserve mention here. As have many students of Victorian social life I have benefited greatly from two collections of essays edited by Martha Vicinus, *Suffer and Be Still* (Bloomington and London, 1972) and *A Widening Sphere* (Bloomington and London, 1977). J.A. and Olive Banks's *Feminism and Family Planning in Victorian England* (Liverpool, 1964) illuminated the English social context for discussions of Britain's redundant women, while Margharita Laski's essay on "Domestic Life" in S. Nowell-Smith, ed., *Edwardian England* (London, 1964) was also important. On the subject of female emigration, one reliable contemporary account is Stanley C. Johnson's *A History of Emigration from the United Kingdom to North America, 1763-1912* (London, 1913; rpt. 1966). Una Monk has provided a very useful history of female emigration societies in *New Horizons: 100 Years of Women's Migration* (London, 1963). Although I have tried to make adequate acknowledgement in the footnotes to the text, my reliance on the work of A. James Hammerton, recently made available in *Emigrant Gentlewomen* (London, 1980) will be evident to those familiar with this book.

Two bibliographies require special mention: Bruce Peel's indispensable *Bibliography of the Prairie Provinces to 1953* (Toronto, 1956; 2nd ed. 1973), and the no less essential compilation of sources for Canadian women's history produced by Beth Light and Veronica Strong-Boag, *True Daughters of the North* (Toronto, 1980). I am also grateful to Georgeen Klassen, Assistant Chief Archivist of the Glenbow Museum in Calgary, for her help in selecting photographs.

Publishers have been uniformly cooperative in according permission to reprint selections not yet in the public domain. The pages from Mary Georgina Hall's *A Lady's Life on a Farm in Manitoba* are reprinted from the text published in 1884 by W.H. Allen & Co., London. *What Women Say of the Canadian Northwest* was issued by the C.P.R. in 1886. "Women Wanted" comes from Jessie M. Saxby's *West Nor'-West,* published by James Nisbet & Co., London, in 1890 and reprinted with their kind permission. Blackwood's of Edinburgh has given permission to reprint "A Lady's Life on a Ranche" by Moira O'Neill (Agnes Skrine) from *Blackwood's Magazine.* Elizabeth Lewthwaite "Women's Work in Western Canada" originally appeared in the *Fortnightly Review* for October 1901. Marion Cran's *A Woman in Canada* was originally published by W.J. Ham-Smith in London in 1910. The writer wishes to thank D.A. Jenks for permission to reprint the four selections by Georgina Binnie-Clark. "Hilaria's Adventures" first appeared in the book *A Summer on the Canadian Prairie,* published by Edward Arnold in 1910, who also gave permission to reprint the chapter. "Are Educated Women Wanted in Canada" appeared in the *Imperial Colonist,* February-April 1910. "Conditions of Life for Women in Canada" was originally a speech to the Annual Meeting of the National Union of Women Workers on 20 October 1909 and was published as part of that conference's proceedings. "Land and the Woman in Canada" first appeared in *United Empire,* 1913. Bell and Hyman has granted permission to reprint the selections from Ella Sykes's *A Home-Help in Canada* published by G. Bell and Sons in 1912, and Western Producer Prairie Books of Saskatoon has given rights for the extract from Elizabeth Mitchell's *In Western Canada Before the War.* Emily Weaver's "The Woman Canada Needs" is from her *Canada and the British Immigrant,* published by the Religious Tract Society in 1914, for which permission to reprint was received from Lutterworth Press.

Every effort has been made to contact authors and publishers to obtain permissions. If the publisher is made aware of any errors which may have been made in obtaining permissions, the publisher will take steps to ensure that proper credit be given at that time.

Finally, and all too briefly, my love and my thanks to David, and to Cathy, Brian, and Chris, who have lived with this project and its progenitor, and have seen the whole thing through with grace and good humour.

S.J.
February 1982

INTRODUCTION

"England is glutted with female labour, Canada faints for want of it. It looks like the simplest problem in the world to solve. In reality it is bristling with difficulties." So wrote English journalist Marion Dudley Cran in her travel book of 1910, *A Woman in Canada*. Mrs. Cran had spent six months travelling across Canada in 1908 at the request of dominion government officials, who wanted her help in sorting out certain perplexities that England and Canada shared with regard to female labour. Parts of Mrs. Cran's book are reprinted in this volume, along with selections from other books and articles that originally appeared in print between 1880 and 1915. During those years, the opening of the Canadian West to settlement gave rise to an outpouring of publications addressed to readers overseas, describing Canada and inviting immigration. Drawing liberally on these publications as source materials for their research and writing, Canadian historians have looked from a variety of standpoints at the movement of people to the broad expanses of the West. Yet the story of prairie settlement, although told so many times, still has a few chapters missing.

One of the missing chapters concerns middle-class women from the British Isles. Mrs. Cran was only one of many writers to put the spotlight on Western Canada's offer to the thousands of women who, largely by virtue of their genteel upbringing, were declared surplus — "superfluous," "redundant" — in Great Britain. Hence the terms of her assignment from the Canadian government. "I was asked," Mrs. Cran explained in her foreword, "to regard the country from a woman's standpoint as much as possible; to study the lives of the Englishwomen settled there; to form my own opinion as to their happiness, their usefulness, their success or failure as settlers and the wives of settlers; to discover if possible in what ways they could make money for themselves without having to wait for menfolk to bring them or send for them. For the Dominion Government is aware that England is overcrowded with women, and that her own prairie lands are crying for them by the thousand." The prairie West from a woman's standpoint, then, was Mrs. Cran's guiding perspective in *A Woman In Canada,* and the same perspective governs this volume of documents reprinted from the turn-of-the-century British and Canadian press.

In these documents, the student of English-Canadian social history will encounter viewpoints on western settlement that, if not running directly counter to accepted historical interpretations, nevertheless suggest the need for some re-thinking of the period. At the very least, they provide glimpses of the pre-war prairie provinces to supplement an already rich store of published observations on the social side of settlement. More importantly, they point to ways of understanding how certain beliefs and prejudices took root in the West and why some social, economic, and cultural issues have always seemed more urgent than others in the minds of western Canadians. Finally, they demonstrate the value of conducting historical study within the broadest possible context. No fully satisfactory account of Canadian development can result from an exclusive focus on events and currents of thought within our national borders; nor should boundaries more cultural than geographical or political be allowed to limit or obscure the picture. There was for a long time a marked disinclination among the historical profession at large to look attentively at this or any country from a woman's standpoint. That time is now past, and the study of history is the richer for it.

When Mrs. Cran wrote of a "glut" of female labour in the England of her time, she was scarcely overstating the case. The whole of the British Isles was indeed overcrowded with women in the early years of this century — overcrowded, that is, not just in the usual sense of uncomfortably high population densities, but meaning as well that at all levels of British society, females far outnumbered males. Yet at the very same time, Canada complained of a shortage of women, "shortage" again not only in absolute but also in relative terms. The problem was particularly acute in the prairie West, where in most newly settled districts men might outnumber women by ratios of two, five, even twenty or more to one. It looked, as Mrs. Cran said, like the simplest problem in the world to solve. Surely there need only be a concerted effort to bring Englishwomen to the Prairies, and the numerical imbalance between the sexes would be relieved in both countries at once. But the formula that looked so logical and straightforward on paper was immensely complicated in practice, as thousands of emigrant Englishwomen found out over the years. Difficulties there were in abundance; yet there were discoveries and benefits as well. Both the obstacles and the rewards attending British female middle-class emigration to Canada are fully evident in the documents that follow. Because the precise circumstances surrounding their original publication are not generally known to students of Canadian history, however, it may help the reader to have access to some relevant background information.

Of central importance is the fact of Britain's chronic oversupply of women, a continuing feature of British society from Napoleonic times to the present day. The long years of war or threatened war in Europe between 1790 and 1818 took their toll on the male sector of the population, while the emigrations of the following decades took yet more men away. Not until the census of 1851, however, was the magnitude of the problem established beyond dispute. The figures were truly startling: out of a total population in England, Scotland, Ireland, and Wales of 27 million, said the census-takers, there were some 650,000 more females than males.

By 1861 the surplus of women had risen to 800,000.[1] Clearly a trend was developing, and perplexity and concern by the British public at large began to find voice in the leading newspapers and journals. "What Shall We Do with Our Old Maids?" asked Frances Powers Cobbe in an article for *Fraser's Magazine* in 1862. "Why Are Women Redundant?" queried W. R. Greg in the *National Review* that same year.

Why indeed? Explanations were gradually forthcoming from the keepers of statistics. Differing mortality rates during childhood was one (more girls than boys survived to the age of fifteen), while another hinged on the enlistment of boys and men in the army, navy, and merchant marine. More significant than either, however, was emigration to the colonies. Between 1850 and 1914, some 200,000 Britons per year, on average, left their homeland for greener pastures overseas, and all through this exodus male emigrants outnumbered female emigrants by a ratio of three to two.[2] Thus the trend of mid-century continued, until by 1911 there were over 1.3 million more females than males among the United Kingdom's 45 million people. Statistically, these 1,328,625 females were "excess"; economically and socially they were "superfluous," "redundant," for the simple reason that women who could not marry — and clearly there were not enough husbands to go around — stood an excellent chance of permanent unemployment.

Among working-class women the prospect of redundancy was not looked on happily, perhaps, but at least it did not spell disaster. A century ago as today, girls of the working classes in Britain took for granted their participation in the paid labour force, for a few years before marriage at least, but often for most or all of their adult lives. They worked on farms, in factories, behind shop counters, and everywhere throughout the growing field of domestic service. As the nineteenth century went on, they also began to enter the lower ranks of teaching, nursing, and clerical work. Accustomed to looking to their own energies and skills for the necessaries of life, England's wage-earning women — some 4 million in number by 1901 — could, if the need arose, face widowhood or spinsterhood without despair.

Paradoxically, the daughters of England's "privileged" classes were in some ways not so fortunate as their working-class sisters. Raised to a life of leisure, the gentlewoman was by definition someone who did not work for pay. Instead, her job was simply to make sure that she married well, so that she might then lend her carefully instilled graces and accomplishments to the running of a well-ordered, tasteful existence for her family. For the middle-class woman, her social standing, her self-respect, her whole provision in life depended on her success in the marriage market, and society was unpitying in its treatment of those who went unchosen. "Failed in business" was the cruel phrase used of the genteel spinster, and where marriage was so emphatically a business, a means to status and support, failure brought penalties ranging from ridicule to outright destitution.

"Distressed gentlewomen," as impoverished middle-class women were called, was no mere phrase, therefore; the privations of these women when male bread-winners died or lost their incomes were very real, and they were not only material, but psychological and emotional as well. Consequently, the plight of the single educated woman without means became one of the most widely debated social issues of nineteenth-century Britain.

Beginning in the 1850's and continuing well into the present century, a variety of reform measures were proposed to rescue the distressed gentlewoman, whether widow or spinster, from her marginal position in British society. Undoubtedly the most sensational phase of this reform movement was Josephine Butler's campaign in the 1870's and 1880's to overturn legislation for the compulsory inspection of prostitutes, among whom were found to be a scandalously large number of former gentlewomen. The revelation that so many middle-class women were driven by poverty into prostitution lent fuel to the demand that employment in office-work and the professions be opened to the widows and daughters of gentlemen. But such demands in turn raised the question of training and so reinforced the concurrent movement to raise the standards and extend the facilities for the higher education of women. So the impulse for reform broadened and deepened, the assorted remedial measures sometimes overlapping, sometimes working at cross-purposes, but at all times aimed at stemming the social and economic decline of the single middle-class woman facing a future for which her upbringing had left her totally unprepared.

Even as middle-class reformers urged their demands for change within Britain, however, the numbers of destitute gentlewomen continued to grow. Reform was slow and haphazard, and not everyone was content, or could afford, to await the outcome. Not surprisingly, then, an alternative solution began to gain popularity among those concerned about the country's oversupply of women. Emigration had helped to cause the problem in the first place; might not emigration be used to solve it? It seemed a possibility at least, especially in view of the fact that in colonies like Australia, New Zealand, South Africa, and Canada, the imbalance between the sexes ran the other way. Since in these countries, males outnumbered females, women were being actively solicited as prospective colonial settlers.

With this possibility in mind, several privately sponsored philanthropic societies devoted to the resettlement of British women abroad were formed. Pioneers in this work were Jane Lewin and Maria Rye, who founded the Female Middle-Class Emigration Society in 1862. Rye had read Susanna Moodie's *Roughing It in the Bush,* published in 1854, and was impressed by Moodie's account of genteel emigrants in a Canadian backwoods setting. Rye apparently overlooked (or discounted) Moodie's warning that prospective middle-class emigrants should think twice before following her example. Instead, Rye and her associates saw abundant promise of material and social betterment for women courageous enough to give colonial life a try.

Those involved in the work of female middle-class emigration soon discovered, however, that no matter how simple and straightforward the theory, the actual practice of exporting gentlewomen was fraught with complication. Needless to say, not everyone was suited for taking up life in a frontier settlement. Youth, health, adaptability, and a willingness to work hard were what counted in the successful settler; genteel accomplishments could be dispensed with, and usually were. Yet it was the educated gentlewoman, not the artisan, farm worker, or skilled domestic servant, who was most clearly redundant in nineteenth-century British society. In short, supply and demand were out of joint: despite the widely publicized need for women in the colonies, and their evident oversupply at home, gentlewomen were seldom the best candidates for sending abroad. The gender was right, but the training was all wrong.

In response to this dilemma, two rather different arguments took shape in favour of persisting with the emigration of gentlewomen. One concentrated on the gender; the other, on the training. The first drew on the premise that a woman's destined role in life was to marry and have children. If women were redundant in Britain, the fundamental problem was their unmarried state, not their imperfect training for other employments. Similarly, if colonial societies were notoriously crude and disorderly in their day-to-day conduct of affairs, the antidote likewise lay in the stabilizing and moralizing influence of family life, an institution increasingly interpreted in the light of Victorian middle-class respectability. Thus, the shipment of superfluous gentlewomen to the colonies would serve several eminently worthy purposes at once. First, it would clear the way to marriage between women otherwise condemned to unnatural spinsterhood and men otherwise at liberty to persist in their (probably immoral) bachelorhood. Secondly, it would cement the bonds of Empire. Thirdly, it would raise the tone of colonial society, for women were widely acknowledged to be the culture-bearers. Finally, it would ensure the future growth of an indigenous colonial population, springing from the purest British stock and raised to the highest standard of British discipline, loyalty, and refinement. Thus the twin stands of matrimonial colonization and woman's civilizing mission were firmly woven into this essentially conservative rationale for the emigration of middle-class women.[3]

Predictably, opposition to this stand arose from reform elements within Britain that saw all emigration as an escapist solution to the nation's underlying ills. Female middle-class emigration was the safety-valve theory at work again in a new guise. Feminists, too, were quick to repudiate the automatic identification of women with marriage and motherhood. On the contrary, they wanted women of all classes, but especially middle-class ones, to turn away from the assumptions about female dependency that, in their view, lay at the root of the distressed gentlewomen's plight. To this end they downplayed talk of woman's proper sphere, emphasizing instead the careful selection of candidates for emigration based on individual qualifications and potential. As they saw it, proper preparation, not biology, was the key to colonial success, in women as well as men.

W. R. Greg's much-reprinted article, "Why Are Women Redundant?", spoke for the extreme conservative position; Frances Powers Cobbe, among numerous others, voiced the feminist counter-argument. Both sides supported the emigration of gentlewomen to the colonies, but for different reasons. Neither side could ignore the patent realities of the situation, however: all theory aside, the most pressing demand from the receiving societies was for women who would engage from the outset in farm and household labour, whether as wives or as servants. Marriage offered security and status, while servants could look forward to relatively high wages, but in either case the work would be essentially the same. As a result, even the feminists found themselves urging candidates for emigration to cast aside their prejudices against what, in the middle-class British household, was commonly regarded as "menial" work, the routine chores of house and garden. Such tasks, after all, were women's work; or so all but a handful of radicals assumed. Hence there is an air of merely stating the obvious when, in *A Woman in Canada*, Marion Cran justified domestic service for gentlewomen immigrants to the prairies by saying, "Every woman is a servant where labour is so scarce" (p. 163).

The fact that in its first twenty years of operation the Female Middle-Class Emigration Society assisted only 302 women to emigrate, most of them teachers and governesses, is a measure of the contradictions and difficulties inherent in the export of gentlewomen to the colonies during the 1860's and 1870's.[4] The long distances to travel, the rumoured hardship of back-country life, the continuing hope that somehow things might be made to improve in England all took their toll. Around 1880, however, the climate of opinion began to change, and female middle-class emigration came into its own. Even as the FMCES wound up its affairs, a host of new societies sprang up: the Women's Emigration Society (1880-84), the Colonial Emigration Society (1884-92), the United Englishwomen's Emigration Association, soon re-named the United British Women's Emigration Association (1884-1919), and the British Women's Emigration Association (1884-1919), among many others. While the phrase "middle-class" was seldom included in their official titles, all of these societies focused their energies on assisting women of the "educated" classes to relocate abroad.[5]

For a variety of reasons these later societies were considerably more effective than the FMCES had been. Steamships and railways had lessened the horrors of travel, and colonial frontiers everywhere were becoming more settled. Furthermore, the new agencies knew better than their predecessors where the shoals and pitfalls lay. It is impossible to arrive at exact numbers, but one authority has estimated that three societies alone, the British Women's Emigration Association, the South African Colonisation Society, and the Colonial Intelligence League, helped over twenty thousand women to emigrate between 1884 and 1914. This same writer finds it reasonable to assume that many thousands more emigrated independently, their only debt to the organized societies being the general respectability these groups lent to the whole idea of genteel female emigration.[6]

The destinations of these women varied over the years. Canada had attracted considerable middle-class emigration in the 1820's and 1830's, but it was to Australia and South Africa that the majority of emigrant gentlewomen were directed under the FMCES. In 1870 the newly formed Dominion of Canada gained control over the huge territories of Rupert's Land, and while only a tiny portion in Manitoba was immediately thrown open to settlement, by the early 1880's the golden lure of free prairie land began to exert its influence in the minds of intending emigrants from Britain. Thus, by the end of the century the majority of the emigrant societies' work was directed towards Canada. In 1910, for example, the British Women's Emigration Association sponsored 902 female emigrants to Canada, as compared to some 130 bound for New Zealand, Australia, South Africa, and the United States combined.[7]

In the main, the work of these agencies consisted of screening applicants for suitability, raising funds to assist with passage money where needed, and appointing matrons to see that the parties of female emigrants reached their destination safely. This was known as "protected" emigration, and it did much to combat lingering doubts as to the respectability and safety of single women embarking on colonial life. Moreover, consistent with their emphasis on proper preparation, several societies set up in training schools in Britain, the best-known being the Leaton Colonial Training Home in Shropshire, where prospective emigrants could learn the skills that would make them instantly employable in the colonies: cooking, baking, cleaning, laundrywork, and dairywork, as well as how to raise poultry and garden vegetables. By adopting these measures, the emigration societies extended their work until scarcely a town in Britain did not have its local branch, while hostels for receiving women immigrants spread across Canada.

This, in briefest outline, was where matters stood as the great surge of prairie settlement gathered force in the closing years of the nineteenth century. It is safe to say that no one in those years with the least knowledge of public affairs, either in Canada or in Britain, could have remained unaware of the controversy surrounding Britain's oversupply of single middle-class women and Canada's corresponding shortage of women. The country's need for women had provided a running theme in government immigration propaganda since before mid-century, and with the opening of the West, this theme re-asserted itself tenfold. In consequence, the role of women formed an important part of the extended public debate over the shape and character of the coming Northwest society. The fact that part of this debate was carried on through writers, publishers, and readers in Britain does not in the least circumscribe its interest for the student of Canadian social history.

As will be evident from the outset to present-day readers of these documents, the woman's standpoint on which they are based is a very particular and historically conditioned one, into which considerations of nationality and class enter fully as much as the writer's consciousness of her sex. On the question of nationality, it should be observed that the adjective "British," although widely used, is a convenient but rather imprecise term of national designation. It includes people from four main national groupings, the English, the Irish, the Scots, and the Welsh. No one speaks for the Welsh in the present collection, while the Irish and the Scots are definitely minority voices: Agnes Skrine ("Moira O'Neill") represents the former; Jessie Saxby and Elizabeth Mitchell, the latter.

To a degree these sub-categories have significance, for the appellation "English" was not always a term of compliment in Canadian usage, although "British" usually was. Resentment against the English in turn-of-the-century Canada was so marked that "No English Need Apply" became a common sign in notices advertising jobs. Feelings on this score could run highest of all among Canadian-born children of English settlers — see, for example, Emily Carr's *Growing Pains* (1946) for a particularly uninhibited demonstration of this fact. Certainly Sara Jeanette Duncan's novel of 1904, *The Imperialist,* derives much of its comic force from the figure of young Alfred Heskith, who must be educated out of his English condescension towards colonials. Some English travel writers found their reception here decidedly unamusing: Basil Stewart, an engineer who helped to build railways through northern Manitoba, included a long diatribe against Canadian prejudice towards his countrymen in *The Land of the Maple Leaf,* published in 1906. Even so late as 1965, the title of Dennis Godfrey's *No Englishman Need Apply,* a novel, suggests that this prejudice has not altogether died out.

The question that must be asked, however, is whether "no English need apply" was the attitude that greeted all English workers in Canada, or whether Canadians were sometimes capable of being discriminating in their discrimination. The legacy of the much-despised English remittance man was to narrow opportunities for male English applicants seeking jobs as farm hands, office clerks, engineers, warehouses jobbers, and the like. Whether women from England, even middle-class ones, encountered the same blanket hostility is open to question. Admittedly there is evidence of strong national prejudice in Ella Sykes's tale on p. 196 below of the home-help who was turned away from a Canadian door with the rude remark, "We don't want any English here," but in Sykes's view much of the blame for this episode could be laid at the feet of her compatriots, who "will persist in criticising Canada and things Canadian by British standards," in unconscious assumption of superiority. Yet Georgina Binnie-Clark, in *A Summer on the Canadian Prairie* (pp. 226, 231), made a point of drawing a careful line between the helpless, hopeless English, who were all lumped together in the Canadian mind regardless of class background or individual talents, and the English*women* (the italics were hers) whose thorough, patient work on prairie homesteads earned admiration and respect throughout the community.

Whatever part gender played in Canadian feelings toward English immigrants, there can be little uncertainty over the role played by class. Colonial resentment drew its nourishment not so much from the fact of English nationality *per se,* as from dislike of stubborn English weddedness to class distinction. To Canadians, caste and nationality seemed irrevocably joined together in the English mind and psyche. Class consciousness was not unknown in Canada at the century's turn, but it was developing in directions quite distinct from old-country notions of inherited and fixed positions in the social hierarchy. Even yet, it appears that the majority of Canadians still regard class as something that can be changed almost at will, a belief nurtured through observation of considerable social mobility relative to English standards.

In this widely publicized aspect of Canadian society, British gentlewomen of a century ago found their greatest opportunity and their greatest threat. The threat grew out of their existing middle-class identity, so integral a part of their British-born consciousness of themselves as "respectable" individuals. Would they "lose caste," or "sink in the social scale," if they came to Canada and took a job in a factory or shop, or became a servant in a Canadian household? In England such employments were unthinkable, and thousands of distressed gentlewomen endured years of extreme poverty, undernourishment, and severe confinement of movement — a kind of slow suicide — rather than work for pay at "menial" or "vulgar" occupations. Since their whole personal identity was bound up in their position as educated women with a standing to maintain, it was only by physically removing themselves from England, and by so doing effectively relinquishing their national and class connections, that they could reach for economic and social independence and eventually for renewed, if redefined, self-respect.

Balancing and in the end outweighing the hazards, however, were the opportunities and rewards — so, at least, writers like Elizabeth Lewthwaite, Ella Sykes, Georgina Binnie-Clark, Marion Cran, and Elizabeth Mitchell believed. Their testimony should not be taken lightly, for all of them were intelligent, sensitive, serious-minded individuals fully conscious of the responsibility they were taking upon themselves in offering advice to their beleaguered country-women. Sykes and Cran, who each spent six months in Canada, came for the express purpose of thoroughly investigating the openings here for educated women; Elizabeth Mitchell spent her year in the West conducting the same kind of close observation and enquiry. The findings of Lewthwaite and Binnie-Clark are even more convincing, for both had come here intending merely to visit and, after only a few weeks' experience in the country, made up their minds to settle and also to persuade others to do so through writing for the British press. The closing line of Cran's *A Woman in Canada* speaks for their combined conclusions: "If I had to earn my living, I would go to Canada."

This was their message, but how many English women readers heard and acted upon it? Questions like these are central to the exercise of social history, yet the answers are virtually beyond recovery. The records of immigrant arrivals kept by the dominion government during this period of western settlement are scarcely more than a rough guide, as demographic researchers in other fields have long since concluded. Similarly, the records of British emigration are useful for gross estimates only, especially where women are concerned. To illustrate: recording officials at Liverpool made some attempt to keep track of the occupations of emigrants embarking there. So male emigrants were identified as workers in agriculture, commerce and the professions, skilled trades, or labourers; female emigrants were assigned to categories listed as domestics and other services, dressmakers and other trades, and teachers, clerks, and the professions. Three-quarters of male emigrants were occupationally accounted for, leaving only one-quarter to the "miscellaneous and not stated" column. In the case of female emigrants, the proportions were exactly reversed: one-quarter assigned to a definite occupation, three-quarters to miscellaneous and not stated.[8] As a result, these records are small help to anyone seeking accurate figures for either the absolute numbers, or the proportion expressed as a percentage, of middle-class female British immigrants to Canada between 1880 and 1914.[9]

Under these circumstances, even the roughest of indicators becomes of inestimable value. Two such indicators have fortunately been provided by A. James Hammerton in his excellent recent book, *Emigrant Gentlewomen.* Using the annual reports of the British Women's Emigration Association, Hammerton compiles a table (p. 176) which shows that of 6,706 female emigrants assisted to leave the British Isles between 1906 and 1914 by this one leading female emigration society, 5,768, or 86 per cent, came to Canada. Of these, 1,079 (18.5 per cent) were explicitly identified as middle class, a designation that included "ladies," "educated," and so on. Another 2,629, or 45.5 per cent, were unidentified by class; these included girls going out under the Girls' Friendly Society as well as escorts and widows. (A note to Hammerton's table gives the information that nurses were not included in the middle-class column.)

Secondly, Hammerton goes on to provide a second table, based on Ferenczi's *International Migrations,* that deals in occupational or class terms with total adult female emigration from Great Britain between 1899 and 1911. This table is even more pertinent to the question of middle-class immigration to Canada, even though the figures reflect departures only, without any reference to points of destination. Assuming that the 86 per cent figure of Canadian destination for clients of the BWEA holds broadly true of all British female emigration in the immediate pre-war years, with a tolerance for error of even 20 per cent, the figures indicate that the proportion of middle-class female emigrants from British shores rose steadily and even dramatically between 1899 and 1911, a shift in class composition that Canada, as the main receiving society, would have experienced with particular intensity.

Reporting practices by emigration officials improved only marginally during this twelve-year period: while an 1899 there were 36,348 women whose occupation was miscellaneous or not stated out of a total figure for female emigrants of 57,248 — that is, just under two-thirds — in 1911 the corresponding figures were

110,642 of 156,606. The most interesting column here, however, is the one headed "teachers, clerks or professional women." It shows that the number of educated women emigrants rose from 274 in 1899, to 1,812 in 1907, to 3,751 in 1911: a fifteenfold increase in just over a decade.

It was, in fact, in response to this efflux of educated and professional women from Britain that an entirely new female emigration society, the Colonial Intelligence League, was created expressly to find places abroad for educated Englishwomen. This was the society that sponsored Ella Sykes in her investigation of the home-help situation in Canada, whence sprang the book that is excerpted below. In its four years of operation before war broke out, the CIL assisted 269 educated women to leave Britain, at the same time spreading an aura of respectability over the plans and ambitions of those who preferred to emigrate on their own.[10]

The immigration and emigration records, inadequate though they are, when substantiated and illuminated by documentary sources such as the ones contained in this volume, throw into sharp relief a hitherto shadowy element in the settlement of Western Canada. It is now clear that in terms of overall immigration to Canada between 1880 and 1914, there were proportionately and significantly more British women, single but usually of marriageable age and with a higher average level of education, entering the West than would have been the case had expected or "normal" patterns of population movement prevailed.

There is a sense, of course, in which mass migrations are never normal or routine, at least in the modern age. They take place in response to cumulative pushes and pulls, and all these upheavals seem distinctly unsettling and abnormal to those involved. Insofar as the propellant force behind most European and even American emigration to the Prairies, not to mention movement westward by the Canadian-born, had its roots in economic or political pressures affecting heads of families, or single males, the expected pattern of female in-migration would have consisted mainly of the wives and unmarried daughters of male immigrants, with a small sprinkling of mothers, sisters, aunts, and other female relatives and dependents. All blood relatives, needless to say, would have been of identical ethnic stock to the males, while the same would be broadly true of wives and other dependents. Thus the demographic norm for the female component of pre-war western settlement ought, in theory at least, to have closely reflected the male component in national, linguistic, and class origins.

It was precisely this pattern or norm that the influx into the West of single educated gentlewomen from Britain upset. Superfluous at home because they could not marry men of their own kind, they came to Canada prepared to work for a living, but also in most cases hoping to make a suitable marriage here. More often than not their hopes were fulfilled, although once again precise figures are lacking, so that generalization must rest on literary sources like those assembled here. The evidence of these sources is unanimous, however: few immigrant Englishwomen remained unmarried more than a year or two, and those usually by choice. In fact, one of the most durable folk myths among British women of the period involved the crowds of bride-hunting males who were said to congregate at prairie railway stations, ready to propose instant marriage before' girls even had time to collect their baggage from the station-agent. Comic embellishments aside, the main point remains: either as independent workers or as the wives of established settlers, British middle-class women, even if their numbers ran only to the tens rather than to the hundreds of thousands, introduced a perceptible skew into the demographic makeup of Western Canada at a crucial time in its social formation.

Thus the significance and impact of these women extends far beyond the question of numbers. For example, English suffrage leaders, even the most notoriously militant ones, were readily and frequently invited to Canada to make speaking tours between 1910 and 1916. Travel writers of the period often remark on the widespread interest here in the visits of the Pankhursts and others, and Canadian newspapers of the time confirm it. It is unlikely that audiences at Canadian suffrage forums were uniformly Canadian-born or that the touring arrangements rested solely in the hands of native Canadian suffragists. Analysis of the memberships of Canadian women's organizations on many fronts would almost unquestionably reveal a significant proportion of British-born women of primarily middle-class origins, just as examination of the leadership of women's unionization here would probably turn up many veterans of the British trade union movement (Helena Gutteridge of Vancouver is a case in point). That the swift rise to prominence of individuals like Irene Parlby and Violet McNaughton, both English, was the outward and visible sign of a pervasive if utterly informal network of former British gentlewomen is a hypothesis that invites further examination.

In the second place, it is difficult to imagine an immigrant group more certain to be conscious of the interdependence of education, economic independence, and social mobility. Schools, universities, and university extension services occupied a central place in the thinking of these women, as did the whole question of access by girls and women to the widest possible range of occupations. Housing, nutrition, sanitation, medical care, and cultural facilities were scarcely lower on the list, reflecting girlhood exposure to the raging controversies in England over the health and welfare of Britain's burgeoning but increasingly misery-ridden industrial proletariat. Canadian scholarship includes numerous careful and serious studies of the marked western consciousness of social issues and programmes throughout the region's brief history. Future studies along these lines would do well to take more fully into account the political culture of the prairie provinces' first women settlers, especially those English-speaking ones of some education who took as normal and proper an informed awareness of the controversies of their day. If nothing else, recognizing their presence would help to throw light on the vexed question of WASP dominance in the West, as well as on the strong middle-class cast of Canadian reform movements, including but also going well beyond the overtly feminist ones.

Thirdly, one can speculate on, and I believe in time more accurately chart, the legacy of educated Englishwomen of independent mind to the present-day culture of Western Canada, through their influence on their children and grandchildren in some cases, and on protegées and intellectual beneficiaries in others. Culture is a broad and amorphous term and can be interpreted in a number of ways. Among social scientists, culture often signifies such characteristic group activities as rural clubs, Sunday Schools, women's auxiliaries, and Girl Guides. Here the work of Eva Hasell and Monica Storrs comes immediately to mind; both these women philanthropists are legends in parts of the West, and they were only two of many pursuing their civilizing mission among Western Canada's more isolated settlements. Visiting and cottage nurses were another means by which books and magazines as well as medical and even religious services reached frontier districts, while Lady Aberdeen's much-publicized scheme for distributing reading matter to western homes was only an institutionalized form of a complex system of linkages that kept British ideals and usages alive on countless prairie home-steads and ranches.

The mention of books and other reading matter introduces other dimensions of culture. Sceptics who see the *Girls' Own Annual* as being cultural only in an anthropological sense might more readily warm to evidences of direct or indirect contributions to the mainstream of literature, painting, music, theatre, and the like. Without becoming enmeshed in the absorbing and complex feminist debate over the cultural mainstream as traditionally defined, chiefly by men, one can nonetheless point to a handful of such legacies as examples of Englishwomen active in the shaping of the arts in Canada. Gertrude Balmer Watt, for instance, made a name for herself in journalism in Edmonton, publishing collections of short pieces under the titles *A Woman in the West* (1907) and *Town and Trail* (1908), while Emily Weaver, who is represented in this collection on pp. 222-29. below, was once widely known and respected in Canada as an author of books of history and fiction. Then there is Elinor Marsden Eliot's *My Canada* (1915), like Georgina Binnie-Clark's *A Summer on the Canadian Prairie,* a lively and inventive merging of semi-fictional plot and character with generous doses of useful advice for intending settlers. Mary Hiemstra's attractive fictional rendering of the Barr Colony episode in *Gully Farm* (1935) is also well known.

Turning to the descendants, the name of Emily Carr has already been mentioned. It is also intriguing to encounter the 1979 reissue (by New Star Books) of Christine Van der Mark's novel of 1947, *In Due Season.* Dorothy Wise, the novelist's daughter, begins her brief biographical afterword to this reissue by writing, "My mother's mother grew up in the north of England, training as a secretary, and emigrated on her own to Canada" (p. 365) — this apparently taking place just before World War I. According to Wise, her English grandmother, Mary Van der Mark, wrote "many stories and poems, some of which were published," thus establishing in the mind of her daughter Christine the normalcy of literary interests and achievement.

Finally, there is the incalculable but nevertheless immensely important question of how far the collective psyche of Western Canada has been shaped by the accumulated impact of the immigrant experience among all its ethnic groups, educated English gentlewomen not excluded. In this connection, it is less facile than it might seem at first glance to draw particular attention to the combination of geographic amplitude and social indeterminateness that was the Canadian Prairies at the century's turn. Discovering seemingly unbounded space in physical terms in the western provinces, emigrant gentlewomen found abundant psychic space as well. "There is so much *room* here!" is the exultant cry of more than one of the writers in this collection, as she prepares her report on Canadian opportunities for the benefit of her distressed countrywomen at home. Space, latitude, movement: to the educated gentlewoman chafing under intense economic, psychological, and intellectual constraint in England, these were magic words — no less magic, probably, than were the words "land" and "property" in the ears of English men. So these women, in coming to the West, acted out what one feminist scholar of literature has called the "archetypal female success story, a passage from imprisonment to freedom."[11]

Generally sceptical of archetypal patterns as adequate explanations of historical phenomena, most historians will want to concentrate on the discrete individual experiences that sustain and define an interpretive generalization of this nature. And it is certain that not all gentlewomen — indeed, perhaps not even a majority — who made the passage from England to Western Canada found either success or freedom here. Only a fraction of the evidence is in, and there are enough unanswered questions to keep a generation of historians in this field fully occupied.[12] All that can be asserted in the meantime is that the documents in this collection support the conclusion that emigration to the Prairies was a liberating experience for a significant number of British gentlewomen. In the spaces of the West, they were able to arrive at a clearer and more just estimation of their hitherto repressed and unarticulated selves — their abilities, their special competences and limitations, their efficacy and worth in the daily run of human affairs.

Elizabeth Mitchell, contrasting English and Canadian town life in 1914, remarked in *In Western Canada before the War* on how the inhabitants of small prairie cities were "like trees in a well-thinned plantation, each counting individually, not indistinguishably crowded together." She went on: "In England, 7,000 souls would make a small, unnoticeable town, but in England an enormous mass of the population does not seem to count — the distinguished citizens are a very small percentage; while here every man is a possible Mayor or Minister of State. Just as the buildings in the Western towns are scattered over a vast area, and make a tremendous show in proportion to their numbers, so a few people seem like a great many, because none are negligible" (p. 9). To the extent that this observation was true of prairie society as a whole in 1914, it was true of women as well as men — as Mitchell herself went on to make clear in her thoughtful comments on the women of the West, a few pages of which are reprinted below.

Simply to count for something was more than the majority of superfluous Englishwomen had been brought up to expect from life, while to achieve a clearer understanding of just what it was they counted for, as individuals and as members of society, was an added and unforeseen bonus. "I owe one debt to my life on the prairie, and that is a fair appreciation of my own sex," wrote Georgina Binnie-Clark in *A Summer on the Canadian Prairie* (p. 278), suggesting even further the birth of a feminist consciousness through her personal struggles as a woman prairie farmer. And the same writer told readers of the *Imperial Colonist* in 1910, "Rich and poor, gentle and simple, Canadian or immigrant, we are all of us working women" — that "we" speaking volumes for the growth of a collective identity among Canadian women of the time.

1. Great Britain Central Statistical Office, *Annual Abstract of Statistics* (London: His Majesty's Stationery Office, 1914; Kraus rpt., 1966), vol. 61-62, 1899-1914, p. 407 (figures rounded).
2. Stanley C. Johnson, *A History of Emigration from the United Kingdom to North America, 1763-1912* (London: George Routledge and Sons, 1913; rpt. London: Frank Cass, 1966), pp. 348, 311.
3. A. James Hammerton, *Emigrant Gentlewomen* (London: Croom Helm, 1979), chapter 6, "Feminism and Female Emigration," especially pp. 129-30.
4. Ibid., p. 125.
5. Ibid., p. 151.
6. Ibid., pp. 175-76.
7. Johnson, *History of Emigration*, p. 259.
8. Ibid., p. 349.
9. For figures on gross British emigration to Canada, however, and to the prairie provinces in particular, see p. 123 below.
10. Hammerton, *Emigrant Gentlewomen*, pp. 174, 177.
11. Mitzi Myers, "Harriet Martineau's Autobiography," in *Women's Autobiography: Essays in Criticism*, ed. Estelle C. Jeninek (Bloomington and London: Indiana University Press, 1980), p. 59.
12. Marilyn Barber of Carleton University is currently engaged in research on British home-helps in Canada; Eliane Silverman at Calgary is preparing for publication conclusions based on her large-scale oral history project on the frontier experiences of Alberta women. Meanwhile, women's history courses are now well established at the majority of Canadian universities and community colleges. The next few years will see extensive and important additions to our knowledge of the historical experience of women in Canada.

PART ONE

The Beginnings:
The 1880's

From *A Lady's Life on a Farm in Manitoba*
Commentary

Before the great rush of settlement took place at the century's turn, there were more than thirty years of alternating expectation and disappointment for proponents of Canadian expansionism. Railways were grandly projected and then delayed or not built at all; great masses of landseekers, predicted and then despaired of. Manitoba, opened to settlement in 1870, proceeded quietly through the 1870's to draw small but steady numbers of farm families and single men from Ontario and the British Isles. The province's population grew from 11,963 in 1870 to 65,954 in 1881.[1] There was intense excitement for a short time as the province basked in the glow of Manitoba fever, but then in 1882 the over-heated speculative boom collapsed.

Accompanying the ebb and flow of Manitoba's fortunes, and in some measure shaping them as well, was a growing body of published commentary and report on the Northwest's attractions to immigrants. Much of it emanated from more or less interested parties, land agents, railway companies, and the like. As counterweight to this sometimes less than candid literature, however, there soon appeared an alternative viewpoint on the province, often with London or Edinburgh as the place of publication. Many elements of Britain's population were under stress, both economic and social, during the middle decades of Victoria's reign, and there was a ready-made audience on that side of the Atlantic for authoritative, first-hand accounts of travel and experience in the new Northwest of Canada.

For example, tenant farmers throughout England and Scotland who had suffered two disastrous harvests in a row in 1878 and 1879 sent delegates to Manitoba to report back to local tenant farmers' associations. Their responses were favourable and occasioned much comment in county newspapers throughout Britain. Readers of these reports made up a significant proportion of British emigration to Manitoba and the Northwest Territories during the 1880's. In other instances, public-minded citizens like Captain Richard E. W. Goodrich, mindful of narrowing opportunities for the sons of army officers, clergymen, and others of the middle classes in Britain, offered the reading public detailed accounts of their experiences as Manitoba settlers. Goodrich's two contributions to this genre were *A Year In Manitoba,* published in London in 1882, and *The Colonist at Home Again,* 1889. And there were others, books and pamphlets of the I-was-there variety, for the most part written by men with a predominantly male readership in mind: the adventurous younger son or the harrassed head of a family grown too large for his shrinking resources at home in Britain.

Set in this context, one little book published in London in 1884 stands out. The title of this book is *A Lady's Life on a Farm in Manitoba,* written by Mary Georgina Hall. About Mary Hall nothing more is presently known than can be guessed at from her writing. She was probably unmarried, and probably under middle age, when she landed in Canada for a visit to her brother A———. That she was of genteel background is evident both in her title and in the text of her book, while the level of prose suggests more than a minimal education.

Travelling with a companion identified only as E——— (perhaps a sister, perhaps a cousin or friend), she reached Winnipeg by train from St. Paul on May 18, 1882. There they were met by a friend and conveyed to A———'s farm near Headingly sixteen miles to the west of Winnipeg. The two women stayed on the farm until late August, at which time they resumed their travels, first to Denver, Colorado, and then home to England. The excerpt that follows here consists of just over half of Mary Hall's *A Lady's Life on a Farm in Manitoba.*

1. W.L. Morton, *Manitoba: A History* (Toronto: University of Toronto Press, 1957; second edition, 1967), pp. 145, 177.

Mary Hall

A Lady's Life on a Farm in Manitoba

Winnipeg, May 18th [1882].

Here we are, and we do feel ourselves really landed in the far North, after a most prosperous journey the whole way. We arrived "quite on time" last night, rather an unusual thing with these trains, particularly since the floods, when the passengers were dependent on the steamer, we saw yesterday as we passed high and dry on the prairie, which had to convey them from one train to another across the floods close to St. Vincent.

O the prairie! I cannot describe to you our first impression. Its vastness, dreariness, and loneliness is appalling. Very little is under cultivation between this and St. Paul, so that only a house here and there breaks the line of horizon. There are a few cotton and aspen trees along the Red River Valley, but with that exception the landscape for the last fifteen hours' travelling has been like the sea on a very smooth day, without a beginning or an end.

We were met at the station here by one of A———'s friends, who drove us out about a mile and a half from the town across the Assiniboine over a suspension bridge built exactly opposite the old Fort Garry, and somewhere close to the spot where our first English pioneers must have landed from the river steamer some twelve years ago to a very comfortable house belonging to another mutual friend, a dear kind old gentleman whose wife and daughter being away has placed the whole house at our disposal until we can get out to the farm, which we find is sixteen miles off.

It will be very difficult to describe everything to you. To begin with, the depot or station presented a curious appearance, such crowds of men loafing about with apparently no other object but to watch the new arrivals; so different to English stations where everyone seems in a hurry either coming or going. And then the roads we had to drive along defy description. The inches (no other word) of mud, and the holes which nearly capsize one at every turn. Even down Main

Street the roads are not stoned or paved in any way. We bumped a good deal in our carriage, and for consolation at any worse bumping than usual were told, "This is nothing, wait until you get stuck in a mud-hole out west." Then our route, thanks to the floods which have been very bad this year and are still out enormously — the upper floors of two-storied houses only being visible in many places — was most intricate. We had to be pioneered over a ditch into a wood, supposed to be cleared, with the stumps of trees left sticking about six inches out of the ground for your wheels to pass over, on to a track, and then through a potato garden to the house.

We were quite ready for our supper, it being about 8 o'clock when we got here; and the food at Glyndon, where we stopped twenty minutes in the middle of the day to "put away" the contents of sixteen dishes of some various mess or another, had not been of the most inviting of meals; and though the chops here were the size of a small leg of mutton and had the longest bones I ever saw, hunger was the best of appetisers, and we did credit to our meal, which had been cooked by our host.

This morning we were awoke by the same kind person depositing a can of water at our door for our baths. He gets up very early, as he has to fetch the water, milk the cow, feed the calf, etc., all before breakfast and starting off for his office.

There is a man-servant here who gets £5 to £6 a month, apparently to do nothing, as he is the only one on the premises who can afford to be idle and smoke his pipe of peace; but servants are so difficult to get in this country, and our host being on the move, having got a better Government appointment at Perth, is anxious not to change now, so, like everybody else, puts up with anything. The last servant they had in this house was the son of a colonel in the English Army, who was described as "a nice boy but very lazy"; but this man-servant hasn't even the recommendation of being nice. He was out at the farm working for his board and lodging, and no wages for some months, but A——— could not stand his idleness.

We all had to cook our breakfasts this morning, and as everyone was, by way of helping, either making toast, poaching the eggs, cooking hunks of bacon, or mending up the fire, the stove was pronounced much too small. The moment we had finished our meal we had to retire upstairs and make the beds and tidy up a little; a half-breed woman living about half-a-mile off is supposed to come in for an hour and wash up and clean the house, but if it is bad weather she is unable to get through the mud; therefore when the ladies of the establishment are away the house is left a good deal to its own devices, the dust and cobwebs not often disturbed.

C——— Farm, May 21st.

Our last letter to you was written with the first impression of our colonist life whilst in Winnipeg, where we had a very good insight of the way English people will rough it when they come out. It would horrify our farmers to have to do what gentlemen do out here. They are all their own servants. That lazy servant in Winnipeg, we were told, gave notice to leave, because one night he was requested to keep the kitchen fire in so that we might have a kettle of hot water when we went to bed.

We spent as little time as we could at our suburban residence, so as to save him any extra trouble, always lunching and sometimes dining in Winnipeg; and though all the restaurants are bad, still the food was almost as good as what we cooked ourselves. Our chief mistake for our first meals was that we put everything on the fire at the same time, and, funnily enough, our fish boiled quicker than the sausages, and they again much quicker than the pudding. Once there was a bread-and-butter one, about which there has been a good deal of chaff, as it was supposed to be first cousin to bread-and-milk!

The weather was very bad, constant rain, and we had a fair specimen of Winnipeg mud. To these buckboards (which is a buggy with a board behind for luggage), or to any of the carriages, there are no wings to protect one from the mud, so that we always came in bespattered all over, a great trial to our clothes. But in spite of the rain and bad weather we were determined to come out here on Friday. We hired a democrat, a light waggon with two seats, and started during the afternoon in the rain, hoping it might clear which it eventually did when we were about a third of our way. It was awfully cold, and the jolting of the carriage over the prairie so fearful that our wraps were always falling off. I had always understood the prairie was so beautifully smooth to drive over; but found it much resembling an English arable field thrown out of cultivation, with innumerable mole-hills and badger-holes, and natural cracks about an inch wide, which drain the water off into the marshes. If your carriage is heavily weighted it runs pretty easy; but woe betide you if driving by yourself — you bump up and down like a pea on a shovel.

We nearly upset, shortly after leaving Winnipeg, as a house was on the move, or, more properly speaking, had been, as it was stuck in a mud-hole; a load of hay, trying to get round it, had stuck as well; and the only place given us to pass was fearfully on the slant down to a deepish dyke, into which a buggy had already capsized. We caught the first glimpse of our future home eight miles off, the house and stables looking like three small specks on the horizon. It is very difficult to judge distances on the prairie, and the nearer we seemed to get to our destination the further the houses were removed. The farm had an imposing appearance as we drove up to it. Mr. B———, who met us at the gate, was most anxious that on arrival we should be driven to the front door and not to the kitchen one, which, being the nearest, is the handiest. He, poor man, has given up his bed and dressing-room to us, and we find ourselves very comfortable.

C—— Farm, May 24.

The two young men, Messrs. H—— and L——, who inhabit a tent about two miles from here, and who are building themselves a stable, are going into Winnipeg to-morrow for more lumber; and as I don't know when I shall have another opportunity of sending letters in, I send you a few lines. These two men have been living with A—— all the winter, and only turned out for us the day we arrived. It was such bad weather they hoped and speculated on our not coming; so that when we were seen in the distance there was a general stampede to clear out. I must say I should have been very loth to turn out, during this cold weather, of a comfortable house into a tent, and, had I been they, should have wished us somewhere. We have already had a taste of the cold in these regions. Friday, when we drove out here, was bad enough; but on Saturday, when E—— and A—— went into town again to take our carriage back, they were nearly frozen with the biting wind and sleet they had to face the whole of the sixteen miles home. On Sunday the thermometer was down to 22, or ten degrees of frost, with a bitter north-west wind, and we had an inch of snow on the ground; and though the sun melted most of it, the thermometer at night went down again to 24. I don't think I ever felt so cold in bed, in spite of a ton weight of clothes. Luckily the stoves are still up in the house — in summer they are generally put away in the warehouse to give them room — so that we have been able to make a light both night and day. We are told the weather is most unusual; anyhow, it is mighty cold. Those poor men in the tent have suffered a good deal; one night the pegs to the windward gave, and the snow drifted against their beds as high as their pillows. They luckily have got a stove, but are obliged to leave their door open to allow of the pipe going out; unfortunately they have no extra tin or iron to put on the canvas round the pipe, which is the usual way to prevent it catching fire.

To describe our life here will take some doing, and, after the novelty has worn off, it will not amuse us quite so much; nor shall we be so keen of helping our Abigail, who is the wife of the carpenter and maid-of-all-work, in everything, excepting that she must always have a great deal to do for a large household like ours, consisting of four men and our two selves, and we shall always want employment, and I don't think we shall either of us care to ride or drive much.

We have fallen into it (the life) wonderfully quickly; completely sunk the lady and become sort of maids-of-all-work. Our day begins soon after 6 o'clock by laying the breakfast, skimming the cream, whilst our woman is frying bacon and making the porridge for the breakfast at 6:30. Mr. B—— and A—— are out by 5 o'clock, in order to water, feed, and harness their horses all ready to go out at 7 o'clock, when we get rid of all the men. We then make the beds, help in the washing-up, clean the knives, and this morning I undertook the dinner, and washed out some of the clothes, as we have not been able to find a towel, duster, or glass-cloth, whilst Mrs. G—— cleaned out the dining-room. The dirt of the house is, to our minds, appalling; but as Mrs. G—— only arrived a few days before we did, and all the winter the four men were what is called in this country "baching it" (from bachelor), namely, having to do everything for themselves, it is, perhaps, not surprising that the floors are rather dirty and that there is a little dust. The weather is much against our cleaning, as the mud sticks to the boots and, do what you will, it is almost impossible to get it off; not that the men seem to have thought much about it, as, until we arrived and suggested it, there was no scraper to either door. Poor Mr. B——— was rather hurt in his feelings this morning on expressing some lament at the late sharp frosts, that all his cabbages would be killed, when we said that it was a pity he had sown them out of doors, as he might almost have grown them on the dining-room carpet. He also amuses us by lamenting that he did so much cleaning and washed the floors so often; he might just as well have left it until we arrived. Our time is well filled up until dinner, at 12.30, at which we have such ravenous appetites, we are told, no profits made on the farm will pay our keep. At half-past 1 when the men turn out again, we generally go out with them, and some out-door occupation is found for us; either driving the waggons or any other odd jobs. There is a lot of hay littered about, and that has to be stacked; also the waste straw or rubbish which is burnt, and the fires have to be made up. Three-quarters of an hour before either dinner or supper (the latter meal is about half-past 6) a flag, the Union Jack, is hoisted at the end of the farther stable — if neither A——— nor Mr. B——— is about, we undertake to do it — to call the men in; and they declare the horses see the flag as soon as they do and stop directly. The class of horse here is certainly not remarkable for its good looks; but they are hard, plucky little beasts, and curiously quiet. The long winter makes them, as well as all the other animals, feel a dependence upon man, and they become unusually tame. The cows, cats, and everything follow the men about everywhere. They used to have to keep the kitchen door shut to prevent one of the cows walking in. A——— has got a jolly old cat who follows him like a dog, sleeps on his bed, and sits next to him at meals. Mr. B——— has a dear colley with whom he carries on long conversations, particularly on the subject of the coolness of the morning and the water in his bath; so you see we have plenty of animal life about. The men at the tent have a black water-spaniel, which greatly prefers our fare and warm house to the tent, so is nearly always here.

May 25th.

We over-slept ourselves this morning, it being a dull day and no sun to wake us up, so that it was past 6 before any of us made our appearance. The way we work here would rejoice Uncle F———'s heart and amaze some of our farmers' wives and daughters. My advice to all emigrants is to leave their pride to the care of their families at home before they start, and, like ourselves, put their hand to everything. We have had some funny experiences; but for all our hard work we get no kudos or praise, it is all taken as a matter of course. I would not live in such a place for worlds, but while it lasts it is great fun; and I think we have done good by coming out, if only to mend up all the old rags belonging to these four men. We were much in want of dusters, etc., the first days, and were told that when the three months' wash which was in Winnipeg returned we should find everything we wanted, instead of which there was a fine display of torn under-linen, and stockings by the dozens, which we have been doing our best to patch up and darn, but no house linen. We shall do as much washing as we possibly can manage at home, I expect, as the prices are so fearful, to say nothing of the inconvenience of being ages without one's linen. I will just quote a few of the prices from our bill of the Winnipeg Steam Laundry. Shirts 15 cents, night ditto 10 cents, vests and pants 25 to 50 cents, blankets 50 cents, counterpanes 35 cents, table-cloths 15 to 35 cents, sheets 10 cents, pillow-slips 5 to 15 cents, night-dresses 15 cents to 1 dollar, petticoats 30 cents to 1 dollar, etc., everything in proportion. We thought one dollar per dozen all round was exorbitant, but when hardly anything is less than eightpence (as a cent, according to the exchange, is more than a halfpenny) it seems ruinous.

We get 4 dollars 80 cents only for the sovereign here, being tenpence short of the five dollars.

May 28th.
Our weather is improving, to-day has been lovely; but alas! with the warmth have come the mosquitoes. I don't believe you will ever see us again; they (the mosquitoes) bite so fearfully, even in the day-time, that they will devour us up entirely. A——— is having wire coverings made for the doors and windows; but, unfortunately, owing to the floods after the melting of the snow, all the stores which ought to have arrived in Winnipeg a month ago have been delayed, and the shops are very short of goods of all sorts and kinds. There are said to be 4,000 cars with provisions, etc. between this and St. Paul. A——— and I spent an afternoon at the other farm, "Boyd," which he rents of a Mr. Boyd, three thousand acres for £40 a year. It is covered with low brushwood with a few trees here and there, and a good deal of marsh, and therefore unfit for cultivation, so they keep it entirely for their cattle and for the cutting of hay in summer. It is a much prettier place than this, the house being surrounded by trees, whereas here we haven't one within seven miles, though last year they did their best and planted nearly five hundred round the house as avenues to the drive; but only a few survived the drought of last autumn and severe cold of winter, the rest are represented by dead sticks. We tried to see the cattle at Boyd's, but they were away feeding on the marsh and could only be looked at from a distance, as we

neither of us felt inclined to run the chance of being bogged or of wetting our feet.

In coming home we called at the tent, and I was surprised to find how quickly Messrs. H——— and L——— were building their stable, which is to be large enough to hold two stalls and a room beyond, which, when they have a house, will make a good loose-box; but for the time being they intend to live in, either sleeping in the loft or tent.

To build a house or stable is not very difficult; but with no carpenter or experienced man to help it wants a certain amount of ingenuity. You lay out your foundation by putting thick pieces of oak called "sills" on the ground in the shape of your house. In town these "sills" are nailed to posts which have been driven eight feet into the ground; but on the prairie are simply laid on the flat; on to the sills come the joists, planks 2 x 6 placed on edge across, two feet apart. Then the uprights, which stand on the sills two feet apart, form the walls. To these you nail rough boards on each side, with a layer of tar-paper in between if building a stable; if a dwelling-house, on the inside you put against your rough board, laths, and then plaster, on the outside the tar-paper and siding.

The floor is made by nailing rough boards on the joists, then tar-paper, and on the top of that tongued and grooved wood fitting into each other, to make it air-tight.

The roofs, which are almost always pointed on account of the snow, are composed of rafter 2 x 4, two to three feet apart, with rough boards across, then tar-paper and shingles; the latter are thin, flat pieces of wood laid on to overlap each other.

We send you a small sketch of our buildings, which will give you a better idea of these "frame" houses than any description. They can be bought ready-made at Chicago, and are sent up with every piece numbered, so that you have no difficulty in putting them together again.

Our own house is twenty-four feet square with a lean-to as kitchen. The dining and drawing-rooms are each twelve feet square, separated by sliding-doors; A———'s bedroom, the entrance-hall, and stair-case dividing the remainder of the house. Our front-door is not quite in the centre; but thanks to the verandah, one does not perceive it. Above, looking due south, we have a bedroom, dressing-room, and large cupboard for our clothes. There are two other rooms at the back for the men.

The other house is for the labourers, of whom there are eleven, with a woman as cook, the wife of one of them; it is also for a warehouse, where all the spare implements and stores are kept.

Besides these houses we have two good stables, one holding fourteen horses, the other the remaining six (also the cows, pigs, and chickens during the winter); piggeries; and last, but not least, my chicken-house. A——— has presented me with a dozen hens, for which he had to pay thirteen dollars, which with the seven old ones are my special charge, and are an immense amusement and occupation.

His farm here, as he has other land elsewhere besides the Boyd Farm, consists of 480 acres; half of one section and a fourth of another.

All the surveyed country in the North-west Territory has been divided into townships thirty-six square miles, and they again into sections of a mile square, which are marked out by the surveyors with earth mounds thrown up (at the four corners) in the form of right-angled pyramids, with a post about three feet high stuck in the centre. The mounds are six feet square, with a square hole on each side. To the marking of sections a similar mound is erected, only of smaller dimensions.

The sections are numbered as shown by the following diagram:—

N

31	32	33	34	35	36
30	29	28	27	26	25
19	20	21	22	23	24
18	17	16	15	14	13
7	8	9	10	11	12
6	5	4	3	2	1

W   E

S

The Townships are numbered in regular order northerly from the International Boundary line or 49th parallel of latitude, and lie in ranges numbered east and west from a certain meridian line, drawn northerly from the said 49th parallel, from a point ten miles or thereabouts westward of Pembina.

When the Government took over the territory from the Hudson Bay Company in 1870, two entire sections in every fifth township and one and three-quarters in every other, were assigned to the Company as compensation. There were also two sections reserved as endowment of public education, and are called School

Lands, and held by the minister of the Interior, and can only be sold by public auction.

The same was done for the half-breeds; 240 acres were allotted to them in every parish. Their farms are mostly on the rivers, along the banks of which all the early settlers congregated; and to give each claimant his iota the farms had to be cut up into long strips of four miles long by four hundred yards wide.

On every section-line running north and south and to every alternate running east and west nine feet, or one chain, is left for roads. Our farm-buildings are not quite in the centre of the estate, on account of having to make the drive up to the house beyond the marsh on the eastern boundary.

I have drawn you a plan of the farm; the spaces covered with little dots are the marshes: the one on the west extends for miles, and has a creek or dyke dug out by Government to carry off the water. From the drawing it looks as if there was much marsh around us; but this bit of ground was the driest that could be found not already taken up. As it was, A——— purchased it of a man who has some more land nearer Winnipeg, giving him five dollars per acre. The Nos. 30 and 31 mean the sections of the townships.

For emigrants wishing to secure a "homestead," which is a grant of 160 acres given by Government free, with the exception of an office-fee, amounting to ten dollars on all the even-numbered sections of a town-ship, he will now have to travel much further west, as every acre around Winnipeg is already secured, and has in the last two years risen most considerably in value.

The Canadian Pacific Railroad Company, which was given by Government 25,000,000 acres, besides the 25,000,000 dollars to make the line across the country from Thunder Bay on Lake Superior to the Rockies, sell their land (which is on odd-numbered sections of every township for twenty-four miles on each side of the track, with the exception of the two sections, 11 and 29, reserved for schoollands) for two dollars fifty cents, or ten shillings per acre, to be paid by instalments, giving a rebate of one dollar twenty-five cents, or five shillings per acre, if the land is brought into cultivation within the three or five years after purchase.

A man occupying a "homestead" is exempt from seizure for debt, also his ordinary furniture, tools, and farm implements in use, one cow, two oxen, one horse, four sheep, two pigs, and food for the same for thirty days; and his land cultivated, provided it is not more than the 160 acres; also his house, stables, barns and fences; so that if a man has bad luck, he has a chance of recovering his misfortunes.

In one of your letters you ask if a poor man coming out as labourer, and perhaps eventually taking up land as a homestead or otherwise, would encounter many difficulties. I fancy not, as both the English and Canadian Governments are affording every facility to emigrants, who can get through tickets from London, Liverpool, or Ireland at even a lower rate than the ordinary steerage passenger. They can have themselves and their families booked all the way, the fares varying from nine pounds five to the twenty-eight pounds paid by the saloon.

On board ship the steerage have to find their own bedding and certain utensils for use; otherwise everything else is provided, and, I am told, the food is both good and plenty of it. Regular authorised officers of the Dominion Government are stationed at all the principal places in Canada, to furnish information on arrival. They will also receive and forward money and letters; and everyone should be warned and put on their guard against the fictitious agents and rogues that infest every place, who try to persuade the new-comers into purchase of lands or higher rates of wage.

We heard the other day of an English gentlemen being taken in by one of these scoundrels, and giving a lot of money for land which on examination proved to be worthless. Luckily for him, there was some flaw in his agreement, and his purchase was cancelled. Men who intend buying land should be in no great hurry about their investments; the banks give a fair percentage on deposits, and it is always so much more satisfactory to look around before settling.

E——— has been very busy arranging the garden; a most fatiguing process, as she has to cart all her own sods to make a foundation and then heap soil on to them; but having brought a quantity of seeds from England she feels bound to sow them, and hopes they will make a grand show later on, and the place quite gay. You should have seen the beam of delight which shone on the countenance of a stranger who had come out from Winnipeg for the night, when on arrival he was immediately pressed into E———'s service to carry water for these said seeds. The temperature is now at 64°, and, as things grow as if by magic, we hope they will soon put in an appearance. Oats planted only a week ago are now an inch above ground. We have had a nice breeze the last two or three days, so that the mosquitoes have not worried us so much.

The prettiest things to see here are the prairie fires at night. The grass is burnt in spring and autumn so as to kill off the old tufts and allow of the new shoots growing for hay. The fires look like one long streak of quivering flame, the forked tips of which flash and quiver in the horizon, magnified by refraction, and on a dark night are lovely. In the day-time one only sees volumes of smoke which break the monotony of the landscape, though I don't know that it is picturesque. With a slight breeze the fires spread in a marvellous way, even at the rate of eight or nine miles an hour. The other day A——— and Mr. H———, whilst putting up their tent, did not perceive how near a fire they themselves had lighted at some distance was getting, until it was upon them. They then had to seize hold of everything, pull up the tent pegs as best they could, and make a rush through the flames, singeing their clothes and boots a good deal.

The pastures on the burnt prairie are good the whole summer, and animals will always select them in preference to any other. The wild ponies, be the snow in winter ever so deep, by pawing it away, subsist on these young shoots and leaves of grasses, which are very nutritious and apparently suffer little by the frost, which only kills the upper leaves but does not injure what is below.

The mirage is also very curious; the air is so clear that one often sees reflected, some way above the horizon, objects like the river, trees, and even the town of Winnipeg, which we could not otherwise see; we could actually one evening, at sunset, distinguish the gas-lights.

Sunday.

This is a real day of rest, and the men really do deserve it. We all have a respite, as regards breakfast, it being at 9 o'clock instead of 6.30; and do we not appreciate the extra forty winks! The whole day is spent more or less in loafing, we having no regular church nearer than Winnipeg, sixteen miles, though an occasional service is given at Headingley, eight miles off. The men lie stretched on the straw-heaps in the yard, basking and snoozing in the sun. We generally have some stray man out from Winnipeg, and are much struck with the coolness of their ways. Colonial manners, somehow, jar a good deal on one, they take it quite as a matter of course that we ladies should wait on them at table, and attend to their bodily comforts. On the other hand, they never seem to object to any accommodation they get, and are perfectly satisfied with the drawing-room sofa for a bed, even with sheets taken out of the dirty linen bag, which has been once or twice the case when our supply has run short. I don't object to their coming, only that our Sunday dinners have to be in proportion, and as all our provisions come our from Winnipeg it is rather difficult catering. We have no outside larder or anywhere to keep our meat and butter, so have instituted a lovely one by putting all our things down the well, which is nearly dry and is under the kitchen floor. In winter there is never any need of a larder, as the meat is frozen so hard that it has to be twelve hours in the kitchen before they can attempt to cook it.

Our food is very good and we have the best of all receipts, ravenous appetites for every meal. Our breakfast consists of porridge, bacon, and any cold meat, jam, and any quantity of excellent butter and bread. Dinner, a hot joint and a pudding of some sort, finishing up with coffee. Supper, much the same. We have coffee with every meal, and, as the pot is always on the hob, anybody can have a cup when they like. The men have about two cups apiece before breakfast when they first get up. We never mind any amount of coffee, but wage war against the cocktails, taken before meals as appetisers. A cocktail is a horrid concoction of whisky, bitters, sugar and water, which are all mixed together with a "swidel" stick, which stick is always on the wander and for which a search has to be made. Nipping is too much in vogue in this country, but we are told that a lot of support is wanted, the air is so rarefied and the water has so much alkali in it, and therefore not supposed to be healthy, but it is most beautifully clear and delightfully cold to drink.

It certainly does disagree with the horses and cattle when first imported into the district.

June 3rd.

If you happen to know of anybody coming out here, and so many do, and you would like to give A——— a present, I wish you would kindly send him a few table-cloths, dusters, towels, and pairs of sheets; in short any linen would be most acceptable as we are so short. How these men managed when the linen went into Winnipeg to be washed, and was sometimes kept a month ere it came home, is a mystery. These extra men living in the house have none. They facetiously describe their ideas of dirt by saying, if the table-cloth, however filthy it might look, when flung against the wall didn't stick, it went on for another week; if it stuck, was then and there consigned to the dirty-linen bag.

Since we have been here we have instituted a weekly wash, every Monday and Tuesday. E——— and Mrs. G——— preside at the tub all day, and even then our sheets and towels often run short.

Every colonist ought to provide himself with two pairs of sheets, half a dozen towels, two table-cloths, and a few dusters; and as those things and his wearing apparel, if in use six months previously, are allowed into the country free of duty, they might as well bring them over, as everything of that sort in Winnipeg is so fearfully dear I do not like buying anything there. We sent for some unbleached calico the other day, worth twopence-halfpenny; was charged twelve cents or sixpence a yard. Besides the four yards of calico there were ten of bed-ticking, also ten of American cloth; and the bill was six dollars seventy cents, nearly seven-and-twenty shillings. Everything is equally dear, the demand is so much greater than the supply. Beef is tenpence to thirteenpence a pound, mutton about the same, bacon tenpence, pork tenpence, chickens four and twopence each. We use a good deal of tinned corned beef; and very good it is, it makes into such excellent hashes and curries and is so good for breakfast.

A——— also wants a pair of long porpoise-hide waterproof boots sending out; they are quite an essential, as after the heavy rains water stands inches deep in our yards, and he has so much walking into the marshes. In the spring, when the snow has melted, the "sloughs" or mud holes along all the tracks and across the prairie are so deep that horses and waggons are repeatedly stuck in them, and the men have to go in, often up to their waist, to help the poor animals out. The only way sometimes to get waggons out is to unhitch the horses, getting them on to firm ground, and by means of a long chain or ropes fastened to the poles, pull the waggons out which as a rule have previously had to be unloaded. The clothes these men wear are indescribable. A———— at the present moment is in a blue flannel shirt, a waistcoat, the back of which we are always threatening to renew. Inexpressibles somewhat spotty, darned, and torn, and, thanks to one or two washings, have shrunk, displaying a pair of boots which have not seen a blacking-brush since the day they left England. Coats are put on for meals, to do honour to the ladies, but seldom worn otherwise. The coarser and stronger the clothes are the better. A————'s straw hat is also very lovely, it serves periodically for a mark to shoot at with the rifle on Sunday mornings, or when company come out from town. We both of us feel much like our old nurse when we are doing our mendings, cutting up one set of old rags to patch another; but thanks to ammonia and hot irons, we flatter ourselves we make them almost look respectable again. . . .

June 12th

We have had a real visitor lately — I mean one who has brought a change, and a toothbrush; and for the auspicious event we rigged him up a stretcher bed, the most comfortable of things, canvas stretched on to a wooden frame, with a mattress on the top. You could not wish for anything softer. He was one of our ocean companions; his nickname of Mike still sticks to him. On getting to Winnipeg at night he had great difficulty in finding our where-abouts; even at the Club he was told the only W———— known kept a store in Main Street. Luckily from the Club he went to A————'s livery stable, which is exactly behind it, where a man offered to drive him out forthwith, having driven another man here only four days ago; but he preferred waiting till the morning, getting here some-where about 9 o'clock, when he was set down immediately to work to stone the raisins for a plum cake, and when tired of that had to help A———— planting potatoes. He declares he never will come here with his best clothes and a "boiled" shirt on again, as we have worked him so hard.

The accounts he gives, in an exaggerated Irish brogue, of his experiences in Minnesota have kept us in fits of laughter. The description of their first drive, when both he and his companions were all bogged; and how that twenty-seven mules and twenty-eight horses bought at St. Louis all arrived one night at the station about 5 o'clock, after sixty hours' travelling with no food or water, had to be unloaded from the cars, and they hadn't a halter or even a rope to do it with. Eventually they got all the poor beasts into a yard with wooden pailing round, but, something startling them, they made a rush, the fence gave way, for which damage the proprietor charged then ten pounds, and all galloped straight on to the prairie, and it took the men all night getting them together again. One pair of horses disappeared altogether; but were brought back when a reward of thirty dollars was offered; they had wandered nineteen miles.

Mike slept in A———'s room. They talked so much, and told so many funny stories, that we despaired of ever getting them down to breakfast; Mike declaring he would like to bring his bed along with him, as he hadn't slept in one, or been between sheets since leaving New York, six weeks previously. We drove him over one afternoon to fish in the creek about two and a half miles off; but as we had to go in a light waggon, and with only one spring seat, both Mike and A——— had to hang on behind, with a plank as seat, which was always slipping and landing them on their backs at the bottom of the waggon. When we were about half a mile from home E——— made a wager that she would get through the wire fence and home across the prairie before we could get round and the horses be in their stable. We had a most exciting race; the gates, which are only poles run from one end of the wire to another, were a great impediment, and I believe it was really a dead heat, through all the labourers entering into the joke and rushing to unhitch the horses, which were disappearing into the stable as E——— was at the kitchen-door.

I fancy that on the whole, in spite of his hard work, Mike enjoyed his visit, not only for the pleasure of our society, but as he had never seen a piece of meat, nor anything but pork and beans and bad coffee at Warren, nor had a bed to lie on, nor as much water as could be held in a tea-cup to wash in; he must have felt he had dropped into a land of Goshen by some happy mistake.

To give you a clearer insight into our daily life, and as I have nothing really to write about this week, I think I cannot do better than copy out our journals, which we try to keep regularly, though in our monotonous every-day life it is sometimes difficult to find incidents to chronicle.

Monday. — Wash and cook all the morning; E——— and A——— plant willows in the marsh during the afternoon. I wander about the prairie in search of a duck's nest I saw yesterday and thought I had marked; but the tracks, stones, and ridges on the prairie are so alike, that it is almost impossible to remember any place; anyhow, I cannot find the nest. I could not take it yesterday, as I was riding, and the animal will not stand still to let you mount, and had I had to scramble up on to her I should certainly have broken all the eggs I took. An exhausting day with a hot wind blowing; we are craving for rain, and thankful for the slight showers that fell during last night. It is marvellous how quickly vegetation will grow. Some sample wheat planted in the garden, of which there was no sign yesterday, thanks to the rain and sun has grown quite an inch by 6 o'clock this evening. The grass is beginning to look so green and nice.

Tuesday. — E——— and Mrs. G——— finish their wash which they could not get through yesterday. I go up to the tent, with Mr. H——— to drive his waggon, and help to unlumber the wood he brought out yesterday from Winnipeg. Riding on these waggons loaded, and without a spring seat, is anything but pleasant over the prairies, but Mr. H——— is so accustomed to it now that he can stretch himself on the top and sleep soundly; and once or twice, coming out from town, has found himself in quite the wrong direction by allowing the horses to go their own way.

E——— and I spend our afternoon cleaning up the tent.

Wednesday. —A ——— and I drive into Winnipeg. We have had various commissions to do, and A——— had to attend a meeting at the Club. Mr. W. H——— has most amiably put his house, consisting of two rooms and a kitchen below, at our disposal whenever we want to rest; so I spent my whole afternoon there, nominally reading the "St. James's Gazette," but, I fancy, indulging in "forty winks" whilst waiting for A———. We afterward dined with the judge in his very nice pretty house called "The Willows," driving home later. The cold was so great that A———, who had brought no great-coat, was forced to run behind the buggy some way to get warm and produce circulation. The prairie fires quite lovely on all sides, quivering high flames for miles, and the night being dark, they looked very bright.

Thursday. — Was so tired after my day in town that I breakfasted in bed; disgraceful! By the time I get down the family have all dispersed to their various works. After dinner E——— and I drive a waggon over to the Boyd Farm to fetch oats for Mr. H———. The students, who haven't much to do, are enlisted into the filling and loading of the sacks; rather glad, we fancy, of some occupation. On our return we found a friend of Mr. B———'s, who, having heard of our proximity, he living at Headingley, has come over to dine and sleep. Our "parlour" sofa, as usual, is called into requisition. It will soon be worn out, so many sleep on it. I think last week it was occupied nearly every night.

Friday. — We have had very smart company to-day, as the judge, his wife, niece, and another man came over. We hoped they would stay to dinner, and had "killed the fatted calf"; but I fancy the ladies dreaded the prairie by night, and insisted upon returning — we could hardly persuade them to take a cup of tea — fearing that they might be benighted.

Saturday. — Hard at work cleaning all the morning. Mr. B———'s friend leaves after dinner, and I drive the mares in the waggons whilst the men stretch the wire-fencing. E——— rides to the tent with letters. We sustained rather a shock to our nerves to-day; about 12 o'clock a buggy was seen coming towards the house just as we were sitting down to dinner, and as our food was scanty we did not know how we possibly could feed three extra men. Luckily they only came to enquire their route to the tent, and it was a relief when they drove on; though we felt we ought to have given them some food, as the tent could only provide bacon and biscuits.

Sunday. — Mrs. G———, our factotum, has a holiday, and goes over with some of the other labourers to spend the day at the other farm. E——— and I have to undertake the *ménage* for the whole day. Our mutton, a leg, was very nicely done, also our vegetables, rice, and beans; but the "evaporated" apples, which we use much, required boiling previous to being put in a tart, which we neither of us knew. Therefore they were not done, and the crust was all burst. The men from the tent, who generally spend their Sundays here, were allowed some dinner, on condition they washed up afterwards.

June 18.

I am afraid our letters will not be so interesting as the novelty wears off; the monotony of our life may begin to pall upon us. We hardly ever go two miles beyond the farm; to take our neighbours at the tent their letters or parcels brought out from town, is about the limit to our wanderings. We did drive one of the waggons to our neighbour Mr. Boyle to fetch home some oats the other night, and we also have been into town to pay our respects to the Governor and his wife. We happily don't want much outside attraction, for we have so much to do on the farm. The men work us pretty hard, I can tell you; as, besides all our indoor work, we have had three afternoons cutting potatoes for seed, until our hands are too awful to look at, and the water is so hard that we never shall get them a decent colour again. Some "white elephants" potatoes planted three weeks ago (thirty in number we cut into 420 pieces) already make a great show, and will want banking up next week. About ten acres of ground close to the house have been reserved and are called "the garden," in which have been planted turnips, flax, beet-root, lettuce, tomatoes, and potatoes; in short, all the luxuries of the season. But I am afraid none will be ready before we leave, if we carry out our idea of going to Colorado early in August.

We have been craving for rain, and at last, luckily, had a delightful shower a few days ago, which had freshened us up and will make things grow. There is no grass as yet above four inches in height, and this time last year they were hay-making. The men are beginning to fear there will be none; but with a little warm weather and a certain amount of rain everything grows as if by magic, so we may still have hope to have a good season.

Only very few of the garden-seeds have made their appearance, which is disappointing after all the trouble they were; but the wild flowers are beginning to come out on the prairie, small bushes of wild roses are all over; there are also very pretty sunflowers, a tree maiden-hair, several different vetches, sisters, yellow-daisies, & c.; many we cannot name, indigenous to this country we conclude.

June 26.

We quite feel as if we had been here years instead of about five weeks; and though it was prophesied before we left England that, after turning the house up-side down and making the men very uncomfortable with our cleanings we should then go on strike, it has not been altogether fulfilled. We certainly did try to clean up a bit, but we still help in housework, and have to do as the servants at home. If we expect visitors, or on a Sunday, put on a tidy gown; otherwise we generally live in the oldest of frocks (which are more or less stained with either mud or the red paint with which we have been painting the roofs of both the stable and the labourers' house), very big aprons, sleeves to match, and our sun-bonnets. E——— had concocted for herself a thin blue-and-white shirt, and as she generally lives with her sleeves tucked up, her arms are getting quite brown and sunburnt. Our boots are the only things we do not much like cleaning, they get so dirty again; and we have come to the happy conclusion that unblacked boots have a "cachet" that blacked boots have not. When we first arrived the men promised to do them for us every Sunday; which promises, like so many, have partaken of the nature of pie-crusts.

We are both of us delighted to have come, the whole experience is so new, and what we couldn't have realised in England; and I am sure, in spite of the *bouleversement* of the bachelor *régime,* it is a great pleasure to the men we are here. Our Winnipeg acquaintances tell us that A——— is quite a changed man, so cheery and even bumptious, and that everything is now *"What we do* at the farm."

It is all very well, however, in the summer; if obliged to stay through the winter, it would be quite another "pair of shoes." The thermometer often registers forty degrees of frost, though the effects of this extreme temperature in the dry exhilarating atmosphere is not so unpleasant as might be imagined, but the loneliness and dreariness of the prairie with two or three feet of snow would be appalling. The cold is so great that you have to put on a buffalo coat, cap, and gloves, before you can touch the stove to light the fire, and notwithstanding the coal stove which is always kept going in the hall to warm the up-stairs room (through which the pipe is carried), the water in buckets standing alongside gets frozen.

Then the blizzards, which are storms of sleet and snow driven with a fierce wind, and so thick that it is quite impossible to get out of doors, or see at all, would be too trying.

Even to get across the yard to the further stable the men have to have a rope stretched as guide so as not to lose their way; and these storms sometimes, as they did this last year, continue for three weeks consecutively.

The snow on the prairie is never very deep, but it drifts a good deal, and was to the depth of twelve feet on the west side of the house.

No work can be done much in the winter on account of the cold and snow, so that from the middle of April, when the snow begins to go, until the beginning of October everything has to be rushed through and as many hands put on as they can possibly get, who are all discharged at the end of summer and only two or three kept to look after the animals. After threshing, these men have little or nothing to do: digging out the well to water the horses, teaming hay into the town on sleighs, and fetching timber over from the other farm, is about their only outdoor occupation. All the animals in the shape of horses, cows, pigs and chickens are huddled together in the stables for warmth.

July 5th.

We have received our letters most unexpectedly to-day; two of our gentlemen coming out last night from town brought sundry parcels, newspapers, etc., but never thought of turning round to see if all was safe in back of carriage, declaring it was such rough driving they could only think of how to hang on and not be jolted out, so that by the time they got home, letters, a horse-collar, spare cushions, etc. were all gone. It was too late to send after them; but one of the men started back at 3.30 this morning, finding most of the lost things strewn broadcast over the prairie, even to within a short distance of Winnipeg. He went on to feed and bait his horses, at the same time enquiring for letters, finding ours just come in, and which would have lain there until our next opportunity.

Our variety to-day has been the absence of our cook, and we are again left in charge, and we flatter ourselves the dinner was "immense." Stewed beef, rice, mushrooms, (of which some were rather burnt, others not quite done enough, but that is a trifle), yorkshire pudding (baking-powder making an excellent substitute for eggs), and an apple tart. What more could you want? We are quite ambitious now, and have curries, rissoles, etc. A——— used to say he hoped we should not expect either him or his friends to eat our dishes, as they would have to go to bed afterwards for at least three or four hours; but they very much appreciate any change made in the *menu*.

We are longing to make bread, which takes up a great deal of our factotum's time, as it has to be set over night and kneaded three or four times the following day; but are begged to defer that amusement until within a few days of our departure, as it would so entirely upset our American trip if we had to attend A———'s obsequies. The bread is perfectly delicious, so light and so white in colour. The flour is excellent. It is not made with brewer's yeast, but with a yeast gem dissolved in warm water, to which is added a handful of dried hops boiled beforehand for about ten minutes, and strained. To that is added a cupful of flour a teaspoonful of salt, and one of sugar, and the whole is put into a warm place to ferment; when fermented, which takes about twelve hours, into a cool place, where it will remain good and sweet some time.

A Receipt for Bread-Making.

Put ten large spoonfuls of flour in a bread-pan, and add enough warm water to make it into a thin batter, add half a pint of yeast, mix well, and, having covered the bread-pan with a cloth, put it in a warm place near the stove over night. During the night it should rise and settle again. In the morning add enough flour to make it in into a thick dough, and knead it on a bread-board for ten minutes. Put it back into pan for two hours and let it rise again. Grease your baking-tins, knead your dough again, and then fill the tins half full, put them close to the stove to rise, and when they have risen thoroughly, grease the tops of your loaves with a little butter (preventing the crust breaking and giving it a nice brown colour) and put them into the oven and bake for an hour to an hour and a quarter.

As F——— had not Mrs. G———— to wash up with her, she enlisted one of the men, and it was very funny to see him in a hat three times too big for his head, pipe in his mouth, sleeves turned up, drying the dishes and putting a polish on them. Talking of hats, E——— has at last got one and a half, it literally covers even her shoulders, and at midday she declares she is as much in shade as under a Japanese umbrella; for trimming a rope is coiled round the crown, the only way to make it stay on the head. Of her gloves there is only the traditional one left; the other is among the various articles we have left on the prairie, bumped out of the buggy one day when she took them off to take care of them in a shower of rain.

That driving on the prairie is loathsome, but if we want to get about at all we must do it, as we don't like the riding horses. At the present moment we have got one of the plough animals, which is rideable. The poor beast was frightened one night three weeks ago, during a fearful storm of thunder and lightning, and ran into the barb wire, wounding itself horridly on the shoulders and neck. The skin had to be sewn up, and it cannot wear a collar for the present so we have it to ride if we like. It is not a slug like the other two.

The thunder-storms here are frightful; they are also very grand to watch, as we can see them generally for miles before they come up. We, luckily, have about ten lightning conductors on the houses and stables, so that we feel safe. A thunder-bolt fell pretty near the other day, destroying about six posts and the wire of our north fence. Thanks to the rain we have lately had, and the warm sun, we find such quantities of mushrooms all over the prairie. They grow to such a size! We measured two, one was 21½ inches round, the other 21, very sweet and good, and as pink underneath as possible. The labourers have been so pleased with them that last Sunday they began picking and cooking them in early morning, going on with relays more or less all day, so that by the evening they couldn't look another in the face, and it will be some time before they touch them again. We have them for every meal.

Our diaries here are more or less public property, and as we have been nowhere or seen anything at all exciting since we last wrote, I am going to copy down from the journals the incidents, if any, of the last week. You seemed to appreciate it the last time we sent you home a copy, but you must forgive if it is somewhat of a repetition to our numerous letters. The weather, for one thing, is daily chronicled, as it takes up much of our thoughts, so much in the future depending on its being propitious just as this time of year, when the seeds are all sown and the hay almost ready to cut.

Tuesday. — Beautiful day, so warm and nice, without being hot; everything growing, too, marvellously; even the seeds in the garden, which we began to despair of, are coming up.

The men have been very low, on account of the scarcity of rain; but we have had one or two thunder-storms lately which have done good, and in this climate I do not think one ought ever to give up hopes. E——— has been painting wild flowers, which at this moment are in great profusion and variety all over the prairie, most of the day, varying her work by painting the doors of the room, which were such an ugly colour, a pale yellow green, that they have offended our artistic eyes ever since we have been here. I am said to have wasted my whole morning watching my two-days-old chickens, supposed to be the acme of intelligence and precocity. The afternoon was spent in shingling the hen-house. It was only roofed over with tar-paper laid on to the rafters, which answers well if the wind doesn't blow the paper about, or that it has not any holes; but as the hen-house is only a lean-to of the stable, the roof of which we have been very busily painting, it has been trodden upon a good deal in getting on and off the roof, and, in consequence, the paper is much like a sponge, letting any rain in, and drenching the poor sitting fowls; but with the shingles overlapping each other on the tar-paper, the roof will be quite water-tight.

Wednesday. — Our factotum has gone into town, and we are left in charge, E——— parlour-maid, Mr. B——— scullery-man, and I cook. We have heaps of mushrooms at every meal, a most agreeable change to the rice and white beans we have only hitherto had.

Thursday. — Hot day. A——— went into town to some meeting at the Club. We have been dreadfully tormented with mosquitoes today, also the big "bull-dog" fly, which, whenever the kitchen door was left ajar, came into the house in myriads; but we find that Keating's powder most effectually destroys them, and in a very few seconds. We have been busy making a mattress and pillow for Mr. H———, really one does not realise how clever one is until our genius is put to the test in an establishment like this. E——— and I drove up to the tent after supper with our handiwork, and had great pleasure in seeing it filled with hay. Our drive was not of the most enviable: we had a waggon with no spring seat, only a board, which was always moving, to sit upon; one horse would tear along, the other not pull an ounce, in spite of applying the whip a good deal, and we were nearly smothered with mosquitoes, I never saw such clouds of them, and on our return home there was a general rush for the bottle of ammonia, which is the only thing that allays the irritation.

Friday. — Excitements have been crowding in upon us to-day. Bob, one of the labourers, who went into Winnipeg yesterday, only arrived home at 3 A.M. this morning. He left town at 6, but the night being dark he lost his way, and finding himself on the edge of a marsh, having a feed of oats with him, wisely unhitched his horses, tied them to the wheels, and waited patiently for daylight. Just as we were sitting down to dinner, three men who have been surveying the Government ditch near here, came and begged to be fed. Luckily we had soup and plenty of cold meat: but our pudding — the less said about that the better. We always have the evaporated apples as a stand by, and they are delicious; so with quantities of butter and milk we never need starve.

Then in the evening, when Mr. B.——— was going to the stable to serve out the oats for the horses, he came in for the finish of an exciting race between two of the plough horses. The jockeys or riders were told forthwith that a waggon was going into town the following morning, and that their services would be dispensed with in future. Just as we were going to bed we heard A——— coming in, and with him a stranger who turned out to be our cousin, only fifteen days out from England, *via* Canada. He looks very delicate.

Saturday. — We had made no preparation for E. P.——— last night, so he had to occupy the "parlour" sofa, and says he slept like a top; doubtlessly did not require much rocking, as he had travelled through almost without stopping. We were busy all this morning writing letters for the discharged miscreants to take into town. It has been very hot and close all day. I rode up to the tent, and hurried home, seeing a thunder-storm coming up, which was grand; and it was very lucky that I got home, as it began to rain at 3 o'clock, and is still pouring in perfect torrents at 10 o'clock P.M.

Sunday. — The yard is in such a fearful state of dirt, and the water standing inches deep, that it has been nearly impossible to move beyond the door. I put on A———'s long waterproof boots, and managed to get as far as my hen-house, and found two of my chickens dead.

Another sitting hen has been a source of great anxiety, as she will peck her chicks to death as they hatch, and out of a sitting of eleven eggs we have only been able to save five birds. A wet Sunday hangs very heavily on our hands here, as there is nothing to be done.

Monday. — Big wash as usual all the morning, and just as E——— and I were to drive a waggon over to Mr. Boyle for some oats which required fetching, we had quite a scare. A *lady* and gentleman were seen to be riding up. We both of us rushed up-stairs to put on some clean aprons to do honour to our guests, who, with another man, also out from town, remained the whole afternoon. We have never dined as many as nine people in our vast apartments before, but we managed very nicely.

We have had heavy showers with a high wind, and the thermometer down to 50 all the afternoon. We tried to persuade our lady visitor to stay the night, A———

offering to give up his room; but she persisted in going back, and, I am afraid, will have got very wet, in spite of E——— lending her waterproof jacket.

Tuesday. — The household had a long turn in bed this morning, Mr. B——— only getting down at about 7.15, when various things were offered him to prop open his eye-lids when he did appear.

The weather has been slightly better than yesterday, but the wind has been high, and it was really quite cold, varied by slight showers of rain in the morning. In the afternoon we all made hay. I worked my rake until my horse beat me by refusing to move in any direction excepting homewards; and I had to call A———, who was stone getting, to my rescue. He, with judicious chastisement in the shape of a kick or so, made the horse work. E——— and E.P——— loaded hay. Thanks to the late rains the marshes were heavy, and they very nearly stuck once or twice in going through them. There were no mosquitoes, which was a blessing, but one is never troubled with them in a high wind.

July 9.

You should have seen A——— and his equipage start into Winnipeg two days ago. He and the men from the tent had to go in and bring out a waggon and the new "Cortland waggon" (my present), and they had to take in the broken buggy to be mended. So they started with a four-in-hand to their cart, the broken buggy tied on behind, and another pair of horses behind that again. The buggy they say very nearly capsized going over the bridge of the creek when near Winnipeg, otherwise they got on beautifully; but it was a funny arrangement altogether, and they seemed to cover a quarter of a mile of ground as they left here. Winnipeg grows in a most astonishing way; every time we go in, a new avenue or street seems to have started up. Emigrants, they say, are coming in at the rate of a hundred a day. A few years ago the population was about five thousand, in 1878 about ten, now over forty thousand, a fourth of whom are living under canvas.

It was estimated last winter that the building operations this season would amount to four million dollars, but double that amount is nearer the mark, and many are obliged to abandon the idea of building on account of the difficulty of getting timber and bricks. Every house or shanty is leased almost before it is finished. Winnipeg, as you know, was formerly known as Fort Garry, and one of the chief trading stations of the Hudson Bay Company. Of the old fort, I am sorry to say, there is very little left, and that is shortly to be swept away for the continuation of Main Street. The Governor, now occupying the old house, is to have a splendid building, which, with the Houses of Legislature, are in the course of construction, rather farther away from the river.

The town is built at the confluence of two great rivers, the Red and Assiniboine, the former rising in Minnesota, and flowing into lake Winnipeg 150 miles north, navigable for 400 miles. The Assiniboine has many steamers on it; but the navigation being more difficult, the steamers often sticking on the rapids, it is not much in vogue with emigrants going west, particularly now that the railway takes them so much more rapidly.

There is a large suburb of the town the other side of the Red River called St. Boniface, the see of a Roman Catholic Archbishop, possessing a beautiful cathedral and a great educational school for young ladies; for some reason or other we never managed to get over there to see it, though the cathedral is a grand landmark for a great distance.

The railway traffic also is enormous. During the flood 4,000 freight waggons were delayed at St. Vincent; now they are coming in at the rate of 4,000 per week, and still people cannot get their implements, stores, &c. fast enough. We have asked several times for some turpentine at one of the shops, and the answer always given is, "It is at the depot, but not unloaded."

We have been wanting turpentine to mix with the brown paint with which we are painting the dining-room doors. But first of all the paint fails, and then the turpentine, and I fully expect our beautiful work of art will not be finished before we leave.

July 12th.

It is very certain that no gentleman ought to come out to this country, or, when here, can expect to prosper, unless he has some capital, heaps of energy, and brains, or is quite prepared to sink the gentleman and work as a common labourer.

The latter command the most wonderful wages, there is such a demand for them that one can hardly pick and choose. A plough-boy gets from four to six pounds a month, an experienced man from eight to ten pounds, besides their board and lodging; a mechanic or artisan from fourteen to sixteen shillings a day; women servants are very scarce, they get from four to six pounds a month. We were so astonished at the wages in New York; the head gardener in the Navy Yard was receiving one hundred and fifty pounds a year, his underling, seventy-five pounds, the groom one hundred pounds. It is surprising to me that the whole of the poorer classes in England and Ireland, hearing of these wages, do not emigrate, particularly when now-a-days the steerage in the passenger ships seems to be so comfortable, and that for about six pounds they can be landed on this side of the Atlantic. We have nine Britishers and two Canadians on this farm, and the amount of ground broken up does everyone great credit, considering that the whole place is only of a year and a half's growth. Since we arrived we can mark rapid and visible strides towards completion. The house has been banked up and grassed, a fence put to enclose all the yard, and we have actually had the audacity to talk about a tennis ground, which would take an immense deal of making, from the unevenness of the soil. The water, having no real outflow, makes itself little gullies everywhere, which would be very difficult to fill up level; but I don't know that, until we are acclimatized to the mosquitoes, said to be the happy result of a second year's residence, that we should feel inclined to play tennis, as we could only indulge in that diversion of an evening when work was ended, and that is just the worst time for these pests. They spoil all enjoyment, we never can sit out under the verandah after supper, which we should so like to do these warm evenings. They bite through everything, and the present fashion of tight sleeves to our gowns is a trial, as no stuffs, not even thin dogskin, are proof against them, and our faces, arms, and just above our boots are deplorable sights. Ammonia is the only remedy to allay the irritation. I am not drawing a long bow when I say that in places the air is black with them.

The poor horses and cows are nearly maddened with them if turned out to graze, and the moment the poles across the road are withdrawn, they gallop back into their stables. The mosquitoes are great big yellow insects, about half an inch long.

The house and country at Boyd's farm is much prettier than this, from the lot of trees round it, and the ground not being so flat; but we wouldn't change for all the world, it is so stuffy, and the flies and mosquitoes are much worse there than here, where we catch the slightest breeze of wind, which always drives them away. We were dreading making the hay in the marshes on account of them.

I do not think we shall suffer much from the heat, as nearly always, even in the hottest part of the day, there is a breeze; and as yet the nights are deliciously cool, we have never found one blanket too much covering. . . .

C——— Farm, July 30th.

We found the most lovely batch of letters, almost worth being away from home for ten days, on our arrival here at 12 o'clock P.M. on Tuesday, which completely revived our drooping spirits; we were feeling rather limp and tired after a long day in Winnipeg, and losing our way across the prairie coming home. It was very dark, and the only guide we had was when the vivid flashes of lightning reflected the farm-buildings; as it was, we drove through the big marsh, the mosquitoes nearly eating us up; and A——— so worried by them that he couldn't think of the trail, and trusted to the horses finding their way. The joy of coming upon our own fence is better imagined than described. I pictured to myself that we should be like one of our labourers, who, having gone into town just before we started up west, lost his way coming out, unharnessed his horses and picketed them, and sat down quietly, waiting for daylight before he ventured on. It is marvellous that anyone finds their way on the prairie. There are numberless trails made during the hay-

URGENT!

Thousands of nice girls are wanted in **THE CANADIAN WEST.**

Over 20,000 Men are sighing for what they cannot get–WIVES! Shame!

Don't hesitate–COME AT ONCE. If you cannot come, send your sisters.

So great is the demand that anything in skirts stands a chance.

No reasonable offer refused They are all shy but willing. All Prizes! No Blanks.

Hustle up now Girls and don't miss this chance. Some of you will never get another.

Special Application Card from

Plate 1. Women Wanted! Despite the humorous tone of this notice, its message was serious: in many newly settled districts, men might out-number women by as many as twenty to one.

Plate 2. Although these men were probably awaiting more prosaic freight, one of the enduring myths about the period involved the crowds of bride-hunting males said to congregate at prairie railway stations, like this one in Bassano, Alberta, in 1910.

Plate 3. The size of schoolbuildings and the number and ages of the children varied in the West. But the schoolteacher's role was a respected one, and farms competed for the honour of boarding her. Pictured are schoolchildren in Rife, Alberta, c. 1912–13.

Plate 4. When Mary Hall arrived, she discovered that her brother was sending his laundry into Winnipeg at three-month intervals. Ella Sykes gives a vivid picture of the more than four hours spent with the boilers, wringers, and tubs doing the weekly wash when she worked as a home-help.

Plate 5. The interior of Armstrong's store in Nanton, Alberta, 1912, with the tailoress, Mabel Smith, in the centre.

Plate 6. Because of cramped living quarters, many domestic chores, such as churning (pictured here) and washing, were done out of doors.

Plate 7. New inventions such as the typewriter and the telephone extended the range of respectable employment for young, single women beyond the jobs of nursing, schoolteaching, millinery work, and domestic service.

Plate 8. "This is all our own. England could never have given us this. We shall soon be more comfortable" was the comment received by Marion Cran from another English settler living in a log home like this one near Content, Alberta.

Plate 9. Two women homesteaders outside their first dwelling, c. 1912. Small as it is, the house is clearly more substantial than many temporary shelters erected by settlers.

harvest, which may mislead; and in a country which has been surveyed some time back, the section-posts have almost entirely disappeared, the cattle either knocking them down or they having been struck by lightning.

We found our bedroom very full of mosquitoes, so that our sleep was much disturbed, in fact we never slept properly till after the sun rose; but our letters cheered us up and were far more refreshing than ten hours' sleep.

The netting over our windows had got torn from the tacks, so that the mosquitoes had come in by shoals just to show how they appreciated the attention of having things made easy for them. Otherwise, we are not generally much bothered with them in the house, netting being over every door and window.

The cat sometimes thwarts our protection by jumping through them in the morning, and no thumpings seem to impress her with respect for the said net.

We are told the mosquitoes will be gone in a fortnight; certainly the big yellow ones have lived their time and are not so plentiful, but they have been succeeded by a small black species which is quite as venomous, and not so easy to kill.

We went to Church yesterday at Headingley: quite a red letter day. It was only the second time we have been able to manage it in the ten weeks we have been here; and though it was very hot in Church we were ashamed to take our gloves off, on account of the scars.

The Church is quite a nice little building, and the service delightful after so many weeks of not hearing it. We had to take our horse out, tie it to the church-yard paling, and put the dog in the buggy to take care of our goods and chattels.

We are getting quite low at the thoughts of leaving this in ten days' time; being rather like cats, attached to any place where one has heaps of occupation, and where one is kindly treated and well fed, however ugly that place may be.

We have been very busy haymaking since we got home, and a grand stack is in the course of erection nearly opposite the dining-room window. You never saw anything so astonishing as the way the oats, potatoes, etc., have shot up in our absence. Even the puppy, which we left a fluffy ball, seems to have grown inches. Then, all my chickens are hatched, and are an endless pleasure and anxiety. I am supposed to spend hours over them.

We have received four sheets of official paper from Mr. W———, full of directions about our journey to Colorado, describing his home, etc., even to the nickel-plated tap we shall find in his kitchen, which is to supply us with an unlimited amount of water. He tells us we need bring nothing but a saddle and a toothbrush — he will find all the rest; and that we are to make it a note that it is one of the strictest rules of mining camps that guests are never allowed to pay for anything. As we hope he is making a fortune by his mines, we shall not have so much compunction of accepting these terms. We are to sight-see, climb mountains, go into the mines, fish for trout, and do nothing the live-long day but amuse ourselves.

I am afraid A——— will miss us terribly, dear old soul! He is very fond of having us here, and is always bemoaning our departure. I think it will make a great difference to him and to his humdrum hard-working life, as we are always cheery and have never had a difficulty or annoyance of any sort.

August 6th.

We are rejoicing now that we have settled to go to the Rocky Mountains, as the hot weather we speculated on avoiding has come in with a rush, and for a whole week the thermometer has been at 80° to 85°. One morning before a thunder-storm, when it fell forty degrees in a few hours, it was up to 90°. We have had some rain, but not the heavy storms we have seen wandering round, which generally follow the course of the Assiniboine — a relief to out minds, as our hay is still out.

It has been cut nearly all round the property outside the fence, in spite of the risk one runs of having it subsequently claimed by the owner of the section, who is generally a half-breed, a loss only to be avoided by leading it home at once, which we are doing.

This has happened to our neighbour, with whom, I am afraid, we do not sympathise very keenly, as he had taken up the marsh which our men cut last year, and had the full intention of doing again this year, so they looked upon it in the light of their special property.

We have only two waggons working here, as nearly all the men and horses are gone over to Boyd's; and as our hay is a mile and a half away, we don't get much more than five loads a day, so that the stack does not grow very fast.

Our excitement this week has been a cricket match with Boyle's Farm; four of their men we challenged. It really was too amusing. They had a bat and ball, stumps, but no bales, and played on the prairie, which was so fearfully rough that it was almost dangerous, the ball shot in such various directions after hitting the tufts of grass. Everybody fielded, but a ball going into the wheat-field behind the wickets was not counted as a lost ball. The total score of the two innings was only ten, and in one our opponents went out without a single run; so you may fancy the howls of either applause or derision at every ball.

August 17th.

The Farm with all its toils and pleasures is a thing of the past; we were both very low when we turned our backs upon it and its inhabitants just a week ago. We have been in such robust health the whole of our three months, hardly a headache or finger-ache. Our maid-of-all-work life has suited us, and we have acquired such an immense deal of practical knowledge that for those reasons alone we might be gratified and pleased we came.

| *What Women Say of the Canadian North-West*
Commentary

By 1884, when Mary Hall's account of her Manitoba adventure appeared, the prairie section of the C.P.R. was complete. A year later the entire line was in operation, and the railway company was in business — not merely in transport, but also in land. The company directors marked the occasion with an upsurge of emigration propaganda designed to bring settlers into the region. Seven pamphlets were published by the C.P.R. in 1886 alone: *Free Grants of Land; Letters from Actual Settlers; Settler's Index to Golden Manitoba; Upplysninger om Manitoba; What Settlers Say of the Canadian North-West;* and finally, a forty-nine-page booklet of closely printed type entitled *What Women Say of the Canadian North-West.*

What Women Say . . . follows a common pattern in C.P.R. propaganda before the hard sell of later publicity campaigns set in. Like others of its kind in the 1870's and 1880's *(What British Emigrants Say . . .; What Actual Farmers Say . . .),* it consists almost entirely of personal testimony garnered from Northwest residents in response to a questionnaire.[1] Questions were asked on a wide range of topics deemed to be of particular interest to women readers. They included general advice to newcomers, remarks on the climate, schools, and churches, the price of provisions and clothing, the Indian question, the profitability of dairying and poultry-raising, and openings for women in domestic service and trades. The pamphlet concludes with a general question, "Are you contented?" — of 320 canvassed, so the C.P.R. claimed, all but a half dozen said they were. This pamphlet was widely distributed in Great Britain, and testimony from many respondents of English and Scots origin is included. Inevitably there is much repetition in the replies, and all but a few are too brief to be of much help in reconstructing a detailed picture of the lives of these women as settlers. Certainly it is far from clear that many of them were genteel in their social origins. Nevertheless, their combined testimony established once and for all for British readers the urgent need for more women settlers in the West, at the same time addressing issues of great practical concern in a specific, no-nonsense manner.

Responses to only six of the original questions have been reproduced here; they constitute slightly over one-third of the pamphlet as it appeared in 1886. The section on the climate and its healthfulness for children has been included because the image of the Canadian Northwest as a frozen wilderness unfit for human habitation was still dominant in the minds of outsiders. The information on dairying and poultry-raising was also of immediate practical interest to women, for it was often from these sources that settlers derived what small cash income they could count on during the difficult years of getting established. As both the contents of this pamphlet and its very issuance by the C.P.R. make clear, the labour of women was recognized from the start as essential to western settlement. What women said of the Canadian Northwest in the fall of 1885 was that they wanted more women to come: "Girls are scarce" and "We have already too many bachelors." As to their prospects for success, "That depends on themselves."

What Women Say of the Canadian North-West

With the mother, wife or sister, very often rests in a large degree the answer to the first question: "Shall we emigrate?" and also to the second question, "Where shall we make our new home?" And in order to obtain reliable answers to these questions, from actual settlers, letters were sent in the month of September, 1885, to as many women throughout the Canadian North-West as could be addressed with accuracy. No selection was made in sending out the questions, for none was possible; and in the publication of the replies on the various points, every care has been taken to preserve the thoroughly representative character of the pamphlet by giving the replies just as they were received. They tell their own story in simple but forcible language, and the public are earnestly and confidently invited to a careful perusal of what women think of our Great North-West.

SHALL THE FAMILY ACCOMPANY THE INTENDING SETTLER?

This is an important matter, the settlement of which confronts the intending settler at the outset. The question addressed on this point asked, "Would you recommend an emigrant to bring his wife and family with him, or leave them behind till he has a home ready for them?" It will be seen from the replies that many advise that the family shall accompany the new settler, as in a large number of cases they are found a comfort and an incentive to energy and speedy settlement. If the intending settler has sufficient captial to allow of his placing his family in comfortable lodgings in one of the towns or cities of the North-West while he himself is "locating" his farm and erecting comfortable quarters, then it may, in most cases, be advisable to take wife and family in the first instance. If, on the other hand, the intending settler has little or no capital, but intends, by becoming a farm hand, to assist some resident farmer, and thus gain experience and capital, it then becomes a question whether the wife and family are accustomed to farm work, or could be of assistance on a farm. If so, little difficulty should be experienced during the season in securing situations for all — it may be on one farm — and the family circle could thus be maintained until the head of the family has launched out into farming on his own account.

The most representative replies run as follows. They are written from all parts of the country as may be seen on reference to the full names and postal addresses given in the replies to subsequent questions.

Abshead, Mrs. Rachael. — "If they are used to work bring them with him, as expense will be lighter to bring all in one removal."

Anderson, Mrs. M.G. — "I should say come early in the spring (say end of March), bring wife and family; they will be of great assistance in forming a comfortable home quickly."

Ashev, Mrs. E. — "Yes, bring them, as he can rent a house in the country at very small cost, especially if some of them are old enough to be useful."

Begg, Mrs. K.S. — "Let him bring his family, but early in the Spring, so that he can have a home ready for Winter."

Bell, Mrs. Helen. — "I would recommend the wife and family to come with the father. I and eight children came with my husband.

Bethune, Mrs. A. — "If he has money enough to spare to pay for their board while he is looking around, by all means take them with him. Some women have more pluck than men, and are more anxious to get settled."

Brown, Mrs. John. — "I stayed behind, but I would prefer going along."

Brown, Mrs. (Revd.) N. — "If he has a little means it would be better for them to come together, if not, he had better come first and get a home ready."

Butcher, Mrs. G. — "I believe he should bring his wife and family if his wife be fairly healthy, and his children of pretty good size, so that one can help the other to surmount the difficulties of settlement; but come in the Spring."

Campbell, Mrs. R. — "By all means bring wife and family along, as there are too many single men here now."

Cheasley, Mrs. George. — "If the family is small, leave them; if grown up, bring them. There will be lots of work for them."

Cosgrove, Mrs. James B. — "Bring family by all means. A family arrived six weeks ago (August, 1885), from Birmingham, England, and they are well suited."

Creasar, Mrs. William. — If he has some means, he had better bring them; if not, he had better leave them for a year after he comes."

Davies, Mrs. (Revd.) P.W. — "I believe they would do just as well to bring them right along if they come as early as possible in the Spring. They can have a house and be in it before Winter."

Doyden, Mrs. A. — "I came in the Spring with my husband, and think it was the better plan."

Foley, Mrs. R.D. — "Yes, if he has means to make them comfortable, bring them."

Forbes, Mrs. G. — "Certainly, bring them along and do the best till they get a home. A house can be easily got."

Franklin, Mrs. B. — "Bring them if it is warm weather, and camp out till he can build a log-house."

Gowler, Mrs. A. — "I think it would be the best, as a house can be got for a trifle, and food is cheap and plentiful."

Gregory, Annie. — "If he intends to purchase land, bring them with him. If he intends to settle on uncultivated land, leave them behind until he has a home ready for them."

Hall, Mrs. W.B. — "In most cases a home is sooner secured by emigrating together."

Hanson, Mrs. J.D. — "According to his means. If a son and daughter came with the father they could go and work out, and learn the ways of the country, and make friends, so that when the whole family came they would not feel so lonely, and be able to show how things require to be done in the North-West."

Haney, Mrs. A.W. — "I would bring every soul of them."

Huddlestone, Mrs. T. — "My advice is, if the emigrant is a farmer, to bring his wife and family, rent a farm for a year, and look for land, leaving his family on the farm, or if an emigrant has means of support for a year, bring his family with him. House rent is low here."

Jeffery, Lavinia. — "By all means; we have already too many bachelors."

Leech, Mrs. John. — "I think a man with a small capital had better leave his family behind till he gets settled."

McDonald, Mrs. A.G. — "If he has a working family I would advise him to bring them along with him. A man cannot farm alone very well."

McKay, Mrs. (Revd.) M. — "Bring the family with him. A house can easily be secured, when a family can make a home far quicker. Or even a farm, costing next to nothing, might be rented with advantage for a year."

McKay, Mrs. Philip. — "A man should provide a home for his family before they come here. A newly married couple might come together."

McKenzie, Mrs. Jean — "I came here with my father's family from Scotland to Ontario, in 1843, and married there, and came with my husband and family here, so others can do so themselves. Plenty of work to do for them here, if willing, and plenty to eat."

McRayne, Mrs. J.A. — "Anyone having money to keep their family for six months, bring them."

Marlat, Mrs. S.R. — "Preferable, I think to bring his family and leave them in one of our large towns, as houses are plentiful, rents low, and living reasonably cheap."

Proctor, Mrs. H. — "Bring them with him; there are few difficulties now to contend with since the Canadian Pacific Railway has been opened."

Roddick, Mrs. G. — "It is better to come together, as there is difficulty now in obtaining supplies and house to rent at a moderate figure."

Rose, Mrs. H. — "If he has means to provide for them there, most decidedly bring them along, and apply that means in making a house for them here."

Stirton, Mrs. James. — "Bring them by all means. The wife is an important factor in commencing a homestead.

Sumner, Mrs. J.Q. — "If they are all willing to take a hand in making the home they should come by all means."

Sutherland, Mrs. J. — "A strong family, willing to work, should come together but each family should decide for themselves."

Whimster, Mrs. M. — "That would depend upon the means at his disposal. A man with a few boys growing up would do better to take them along with him, if possible with a little capital, and with a thrifty growing family, using strict economy, their success would be ensured."

Yeoman, Mrs. G.M. — "Bring every chick and child, unless there is some strong reason for not doing so; they will all help to pull through, and feel all the better for having done so, even if it is a severe tug. I speak from experience."

ADVICE TO NEW COMERS

The following answers are given to the request "Kindly give any advice that may be of service to incoming mothers, wives, daughters, sisters, and any practical information or any household receipt that may be of service to them." In these answers much will be found of service and value to the intending settler.

Mrs. J. Alexander, of Sourisford, Southern Manitoba — "Bring plenty of blankets and bedding, also body-clothes. A good supply of yarns is useful. Bring no furniture or kitchen furnishings."

Mrs. S. Ballantyne, of Emerson, Southern Manitoba — "Men with means or men without means who are paying rents in the old country will certainly better their condition by coming here. If poor, those of the family old enough to work will find employment, and thus aid the family in getting a start, and our Canadians are very charitable in the way of helping decent poor men to erect buildings without charge, and they also aid such in many other ways. I was born in Scotland, lived there till I was 21 years of age, and emigrated to the Province of Quebec, lived there over two years, came to Ontario, lived on a farm 18 years, in the city 14 years, and in Manitoba over 8 years, and should know of what I speak, and I must say without fear of contradiction, or an attempt at such, by any person who has lived in Manitoba, that for soil, climate, weather and delightful seasons, it stands unrivalled by any country yet known. Our present fall weather cannot be equalled in any country on the globe."

Mrs. N. Bartley, of Wattsview. — "Plenty of good, warm clothing, also bedding, dishes, knives and forks, and any useful article (such as a sewing machine if a good one) that can be packed easily, instead of disposing of it for a trifle, as is generally the way when setting out and leaving their homes."

Mrs. E. Beesley, of Marlborough, near Moose Jaw. — "Would wish all to come who are willing to work. They will soon make for themselves and families comfortable homes, and will be independent, as there is plenty of good land to be easily obtained. It is a healthy climate. I can write from experience, as I came myself in poor health, and since settling here have enjoyed the best of health, and have not paid one cent for medicine."

Mrs. A. Bethune, of Archibald, Southern Manitoba — "Families should first husband their finances to the greatest extent possible, only buying for the first year or two those articles they cannot possibly do without, and don't pay anybody for anything you can do yourself. Be sure your farm is high and dry before you spend a dollar on it. On arrival, get your garden planted with the necessary vegetable seeds, look after your garden well, have your cellar frost-proof, get a few little pigs from your neighbours, and buy nothing that you can raise, buy a cow and feed her well, and if you don't get along well in Manitoba you won't do so anywhere else, I'll assure you."

Mrs. N. Brown (Rev.) of High Bluff, Man. — "This is a splendid country for industrious people, but every one coming here should know how to work. There is nothing here that I consider any drawback to people who wish to make a good home for themselves. Of course they must not expect the same luxuries and social advantages of older countries. Although the winter here is very cold, yet the air is dry and healthy, and (although 25 years of age when I left England, and consequently knowing all about it) I prefer the winters here to those in England."

Mrs. E. Butcher, of Glendinning, Man. — "All the advice I can give to those coming out is not to expect too much the first or second year, but with industry and perseverance, a contented disposition, and a willingness to be cheerful under any difficulties that may arise, and in the course of a few years any family can make themselves a comfortable home. I suppose the cold winter is the greatest objection intending emigrants have to Manitoba. I have now been here four winters, but neither myself nor children have suffered from the cold. We have a comfortable log house, and our stove keeps up and downstairs warm. It is now the 9th of November (1885), and we ploughed up to the 3rd; last year we ploughed until the 16th. I have not felt the cold more than in Ontario, in which country I was born and raised, although we have more degrees of frost; the air being drier, the cold does not seem to penetrate as much. I have been out riding with the thermometer 25 degrees below zero and in a blinding snowstorm, yet did not suffer from cold. Of course I was well and warmly clothed."

Mrs. G. Butcher, of Russell P.O., Shell River, Man. — "Don't be prejudiced in your minds in favour of English methods of cooking, baking, washing, etc., or be too proud to ask advice when you come. You will find new methods here more suited to the country and your altered circumstances. Every housekeeper here learns to be a baker, laundress, tailoress, soap and candle maker, and dairy-woman. New settlers can be taken by the hand by earlier arrivals, and information, receipts, etc., are freely tendered to those desirous of learning. There is great social freedom amongst settlers, so that it would be superfluous to give any recipes. Learn to knit, bring plenty of good woolen underclothing, fishermen's knitted jerseys and boys' good tweed suits. Boys' clothing here is difficult to obtain."

Mrs. S. Chambers, of Birtle, Man. — "Provide yourselves with warm substantial clothing for the winter, strong boots, etc. Do not burden yourselves with heavy articles of furniture. Our houses are small, and all that is necessary can be procured here. I have kept tender house plants blooming in the winter here. The summers are delightful."

Mrs. A.C. Clarke, of West half of Sec. 34, Tp. 1, Range 15 West, Cartwright. — "I would advise mothers and wives to bring lots of girls with them. Daughters and sisters come prepared to go housekeeping for some poor bachelor."

Mrs. C.C. Clitten, of Bird's Hill. — "To women settling in the country would suggest that they pay some attention to gardening, and bring seeds with them; all the small fruits grow in great perfection here. Make a point of setting out raspberries, currants, and strawberries, as soon as possible, these all grow wild here and of very fine flavour, and they also add so much to the comfort of the home. Native hops and grapes are here, and I am told that the cultivated cherry and fine plum do well here planted in bluffs only enough cleared for their growth, the native trees protecting them till they get their growth, then clear away from them."

Mrs. W. Cooper, of Treherne. — "If you intend to help to farm — 1. Bring good, warm, strong, serviceable clothing; study comfort in clothing, more than fashion. 2. If your husband's means are small, be sure to do your utmost to have a cow, some chickens and pigs. 3. Lend a helping hand to the men not supposing it is out of a woman's sphere as the first year brings lots of extra work on the men. 4. Pay as you go, if possible. 5. Bring a few simple medicines with you, or procure them in town, before going in the country on your farm."

Mrs. P.W. Davies (Rev.), of Chater. — "Do not come thinking to have a fortune in a year or so. Many have come expecting this; some have succeeded in it, others have been disappointed. Too many come expecting to commence here just where they left off in some other country where perhaps their parents or friends have been years working away to get the home they are leaving. Of course they will be disappointed, for they cannot have everything at their hands just as they have in old settled places. But come determined that, with the blessing of God, you will have a home for yourself and children, and do not be above work, but rather willing to turn your hand to any respectable work that may present itself, and there is sure success."

Mrs. D.G. Dick, of Dominion City. — "Do not come expecting to find a Paradise. Eve was the only woman that found one, and she was not contented in it."

Mrs. J.D. Hanson, of Oakland Park, Turtle Mountain. — "Bring warm flannels and long stockings or socks — any quantity. Canton flannel garments keep out the wind well, but this clothing is rarely required. Thick strong boots and cork soles, cloth slippers, rubber cloaks and coats, shawls, scarfs and mitts. Chamois leather vests made long over hips, and ulsters lined with chamois or rubber to the waist. Blankets, light and dark colour; railway rugs, warm. Feather beds, if accustomed to them; pillows, leaving out one for each traveller. Bring all kinds of yarn, particularly coarse for socks. For the greatest comfort on a long railroad journey from the sea to the North-West, I would also suggest one or two paper basins, soap, flannel, sponge, towel, comb, brush, small looking glass, etc., put in a bag. Also an extra bag, strong and dark, handy to put in extra things quickly when the train stops before you are quite prepared to leave, and a strap to fasten it with quickly and securely. Each one of course with a shawl and strap, slippers and soft head covering for night, and the pillow can be strapped in shawl. Drinking vessels, and a large mug to convey water safely on cars to your seat. A pound of tea steeped in a quart of water is most refreshing, and easily bottled and diluted; carry sugar, and buy milk at stations and bread and butter also. Strong boxes or packing cases with handles, and well corded to stand long journey and rough handling. Barrels, useful for packing crockery and glassware, and valuables and pictures, thus making a home-like feeling around you at once. Men's underwear best bought here, as being thicker and made suitable to the climate. Good whips and raw hide lashes invaluable in the North-West."

Mrs. A.B. Harris, of Beulah, Manitoba. — "Insist upon getting a good, warm house up the first thing. Bring plenty of warm bed-clothes and flannel clothing. I would suggest that a man should spend his first summer putting up buildings, digging a well, and getting everything into shape for his wife and family. He will save time in the long run. A cold house and no water when it is wanted will make a smiling face look sour and makes her a grumbler."

Mrs. P. Hyde, of Silver Creek. — "As I came from the old country myself, I think for the working class this country is far ahead of the old country."

Mrs. D. Hysop, of Killarney, Manitoba. — "I should suggest that new comers bring a stock of medicines that have been habitually used in the family, as the doctor is difficult always to obtain and his charges are high, and a good stock of warm clothing for winter; also that they obtain a thorough knowledge of bread-making, as that is one of the most important parts of housekeeping out here, because the air is bracing and the appetites good."

Annie Johnston, of Mowbray, Manitoba — "Women as a rule are timid in breaking up their home. I, for one, thought my real happiness gone when we pulled up stakes and started for this country; but on arriving here I found my thoughts were all imaginary, as real happiness commenced here. The thought of having homes for our boys beside us, and keeping our girls at home busily engaged in butter and cheese making, and surrounded by their family, is a great comfort to father and mother. There is plenty of remunerative work for all on their own farm."

Mrs. Kate Lawrence, of Clearwater. — "All I have to say is that there is plenty of homes and situations for all in this country, and no one need be afraid to come if they intend to work, for the old saying is a true one, even in this country,
'Where there's a will, there's a way,'
or rather
'We've plenty of work and good pay.' "

Mrs. Mary Lowe, of Ste. Agathe. — "I have known several Scotch girls who came here some years ago. They are all married, and some of them have done extra well. Smart clean girls can do better here than men."

Alice McConwick, of Fleming, N.W.T. — "Come prepared to farm. Get stock as you can. This is a beautiful place to live in. Bring all you can with you, such as clothes, lots of bedclothes. There were people here yesterday from England; they think there is nothing to hinder people from being rich here."

Mrs. N. McGregor, of Dalton. — "Mothers, do not fret too much. Wives, do your best to help your husbands to make the new home. Daughters, do not wear too much finery, and stick to the young men. Sisters, judge for yourselves; there are plenty of fine single men in this part to keep you smiling all the time."

Mrs. McInnes, of Calgary P.O., Alberta, N.W.T. — "I can give no household receipt, as such can easily be obtained here. I found no difficulty in obtaining anything that I required. As for myself, I am well pleased with the country. Should anyone desire to come to this district, they will find beautiful sections yet vacant."

Mrs. Jean McKenzie, of Burnside, Man. — "Keep cheerful; don't grumble at a few little inconveniences which may occur at first settling; help your husbands and brothers as much as possible, both in work and cheerful advice, and you will soon find yourselves and them in comfortable circumstances, and proprietors of farms with plenty of stock around you, with the finest of wheat and other grains and vegetables of all kinds growing for you. But above all, keep as much as possible out of debt, buy no luxury of any kind on credit that you can do without, and you will soon be prosperous and happy. No rent to pay, and no landowner to turn you out at expiration of lease. Plenty of good land can be got here at low price, and every thrifty man and woman can be their own proprietor."

Mr. A. Johnston, c/o Mr. John Pollock, of Wolf Creek. — "If you have any young girls in your country who would like to start housekeeping, this is the place to come. There are lots of young men who want housekeepers. I would like to give over the job of washing the dishes myself."

Mrs. L. Poyntz, c/o Geo. Armstrong, Esq., Dalton P.O. — "Will be pleased to inform or instruct any such on personal application."

Mrs. Hannah Proctor, of Woodlands P.O., Man. — "Any man or woman of industrious habits, wishing to come here with a view of bettering their position, can do well. If they do not do well, the fault rests with themselves. For example: I have had 14 children to provide for. Up to date, our farm has 100 acres under plough, also 100 sheep, 100 head of cattle, pigs, poultry, and farm machinery and implements, with two yoke of oxen, two teams of horses, which my husband states, taking the stock at fair value, and other articles at cost price, are worth over 12,000 dollars (£2,400), all paid for, with a reasonable amount in the bank. Also a farm of 640 acres, with house and buildings, and other improvements, for which my husband states he would not accept any sum less than 20,000 dollars (£4,000) with many thanks, at present. Compare this with our arrival in 1873, in Winnipeg, with absolutely nothing, for we were provisioned at the expense of the Government till we found employment; and with patience and perseverance, and the industrious habits of the whole family, we have honourably attained our present position to-day; and let me with confidence, say to persons of the right kind, 'Come thou and do likewise.' "

Susan Rhind, of Westbourne, Man. — "They must learn how to bake bread, and keep their spirits up under any little difficulties that may arise. I have kept flowers in the house every winter. If they have singing birds, pets or pictures, bring them."

Mrs. F. Robbie, Birtle P.O. Man. — "Keep your eyes open. Live within your means. Take no notice of grumblers. Make ready for winter. Let the children wear woollen underclothing. Take in the *Nor' West Farmer,* and a weekly newspaper. Settle near a railroad if possible. Go in for mixed farming. Never blame the country for any misfortune you may have. Have a good garden. Exhibit all you can at the Fall shows. Determine that the North West is to be your home."

Mrs. H. Rose, of Minnedosa, Man. — "I would merely suggest that persons having any of musical instruments should bring them if possible; also that girls earning money be very careful who they lend it to, and I think the better way is to put it in some safe bank as soon as it is earned."

Mrs. J.M. Sutherland, of Virden. — "Any one coming with a family needs money enough to keep them for a year least. If they are willing to work, and are not afraid of any kind of work such as milking cows, attending poultry, etc., there is no need to fear that they can make a home here. Bring all your warm clothing. The winter is certainly cold, but healthful and pleasant."

Mrs. J. Taylor, of Headingley. — "Mothers, come with a determination to better your circumstances, and be prepared to meet what disadvantages must necessarily come to you in a new country like this, and you will soon better your circumstances."

Mrs. S. Taylor, Parkisimo, Man. — "Daughters which have been raised to farming need little advice. Others coming to Manitoba can get assistance from older settlers, who are always ready to advise new comers if asked. In our settlement we have a good class of people for that."

Mrs. R.P. Thompson, of Miami P.O., Man. — "They will all want to make up their mind to meet with some disadvantages and difficulties, and to make up their minds to overcome them, and accommodate themselves to their new home. All should come with means enough to buy one or two cows and a few hens, which will soon bring in quite a portion of the living, then in a year or two, they, by careful management, will have some poultry, eggs, butter &c. to sell, and there is always a ready sale for such produce at fair price. I sold a lot of spring chickens at the door a few days ago for 40 cents (1s. 8d.), per pair, and geese for 3 dollars (12s.) per pair. If I can be of any service in giving any information of any kind to intending immigrants, I gladly offer to do so, as I am well aware of the overcrowded state of the old country, especially in the cities. As to any one coming to this part (Miami), I will undertake to help them to find a suitable house. There are places here to rent on easy terms, with buildings, where families could move right in. Then there is a lot of good land to be sold at five dollars (£1) per acre, and some for less. I could find homes for eight or ten good girls on farms at from five to eight dollars (£1 to £1 12s.), per month, according to ability, etc."

Mrs. S.J. Wheatland, of Donore, Manitoba. — "Before making up your mind to come to Manitoba, sit down and consider well whether you can forego the comforts you have been used to for a while, and whether you can stand the isolation from society that you will have to undergo for a time if you contemplate farming in the North-West. Of course all these things will be different if you have money to purchase a farm in a settled part of the country. If you can answer these questions satisfactorily to yourselves, then I think you come and consider that you are safe to get along. Of course, we have had several bad seasons, still, I have good faith in the country, and with the experience we have had we might be able to battle with the seasons successfully. I would recommend mixed farming as most suitable to the country. I do not trust to grain, but keep some cow, poultry, and other stock; pigs are also profitable, and will help to fill the purse and improve the farm."

Mrs. G.U. White, of Foxton. — "I think this is a good country for any person who is willing to work. One of our neighbours came here and had only 45 dollars (£9) when he landed in Winnipeg. He is now in a good position."

CLIMATE

The climate of any country is a matter of importance to an intending settler in that country. It will be seen by a study of the following representative answers that the climate throughout summer and winter is healthy and agreeable for men, women, and children. The questions asked were:—

(1) How does the climate of the North-West suit you, and do you consider it healthy?

(2) Is the climate healthy for children, and will you kindly offer any suggestions to new comers on this point?

Mrs. J. Alexander, of Sourisford, Man. — "1. Admirably. I consider it extremely healthy. 2. They grow like mushrooms. Our children have not had any illness all these years."

Mrs. T. Alexander, of Lowestoft, Man. — "1. Well. Very healthy. 2. Very healthy for children. They need plenty of warm clothing."

Mrs. M.G. Anderson, of Grenfell, Assa., N.W.T. "My health has improved, and I consider the climate very bracing and exceptionally healthy. 2. The climate is decidedly healthy for children. My experience recommends that intending immigrants, both young and old, should be well supplied with flannel underclothing for winter and summer use."

Mrs. S.J. Batcock, of Brookwood Farm, Orange Ridge P.O., Man. — "I don't think there is a healthier country in the world. I have had the best of health. 2. There cannot possibly be a more healthy country for children. Mine have scarcely had a day's sickness. Plenty of warm clothing and wholesome food is all they need."

Mrs. E. Beesley, of Marlborough, near Moose Jaw, Assa., N.W.T. — "1. Suits me well. I consider it very healthy. 2. Yes. We were often sick before residing here; now we could not be more healthy."

Mrs. K.S. Begg, of Fort Garry P.O. — "1. The climate is healthy, both for natives and emigrants; more so than Scotland. My husband is Scotch, and ought to know."

Mrs. A. Bell, of Portage la Prairie. — "1. The atmosphere being so dry, I experience more vigour and vitality than I used to . 2. Exceedingly so; less sickness among them than in other climates."

Mrs. Helen Bell, of Burnside. — "1. It is pretty cold in winter, but very healthy. 2. It is very healthy for children."

Mrs. R. Blight, of Fort Ellice. — "1. I think it a healthy climate. 2. As far as I know, I have not seen any but healthy children here, and in one case I know a child who was delicate before she came here, and is quite robust now."

Mrs. A. Bole, of Regina, N.W.T. — "1. I like the climate well, and consider it very healthy. 2. Children coming from any of the countries of Europe get very fleshy."

Mrs. T. Bowman, of Greenwood, Manitoba. — "1. It could not possibly be more healthy. It is very cold in winter, but a dry cold; it does not thaw and then freeze. 2. It is, if they are warmly clothed in winter. It is very healthy for any consumptive people."

Mrs. A.J. Bridgman, of Medicine Hat, N.W.T. — "1. I love the climate and consider it very healthy. 2. I have one boy eleven months old, who has never been sick a day."

Mrs. Elizabeth Broadguest, of Turtle Mountain. — "1. Have never been in better health, and the climate is perfect as far as sickness is concerned. 2. I have eight children, three of whom have been born here; none of them have been ill at all, and we have never had a doctor inside the house professionally."

Mrs. R.J. Brooks, of Asessippi, Manitoba. — "1. I like the climate. 2. Very much so. My children were very delicate in Ontario, but have been very healthy since I came here."

Mrs. E. Brown, of Drumconner P.O. — "1. I was delicate in Ontario, but since I came to Manitoba my health has been good. 2. It is all that could be desired."

Mrs. N. Brown (Rev.) of High Bluff, Manitoba. — "1. I consider it very healthy, and like it well. Never had as good health anywhere else as I have had here. 2. Yes, it is decidedly healthy for children, but parents coming here should provide them with warm clothing."

Mrs. G. Butcher, of Russell P.O., Shell River, Manitoba. — "1. The weather, I find, tires me, especially the strong winds and thunder, but I am weak and nervous. I consider it a healthy country. 2. My six children have enjoyed the best of health since coming here. The eldest, a lad of 16, was subject to asthma when in England; he is now perfectly free from the complaint. I believe this climate to be well suited to the health of children."

Mrs. R. Campbell, of Bridge Creek. —" 1. Very healthy. 2. I have a family of seven children, and they have never had any sickness since we came here to live."

Mrs. J. Chester, of Otenaw, P.O., Southern Manitoba. — "1. The climate is good, and I consider it very healthy. 2. When I came to Manitoba, I brought three delicate children; they have become strong and healthy."

Mrs. Fannie Clark, of Two Rivers, Man. — "1. The climate of the N.W. suits me perfectly. 2. It is considered very healthy for children. It is very seldom a child's death is heard of."

Mrs. C.C. Clitten, of Bird's Hill, Manitoba. — "1. Admirably. I consider it very healthy. 2. Particularly healthful for children. I know of delicate children walking two miles and a half to school every day, and have not had a day's sickness since coming here."

Mrs. W. Copeland, of Richmond P.O. — "1. It is the healthiest I ever was in; no rain in the fall, and no mud. It is a little cold in winter. 2. When we came to this country, we had a boy we expected to die with asthma, but he has never had it since."

Margaret Corrett, of Springfield. — "1. I consider it very healthy, and not at all unpleasant. 2. I think the climate must be good on that point (children), for I don't see any lack."

Mrs. P.W. Davies (Rev.), of Chater P.O., Man. — "1. I am delighted with the climate, and consider it very healthy. 2. I think it is, and can give my own experience. I have five children, and both my husband, my children, and myself have better health than for several years before coming to this country."

Mrs. A. Doyden, of Ste. Agathe. — "1. Summer I think splendid: the winter is cold, but dry and healthy. 2. The climate is good for children. We have four, and have never required to call a doctor since we came to live here."

Mrs. W.A. Doyle, of Beulah. — "1. I do not like it as well as that of Ontario, but I think it is quite as healthy. 2. For children I find it to be a very favourable climate. We have a family of four, all as strong as could be wished."

Mrs. R. Downie, of Crystal City, Rock Lake Co. — "1. Yes, most decidedly so; the climate suits me quite well; lots of sunshine. 2. I think there is no healthier climate known than this for children. In summer nice bright warm days, and scarcely any spring. Winter turns into summer quickly, leaving little time for the breeding of diseases. Winter is clear, cold, and very healthy."

Mrs. M.M. Drury, of Rapid City. — "1. Admirably; my health has improved very much since I have come here. Yes, very healthy. 2. Decidedly so. They should have plain clothing and wholesome food with plenty of open air exercise in summer; a good warm house, plenty of instructive books, and keep them indoors only when cold in winter. There is no fear of epidemics."

Mrs. A.M. Duenning, of the Anglo-American Hotel, Emerson. — "1. It suits me, as also my husband, very well. Two to three years ago, I suffered very much with rheumatism here, which I got through a severe cold in hunting after my cows in the evening in the fall, through long wet grass and bush, but am entirely recovered. 2. Very healthy; only I believe men, women, and children ought to wear underflannels, winter and summer."

Mrs. R. Dunamore, of Bridge Creek. — "1. Healthy. 2. As far as my experience goes it is very healthy for children. In Ontario our doctor's bill each year was from 30 to 50 dollars, but since coming here they have not cost us a dollar."

Mrs. J.M. Fee, of Melgund. — "1. I like it well, and consider it healthy. My mother, who is over 70, lives with me, and likes it. 2. Yes, healthy for children; bring all you can of them."

Mrs. R. Findlay, of Shoal Lake. — "1. It suits me splendidly; is exceedingly healthy. 2. We have six children, and we have never had a professional call from a doctor yet."

Mrs. S. Finn, of Morris. — "1. The climate is not disagreeable by any means. The winter is cold, but healthy. 2. I know of no country more healthy. Bracing atmosphere is just the thing for young people with weak lungs, and this is free from humidity."

Mrs. Flott, of Strathclair. — "1. Very healthy. 2. Yes, but children should be well wrapped up in winter, and allowed to play out in the snow on all fine days, as the snow is quite dry and powdery."

Mrs. C.H. Freeman, of Elkhorn. — "1. It suits me very well, although the winter is very long and severe, and I consider it healthy. 2. The climate is very healthy for children; I hear every one speak of their children being so healthy here, and I think I can speak well of this country for myself, for I was ailing for four years in Ontario, and I am now well and hearty."

Mrs. L. Gartz, of Red Deer, Alberta, N.W.T.— "1. The finest climate I have ever lived in. 2. Have not had a day's illness in a family of eleven."

Mrs. E.J. Gibson, of Wanche P.O. (Tp. 5, R. 22, Sec. 26), Selkirk Co. — "1. I am pleased with the climate, and consider it very healthy. Mr. Gibson had to give up business because of poor health, and he is here as well as anyone. 2. The climate could not be better for children. I have known some that were delicate who since coming here have grown strong and healthy."

Mrs. A. Gregory, of Ninga P.O., Turtle Mountain. — "1. Suits me well; consider it very healthy. 2. Yes, healthy enough. Let them have plenty of outdoor life; no fear of them taking cold as in England."

Mrs. A.W. Haney, of Wolf Creek P.O., Wolseley, N.W.T. — "1. Splendidly. 2. It is; it far exceeds Ontario, and is indeed very prolific. There is scarcely a house where there is not a baby in it."

Mrs. W. Henderson, of Rounthwaite P.O. — "1. Suits some well, but rather cold sometimes, although healthy. 2. My own children were puny and delicate when I came here; now they are robust and healthy."

Mrs. R.C. Hodnett, of Birtle. — "1. Is healthy, certainly; a little severe in the depth of winter, but very agreeable most of the year."

Mrs. J. Honeyman, of Eden, Beautiful Plains, Man. — "1. Extremely healthy; I have good health, and am entirely free from headaches, which I used to be subject to in the old country. 2. I have never seen more healthy children than there are here."

Mrs. J. Hunter, of Neepawa. — "1. The climate is clear, and very healthy in winter; clear and cold; there are no thaws. 2. I think the climate is healthful for children; some days in winter they are not able to go out — that is, small children. Our eldest boy and girl went to school all last winter."

Lavinia Jeffery, of Minnedosa (Sec. 22, T. 13, R. 18 W), Manitoba. — "1. The N.W. is considered very healthy, and particularly so for me, having a weak chest. 2. Children do well in this country, and the man who brings the largest family will be likely to become the most prosperous, provided he can bring a little capital as well."

Anne Johnson, of Mowbray. — "1. I am well satisfied with the climate, as it is not so changeable as in Ontario, and I consider it very healthy. 2. The North-West is very healthy for children; you seldom hear of a child being ill, and not one death in this neighborhood since I came five years ago."

Mrs. J.H.L. Joslyn (Rev.) of Broadview P.O., Assa, N.W.T.— "1. Climate is fair and healthy. 2. Healthful for children, but all garments should be woollen, not cotton, and if possible furs."

Mrs. M. Lowe, of Ste. Agathe. — "1. I was delicate owing to dampness in

Ontario, and subject to colds, but the dry air here has given me splendid health. 2. I have five children, and they have enjoyed the best of health so far. As the snow is dry in winter, they are not subject to colds from wet feet, etc."

Mrs. L. McDermot, of Dundee P.O., Manitoba. — "1. Suits me well, and consider it very healthy; very little illness. 2. Very healthy for children. I have three; they have never had an hour's illness, with exception of colds."

Margaret McGill, of Carolton. — "1. Cold, but pleasant and healthy. (30th October — there were traces of a shower of rain last night, the only rain for the last two months, I did not see or hear it.). 2. Singularly and exceptionally healthy for children and adults. Comers must obey circumstances when they come."

Mrs. J. McIntyre, of Milton Farm, Regina, N.W.T. — "1. I like the climate, and consider it healthy. 2. It is the country for children. One of our little boys was so delicate in Ontario (15 months ago) we thought the journey would kill him, but every day since we came here he has grown better, and is now strong and healthy."

Mrs. M. McKay, (Rev.), Straithclair P.O. — "1. Find summer delightful and winter cold, though healthy, and yet not as hard to endure as the cold of poverty. 2. Very healthy. Only three or four funerals within 20 miles of us since arrival (summer of 1882); yet winter demands plenty of warm clothing."

Mrs. R. McKay, of Crystal City. — "1. Warmer in winter and a little cooler in summer some days would suit me better. 2. Very healthy for the parents. No fear for the children. Just see them at meal time."

Mrs. J.A. McRayne of Sourisford. — "1. It suits me better than Ontario and I consider it very healthy. 2. Very healthy for children. I had an idea before I came here that infants could not live here, it was so cold; but it is just the place for them."

Mrs. B. Marshall, of Ardpatrick P.O. — "1. I like it, and consider it very healthy. 2. Very healthy. Some of my children were subject to croup and other diseases peculiar to children but since I came to Manitoba it has entirely left them."

Mrs. M. Ogltree, of Portage la Prairie. — "1. Am much pleased with the climate; have not used 25 cents' worth of medicine since coming to the country. 2. Never had the pleasure of raising any children; have grown-up step-children. I think there is not as much sickness amongst children in this country as in Ontario."

Mrs. J. Parr, of Bradwardine, Man. — "I think the climate very nice, and believe it is very healthy. 2. I have five children, and they have never cost me one dollar since I came here. They should have warm underclothing."

Mrs. T.F. Purdy, of Regina (Sec. 12, Tp. 21, R. 19), N.W.T. — "1. Like it well; it is very healthy. 2. Children grow immensely, and are healthy with plenty to eat and warm clothes. I have been here four years, and have never seen a child ill."

Matilda Ramsey, of Stuartburn, Man. — "1. Consider it the healthiest in the world, as there is no form of disease peculiar to this climate. In this respect I consider it unequalled. 2. Judging from the children I see round me, I think it is, as I have rarely seen a sick child. I would suggest that each family should provide a good supply of warm clothing, as our winters are cold."

Mrs. E. Robb, of Calgary, Alberta, N.W.T. — "1. I consider it particularly healthy. 2. My little boy, seven years old, has never had a day's sickness in the North West."

Mrs. A. Robertson, of Erinview, Stonewall. — "1. Very well; I consider it very healthy. 2. Very healthy, but they must wear high, long-sleeved dresses, and long stockings instead of socks."

Mrs. E. Rounthwaite, of Rounthwaite P.O., Man. — "1. Well, it is very healthy. 2. It is particularly healthy for children; ours have not ailed at all."

Mrs. J. Rutherford, of Silver Creek P.O. — "1. Suits me well; I was in bad health before I came to the North-West; have had the best of health ever since. 2. Very healthy. All sickly people and children improve very much by coming out to this country."

Mrs. A. Scott, of Portage la Prairie. — "1. Well. It is healthy; the winter is cold, but with comfortable clothing it is very enjoyable. 2. Very healthy; children grow like weeds."

Mrs. J.A. Senecal, of St. François Xavier P.O. — "1. Climate is agreeable, and very healthy. 2. My children have been in the best of health ever since I came to the country, and I believe the climate beneficial to all children as long as they are properly clad for the seasons."

Mrs. H. Shaw, of Midnapore, Calgary, N.W.T. — "Climate very healthy, and winters within 50 miles of the Rockies by no means severe. 2. Could not be healthier. Having eight children, I speak from experience."

Mrs. O.M.H. Shuman, of Whitemouth. — "1. Very well; and it is very healthy. I have not been ill since I have been in the North-West. 2. My little girl has always been healthy and strong. Children with plenty of outdoor exercise soon become very rugged and strong."

Mrs. C.B. Slater, of Wapella, Assa., N.W.T. — "1. Excellently; exceedingly healthy. 2. Yes, healthy."

Mrs. R.H. Smith, of Ninette, Man. — "1. Climate here is better than in Ontario, and I consider it healthy. 2. I have been three years in this place, and only know of two deaths in the settlement. With plenty of good food and clothing children are all right."

Mrs. W. Smith, of Almasippi, P.O. — "1. I like it well, and it is very healthy. 2. My children were very delicate before we came here, but they have been very healthy since."

Mrs. R.T. Stead, of Cartwright, P.O., Chesterville, Man. — "1. December, January and February rather cold, but the remainder of the year lovely; I think the country very healthful. 2. The climate is all that could be desired for children."

Mrs. H.L. Stewart, of Meadow Lea P.O., Man. — "1. Very well. Yes. 2. Yes, very. I have a large family, and all have been remarkably healthy since we came to Manitoba, particularly myself, as I used to suffer from rheumatism."

Mrs. J.G. Sturgeon, of Stockton, Man. — "1. In ordinary circumstances very healthy. Three doctors at different times have failed to make a living in our district. 2. Yes, children born and raised in this country are strong and sturdy."

Mrs. J. Sutherland, of Kildonan East. — "1. Exceedingly healthy, even more so than the Eastern Provinces, where I have had one winter's experience. 2. Quite healthful; children do not require any different treatment from that practised in Great Britain or the United States. I raised a family of 11 children to man and woman's estate."

Mrs. E. Weighman, of West Hall, Man. (formerly of Edinburgh, Scotland). — "1. I have better health than when in Scotland; there is very little sickness around here. 2. My youngest girl, aged ten was delicate when I settled; she is now much stronger. I find the children very healthy all round; care should be taken in the shape of warm underflannel for winter use."

Mrs. J.M. Wellwood (Rev.), of Minnedosa. — "1. As far as my experience goes as a minister's wife, it is very healthy, except for bronchial and rheumatic affections. 2. Yes. Give them stout boots and warm clothing, with plenty to eat, and they will get on."

Mrs. Amelia B. Wenman, of Souris, P.O. — "1. Suits us all; is enjoyable, and very healthy. Of course the winters are cold, but bright and cheerful. 2. I have never had any cause to think this climate is not healthy for children — indeed I think with common sense people need have nothing to fear. I recommend flannel to wear."

Miss Charlotte Whitcomb, of Craigilea P.O. — "1. Summers are pleasant and suit me. I consider it extremely healthy. 2. The climate is decidedly healthy for children. Children suffering from pulmonary diseases would benefit by living in Manitoba."

Mrs. Wright, of Beaconsfield P.O. — "1. It suits me very well. 2. Children here are the picture of good health."

Mrs. Elizabeth Yeskey, of Pleasant Home, Lisgar County. — "1. The climate suits us better than any other we have tried; we prepare for the cold, and find it very healthy. 2. We find plenty of wholesome food and warm clothing is all the medicine children need in Manitoba or the North-West.

DAIRYING AND POULTRY RAISING

The richness of the natural grasses of the Canadian North-West is now happily being taken more advantage of among farmers. Where formerly the only method of farming was growth of cereals, may now also be seen the general adoption of stock-raising, for which the country is so obviously adapted. Much greater attention is in consequence being paid to dairy farming, and as will be seen by the following replies, the pursuit is generally successful and profitable. Poultry is very generally kept among farmers, and with every success. Fowls are, as might be expected, the most numerous, and are in many instances, according to Professor Fream's report, kept in very large flocks. Turkeys, geese, and ducks are also profitably maintained. Special means are, of course, necessary for housing in winter, for which either underground houses or cattle sheds are used, and this being done no losses are reported. The cheapness of bird food and demand for eggs are other inducements to poultry raising. The questions asked were: —

(1) Do you consider the North-West a good country for producing butter and cheese?

(2) How do poultry thrive, and are they profitable?

Mrs. W.E. Abbott. — "1. Excellent. 2. Well; I have a large poultry yard."

Mrs. G.M. Anderson. — "1. Both butter and cheese are produced of excellent quality. The country offers splendid openings for experienced dairy farmers. 2. Poultry thrive well and are very profitable. Eggs, 8d. to 1s. 3d. per dozen; dressed poultry, 8d. to 10d. per pound."

Mrs. J. Armstrong. — "1. There is a good deal of butter made here (Smith's Hill), but not much cheese. 2. Poultry thrive well, but require great attention."

Mrs. E. Beesley. — "1. Yes; excellent. 2. Thrive well and very profitable. Eggs 2 cents each all the summer."

Mrs. K.S. Begg. — "1. First rate as a dairying country; could not be beaten anywhere. 2. Poultry thrive well, and are very profitable. Geese, ducks, turkeys and hens pay well."

Mrs. J.M. Blythe. — "1. Yes. Excellent cheese, equal to rich Cheshire. 2. Very well, if the poultry are housed well in winter; give little trouble."

Mrs. A.J. Bridgman. — "1. Yes, first-class. I have made the most beautiful butter I ever saw or tasted. 2. Yes, poultry thrive and do well."

Mrs. E. Broadguest. — "1. First class in Southern Manitoba. I know for a certainty more can be produced per cow than I have ever known before. 2. Poultry do very well, and prices for them are very high."

Mrs. J. Brunt. — "1. I think there is no better country in the world, it is far ahead of Ontario for butter. 2. Poultry are about the most profitable thing we have, and they thrive very well.

Mrs. E. Butcher. — "1. Excellent. Cows give more milk than in Ontario, and with our luxuriant grasses make better butter. 2. Poultry do well and profitably."

Mrs. G. Butcher. — "1. I think the dairying industry will be the great work of this country. 2. Poultry thrive well. They require care in winter. They are one of the most profitable investments we have. We began with six chickens in 1882, now we have 80 hens."

Mrs. J. Carvers. — "1. I do; in fact, I think the natural grasses of the prairie far ahead of the same food, even of Ontario, for producing rich milk and splendid butter. 2. First-rate; can raise any amount of poultry. They are very profitable indeed."

Mrs. J.K. Champion. — "I consider it excellent, both are of the best quality. 2. Thrive well; I have chickens hatched 11th June weighing now (October) 5 lbs. (four months old)."

Mrs. J. Connell. — "1. Yes, it far beats Ontario on account of the cool evenings. 2. Poultry thrive and pay well if they have a warm place in winter."

Mrs. J.B. Cosgrove. — "1. The best in the world. The butter is, without doubt, superior to Ontario. 2. I bought one pair of Spanish hens, and this year raised 70 chickens (three summers)."

Mrs. Emma Cowlord. — "1. Yes. 2. They thrive well, but are not profitable on bush farms."

Mrs. J.W. Davidson. — "1. There is no better country in the world. On an average 8 lbs. of milk to 1 lb. of cheese. 2. There is no trouble in raising poultry here."

Mrs. W.A. Doyle. — "Yes, decidedly. It cannot be surpassed for that, provided those who undertake the dairy farming business understand it and are particular."

Mrs. M.M. Drury. — "1. A first-class country for dairy farming and produce. 2. Well; I have 150 fowls, they are very profitable. Eggs readily find a market at Rapid City or Brandon."

Mrs. G. Forres. — "1. Certainly it can't be beaten if people go the right way to work; the grasses are of the best, the climate good. 2. Poultry thrive well; plenty of eggs and hay near towns."

Mrs. J.L. Fraser. — "1. None better. 2. Splendid. My hens continued to lay all last winter. Eggs from 10d. to 1s. 8d. per dozen; chickens 6½d. per lb. dressed."

Mrs. G.B. Gordon. — "1. Yes; though prices for butter at least have been very low this season. 2. Well. Poultry raising is generally profitable."

Mary B. Grierson. — "1. This section of country (Violadale) is more adapted for dairying purposes and stock raising than for crop growing, except so much as can be consumed on the farm. The yield of milk and butter can scarcely be surpassed. 2. Poultry raising is the most profitable branch in the housekeeper's province. I have always been successful, and reared 160 chickens from 11 hens."

Mrs. R. Griffith. — "1. Yes, I consider it ahead of the famous Eastern Townships as I made butter and cheese there for 30 years. 2. With proper care poultry thrive and pay well."

Mrs. C.F. Haight. — "1. The North-West, except in parts where it is all plain, could not be excelled for producing butter and cheese. 2. Poultry do well and are very profitable."

Mrs. R.C. Hodnett. — "1. There are few better countries for dairying of my acquaintance. We produce an excellent article. 2. Poultry do well, and hitherto profitable, but a likelihood of overproduction here (Birtle)."

Mrs. J. Hunter. — "1. It is splendid for butter, but cheese is not made much here (Neepawa). Manufactured rennet is very scarce. 2. Poultry thrive splendidly, and very profitable."

Mrs. J. Kelly. — "1. Manitoba produces more butter and cheese to the pound of milk than Ontario. 2. Poultry do well; are quite an item in farm produce."

Mrs. Elizabeth Kenny. — "1. Yes; cows give better milk and more than in Ontario. Butter classes as A1. 2. Thrive well and are profitable."

Mrs. E. Lawford. — "1. There could not be better, as the milk is far richer than in the old country, and there is plenty of pasture. 2. If they have a warm house in winter they pay well. I know a great many who keep house with their egg-money."

Mrs. M.M. Logan. — "1. I think it cannot be excelled for producing butter. I do not know about cheese. 2. All kinds of poultry thrive well and are profitable."

Mrs. M. Lowe. — "1. There is no limit to the hay or pasture. 2. Poultry do well if fed and are profitable. We kept 100 poultry over last winter, and will keep 150 this winter."

Mrs. T. McGee. — "1. First class, better than Ontario, as the grass is very rich and nutritious. 2. They thrive well and are profitable, the lowest price in summer for eggs is 5d. to 10d. per dozen.

Miss McGill. — "1. Yes, excellent, and because of the dry climate cattle winter more easily and are fatter and stronger in the spring than in Ontario. 2. Poultry thrive well; but must have a house warm in winter."

Mrs. P. McKay. — "1. First class. 2. Poultry thrive well, the profit depends on the price of eggs."

Mrs. Jean McKenzie. — "1. First class for both butter and cheese. I have made both in Scotland and Ontario, and I consider I can make them better here than in either of those countries, which I attribute considerably to our cool summer nights and nutritive native grasses. 2. Poultry thrive well and are both profitable and useful."

Mary M. Muckle. — "1. Decidedly; butter of good quality always commanding a good price. 2. Excellent, and with intelligent management poultry are very profitable. Eggs in winter are worth from 1s. 6d. to 2s. a dozen."

Mrs. A. Naismith. — "1. The best I have ever seen. The cows we brought with us give about a quarter more milk than in Ontario. 2. Poultry thrive well; very profitable."

Mrs. M. Ogletree. — "1. No better country in the world, to my knowledge. I make both cheese and butter. 2. If kept warm and fed well poultry do well and are very profitable."

Mrs. J.W. Parker. — "1. I believe it to be the best in the world. It is certainly better than Ontario, which is famous for its production of these articles. 2. They thrive splendidly, and are very profitable. I have as fine geese, ducks and hens, as I ever saw anywhere, healthy and easily raised."

Mrs. A Pickering. — "1. Yes. 2. Thrive well enough, but I have not made much by them. I think if I had a different breed I should do better."

Mrs. E. Pollock. — "1. I consider it far superior to any other I was ever in. 2. They do very well, and eggs are a good price."

Mrs. H. Proctor. — "1. No better in the known world for good butter and cheese. This I know by 20 years' experience in England as a butter-maker. 2. Poultry thrive well, and have been very profitable with us."

Mrs. Susan Rhind. — "1. Yes, first rate. 2. Very well and profitable. I have a large number of poultry."

Mrs. J. Rutherford. — "1. The North-West produces the best butter and cheese on this continent. 2. Poultry thrive well if cared for, and they are the most profitable things on the farm."

Mrs. T.A. Sharpe. — "1. None better. 2. They thrive well. Our hens laid all last winter, with a moderately comfortable house and good feed."

Mrs. J.M. Sherk. — "1. Excellent. Butter made here being fully as good as can be made in any part of Ontario. 2. Poultry thrive well with suitable winter quarters, and are profitable."

Mrs. O.H.M. Shuman. — "1. I have seen very fine butter produced in the North-West, and there are great facilities for cheese factories. 2. Poultry do as well here as anywhere."

Mrs. J.G. Sturgeon. — "1. With butter at ten cents (5d.) per pound here (Stockton), scarcely. Cheese would pay well. 2. Most kinds of poultry do well."

Mrs. J. Sutherland. — "1. Excellent; by a careful test it has been shown that 9½ lbs. of our milk are equal to 11 lbs. of Ontario (for cheese); butter equally excellent. 2. Poultry thrive well, and are in good demand."

Mrs. R.P. Thompson. — "1. Yes, most excellent. We milked nine cows this last summer and made a lot of fine butter, which sold at 20 cents (10d.) per lb. in Winnipeg, and cheese sold at 14 cents (7d.). 2. They thrive well, and are very profitable."

Mrs. W.E. Tisdale. — "1. Yes; and we find by experience that cattle will produce 25 per cent more here on the natural pasturing than on the best fields of the Eastern provinces. 2. Poultry thrive well, and are very profitable."

Mrs. Turnbull. — "1. Yes. 2. Poultry thrive well, though this year has not been so good for them."

Mrs. E. Wrightman. — "1. Very good butter. Cheese has been made by a good many people this summer, and sold well. We expect to do more in that way next year. 2. My poultry do well; turkeys and hens are all I have as yet tried."

Mrs. A.B. Wenman. — "1. I think this a fine country for both butter and cheese. I know our butter is splendid. 2. Poultry do pay well; our hens lay all the winter."

Mrs. M. Whimster. — "Yes, I do, and I have had long experience. This is the best butter country I have ever seen. 2. Poultry thrive well, and are profitable."

DEMAND FOR SERVANT GIRLS

The following answers, from nearly all districts of the Canadian North-West show conclusively that a large demand exists for "hard-working honest girls" as farm help or as general servants. Of course, with girls, as with those of the male sex, there must be a determination to apply oneself with cheerfulness and industry to the kind of life met with on the prairie. The questions asked were: —

(1) Can hard-working honest girls easily obtain situations at good wages on farms or households in the North-West, and what advice, in this respect, would you give to young girls who contemplate making the North-West their home?

(2) Please state, if possible, the general wages paid to girls as cooks, house-maids, and farm helps?

Alameda. Mrs. G.S. McCaughey: — "1. A few girls can obtain good wages here, but there are not many required yet. 2. 32s. per month is generally what is paid." Mrs. C. Troyer also says writing from Alameda: — "1. Yes, and girls who never worked. 2. From £1 to £3 a month."

Alexandria. Mrs. G. Cheadey: — "1. There is a lot of work at good wages for girls, but it is as well for them to keep out of towns, and particularly not to hire at hotels and boarding-homes after coming here. 2. From 10s. to 32s. per month for farm help; mostly about £1 per month." Mrs. T.D. Elliott says: — "1. Good girls can get plenty of good places at good wages, then marry good young men with good farms. 2. From £1 to £2."

Alamsipp: Mrs. Smith: — "1. Girls can find good situations. Wages on farm from £1 to £2 per month, and in cities from £2 to £20 per month. They are in great demand."

Archibald: Mrs. B. Ownes: — "1. Any decent girl who is willing to work can obtain fair wages the year around. 2. Cooks, £3; housemaids, £2 8s.; and for farm helps 32s. to £2 per month." Mrs. A. Bethune: — "1. Good girls are very scarce here, at from £2 to £3 per month. My only advice would be to them, keep good company, be willing to work, have a knowledge of cooking and housework in general, and not to get *married* the minute their first month is finished."

Assiniboine: Mrs. A. Gowler: — "1. Yes, very easily. Any amount of work, and good wages. 2. From 32s. to £1."

Austin: Mrs. H.M. Hall: — "Situations are easily obtained here, and good wages. 2. From £2 to £4 a month."

Bain St. Paul: Mrs. M.J. Taylor: — "1. There is a great demand for the kind of girls you speak of with a prospect of bettering themselves very shortly. 2. Cooks £4 per month, housemaids £2; and farm helps £1 12s."

Balgume: Mrs. B.N.L.: — "1. From £2 to £3 a month. Should advise them to bring their mothers with them. 2. £3 4s. a month for cooks."

Beautiful Plains. Mrs. E.J. Gardiner: — "1. Good honest girls can do well in this country, and can obtain good wages. This is a fine country for girls who want to work. 2. The general wages for girls are from £1 12s. to £2 per month."

Beulah. Mrs. A.B. Harris. — "1. I think many farmers would employ female labour if good girls could be got for say 16s. to £1 2s. per month, but at present £2 to £4 is what good girls are asking per month. As the country is largely settled with bachelors, good girls do not require to be long at service as they can soon get homes of their own. 2. In cities £2 to £4, in country £1 12s. to £3 8s."

Black Hill. Mrs. C.C. Clitten: — "1. Girls can easily get good situations and good wages. Would again advise young girls to learn general domestic work; that in the great demand, and brings good pay. 2. From £2 per months to £3, according to their ability."

Birtle. Mrs. C.E. Minten: — "1. Good working girls are in great demand at all times. None but the strong and healthy should come. If possible they should comes as the daughters or sisters of other immigrants, and in all cases provided with a letter to a clergyman from their former clergyman." Mrs. F. Robbie says: — "1. Good girls are wanted in towns and cities, sometimes on farms. There are lots of well-to-do bachelors who are wanting wives, and good, honest hardworking girls can soon find homes of their own. 2. Cooks, £3 to £4, housemaids and farm helps, £1 to £3 4s., according to age and experience."

Blithfield. Mrs. J.W. Parker: — "1. Such girls are in great demand always, in fact the want of such help is one of the greatest drawbacks to the life of farmers' wives in this country. Their future here would be assured. The country is full of good homes and good situations for such girls. 2. From £1 4s. to £3 4s., according to qualifications."

Bradwardine. Mrs. J. Parr: — "1. Yes, any number of them; come, right here and they will get good wages. 2. Farm helps, from £2 to £3 8s.; cooks, from £3 to £10; housemaids from £3 to £4."

Brandon. Mrs. H. Bartlett: — "1. Good girls can obtain good wages, from £2 to £2 4s. in town, and £1 12s. to £2 in the country." Mrs. G. Roddick says: — "1. Yes, very readily. Bring a note of introduction to some minister, and there will be no difficulty. 2. They receive from £1 12s. to £2 8s. per month."

Broadview. Mrs. J.H.L. Joslyn (Rev.): — "1. There is demand, but few would supply the need. The bachelors want wives the rather. 2. Cooks £3 per month; housemaids, £2 and farm helps, £2."

Burnside. Mrs. J.R. Fox: — "1. They can obtain situations easily anywhere, but wages are not as high as they were two years ago. 2. Wages of housemaids and farm helps £1 to £2 per month; cooks higher." Mrs. S.J. Smith: — "They can get good situations and big wages. I would give a good girl, for the year round, £3 a month. If a girl has any friends, she had better go to them and they will get her a good place, or if she has none, let her come to Burnside, I will get her a good place. 2. For good cooks, from £2 to £3.

Calgary. Mrs. E. Robb: — "1. Good servants girls are scarce, and can easily obtain good places at good wages (£3 to £5 per month), and finally good husbands. 2. Cooks, £3 to £4 per month; housemaids and farm helps, £3 to £5 per month."

Carberry. Mrs. L.J. Lowes: — "Good girls can obtain situations at from £2 to £3 per month on farms and stand good chances of making homes for themselves. 2. Cooks, £3, housemaids £2 8s.; farm helps, £2.

Carman. Mrs. L. McKnight: — "Plenty of work for girls and good wages. Girls do not commonly work out doors, there being sufficient housework for them to do. It is, however, advisable for them to marry, as there are many bachelors in this new country. 2. Housemaids, from £1 12s. to £3 per month."

Cartwright. Mrs. J. Grimby: — "1. Yes, girls are scarce, great demand and good wages. We want a large number of working girls. 2. From £1 12s. to £2 per month."

Chatex. Mr. P.W. Davies (Rev.): — "1. General servants are in good demand in many parts of the country, and I would advise girls coming out with the intention of going out to service to advertise in the *Manitoba Free Press*, or have some friend to make it known where they may be found."

Clearwater. Mrs. K. Lawrence: — "1. The great trouble in this country is there are not enough girls to do the work, and I often wonder, if there is such a lot of girls in England out of work, why they don't come here, as here a good girl would not be one day without a place. I would gladly answer any girl who wishes to come out here and even get her a position. All the talent she needs is to be respectable and industrious. 2. Farm helps, from £1 10s. to £2 and £3."

Crystal City. Mrs. W. Parr: — "1. The girls are very scarce. If they cannot obtain situations as servants, I think they can as Mrs. for some lone bachelor. 2. From £1 4s. to £2 and £3.

Dalton. Mrs. O.M. Yeomans (Rev.): — "Yes, and any who wish to settle down as farmers wives, they can certainly do so by working in some farmer's family."

Dominion City. Mrs. R.W.D.: — "1. Yes. 2. From £2 to £3."

Dundee. Mrs. L. McDermot: — "1. Good working girls can easily get employment at fair wages on farms, as girls are scarce. 2. Cooks in hotels, £2 to £3 per month, farm helps £1 to £2 per month."

Edmonton. Mrs. H.T. Taylor: — "1. Yes, there is a great demand for servants; there are not any girls here, consequently housekeepers have to do their own work. 2. No scale of wages, but £2 a month is generally paid to native girls."

Elkhorn. Mrs. A.M. Duensing: — "1. They can easily obtain situations at good wages, and I would advise them that when they have a good place, that is, good treatment, good and plenty to eat and drink, and a good bed, to stay in their place and not to follow the example of the majority of the Canadian girls, to think that they are ladies and that work is a disgrace. 2. At present cooks from 12 to 20 dollars (£2 to £4) per month; housemaids, 8 to 12 dollars (£1 12s. to £2 8s.) the month."

Fairmount. Henrietta McGill: — "Yes, young girls that understand milking and doing general housework can obtain situations easily at good wages. They will do even better on farms than in towns, as the dangers are less. 2. Cooks, from 15 to 20 dollars (£3 to £4) per month; housemaids, 8 to 20 dollars (£1 12s. to £2); farm helps from 6 to 8 dollars (£1 4s. to £1 12s.)"

Gladstone. Mrs. D.J. Gerow: — "1. Girls can find work at good wages, and so come along as many as can. The only trouble is they are sure to be picked up by our numerous bachelor neighbours."

Glenboro. Mrs. Duncan: — "1. They can. I would say let them not be afraid to put their shoulder to the wheel and all will be well. 2. General servants, in town, 12, 15 and 20 dollars (£2 8s., £3 and £4) a month. In country 10 and 12 dollars (£2 and £2 8s.)."

Grange. Mrs. Gardiner: — "1. Yes, I think it is a very good country for working girls, far better than in Scotland. 2. Girls from 12 to 15 dollars (£2 8s. to £3) per month, and are always in great demand."

Greenwood. Mrs. T. Bowman: — "1. It really could not be beaten, for good girls can get almost any wages they ask, they can easily get 15 dollars (£3) per month. Would advise any girl to come that can, for she will make as much in one month here as in three elsewhere. 2. As cooks, men can get 60 dollars (£12) per month, a female 20 to 25 dollars (£4 to £5), housemaids 12 to 15 dollars (£2 8 to £3). For farm helps 10 to 15 dollars (£2 to £3)."

Grenfell. Meta G. Anderson. — "1. Hard working and honest girls can easily obtain situations at good wages on farms and otherwise, and bachelors abound. My advice to them is 'Be ye humble.' 2. Wages of servants: Good cooks at hotels £4 to £5 per month, in private families £2 to £3. Housemaids from £2. Farm help £1 to £2, according to age and experience. Middle-aged women understanding farm work can obtain good homes and good wages."

Headingley. Mrs. A.C. Dawson: — "1. Yes, wish I could get one. Let them take places in the country even at small wages rather than in towns. 2. In Winnipeg a cook received from 20 to 30 dollars (£4 to £6). Housemaids 10 to 15 dollars (£2 to £3). Farm helps 5 dollars (£1) upwards."

High Bluff. Mrs. N. Brown (Rev.): — "1. There are plenty of good places both on farms and in towns where girls can get good wages. I consider that good girls have a better chance to get on here than in any other place in the world. 2. On farms, from 8 to 12 dollars (£1 12s. to £2 8s.) per month, and in towns from 10 to 20 dollars (£2 to £4)."

Kildonan East. Mrs. I Sutherland: — "1. Honest working girls are in great demand, not only as help, but the country being overrun with bachelors no one can hope to keep a girl more than a few months, and in many cases but a few weeks, when she is married and away. 2. Cooks £3 per month. Housemaids £2 10s. Farm helps £1 12s.. These are the average wages."

Killarney. Mrs. D. Hysop: — "1. Think that good honest girls will always find employment here at good wages. 2. General servants out here get from 8 to 15 dollars (£1 12s. to £3) per month."

Lake Francis. Ann Hoard: — "1. Plenty of employment at good wages for right kind of girls, that is those who can cook and do general housework. From 8 to 15 dollars (£1 12s. to £3) in country for good general servants."

Manitou. Mrs. R.D. Foley: — "1. Yes, very good wages can be had, and plenty of demand, in fact good girls are scarce. 2. From 8 to 10 dollars (£1 12s. to £2) in private families."

Meadow Lea. Mrs. W.J. Bodkin: — "1. Yes, girls, that is good girls, are in great demand, and command good wages. My advice is to stop as long as they can in one place and save money, instead of racing about the country, looking for higher wages. 2. Housemaids and farm helps from 8 to 12 dollars (£1 12s. to £2 8s.) per month, with board."

Medicine Hat. Mrs. A.J. Bridgman: — "1. Yes, they can easily get situations. I would advise them to get in private families if possible. 2. Cooks get from 25 to 30 dollars (£5 to £6) per month, housemaids get from 15 to 20 (£3 to £4)."

Millford. Mrs. J.B.K. Wilson: — "1. Yes, they can always get place and fair wages, and marry more promising young men than from where they come from, for it is ambition that brings them here, and it will not be cast down. 2. Hotel cooks, from 10 dollars (£2) and upwards; housemaids and general servants on farms, from 5 to 10 dollars (£1 to £2) a month, according to strength and understanding."

Minnedosa. Lavinia Jeffery: — "1. Boys are in more demand than girls; few girls will accommodate themselves to the work of a N.W. farm and the towns and cities are at present oversupplied. 2. From 9 to 20 dollars (£1 16s. to £4) per month." Mrs. J.M. Wellwood (Rev.): — "1. Yes, get the address of some good families, come direct and stick to their place. They will get from 6 to 12 dollars (£1 4s. to £2 8s.). As a rule, only one servant is kept, who is supposed to do general work."

Moose Jaw. Mrs. E. Beesley: — "1. Plenty of work in town for industrious girls. 2. 15 to 25 dollars (£3 to £5) per month."

Nelson. Mrs. T.N. Wilson (Rev.): — "1. Honest willing girls are much needed all over the country, and it would be well for girls coming out to realize their true station, and understand that they have to work honestly and not be carried away with too high ideas, coming into a new country, which too often unfit them for their work. They will be much appreciated and sought for. 2. Cooks £36, housemaids £20 to £30, farm helps £18 to £25 per year."

Niverville. Mrs. G.W. Craven: — "1. Yes, my advice to young girls would be when they get a situation to stop, and not expect too much until they get acquainted with the country and not want to go from one place to another. 2. Housemaids and farm helps would get about 10 dollars (£2) a month."

Oakburn. Mrs. J. Menzies: — "1. Yes, good girls can easily obtain situations at good wages and I think any young girl will be happy here. 2. Cooks, I think, 12 dollars (£2 8s.), housemaids 6 to 8 dollars (£1 4s. to £1 12s.) per month."

Oak Lake. Mrs. A. Malcolm: — "1. There are any amount of situations here for good honest girls. 2. Housemaids and farm helps, 8 to 15 dollars (£1 12s. to £3) per month."

Oak River. Mrs. D.D. Fraser: — "1. They can, quite easily. Come at once, as girls are scarce. 2. Cooks as high as 40 dollars (£8); farm helps 10 to 15 dollars (£2 to £3)."

Pendennis. Mrs. T.R. Horner: — "1. Good girls can easily find good situations at good wages as good girls are scarce. 2. Farm helps, from 8 to 10 dollars (32s. to £2) per month, and cooks in hotels have from 25 dollars (£5) upwards."

Pilot Mound. Mrs. J. Farquharson: — "1. Hardworking, honest girls are much required for household work. 2. I think perhaps from 6 to 10 dollars (24s. to £2) per month, board included."

Pipestone. Mrs. W. Lothian: — "1. There is a good demand for such. The wages (especially in the towns) are better than at home. 2. Cooks, 15 to 25 dollars per month (£3 to £5); housemaids, 12 to 15 dollars (£2 8s. to £3): farm helps 8 to 12 dollars (32s. to £2 8s.)."

Pleasant Home. Mrs. E. Yeskey: — "1. Good girls willing to work are needed all over the country. I would advise them to bring all the serviceable clothes they can and if they have friends to have some place ready to come to. 2. On farms, from 6 to 10 dollars (24s. to £2). I cannot state the wages for anything else."

Poplar Point. Jane Stainger: — "1. Unless they have friends here or places appointed to go to, I would not advise them to come. 2. All the way from 5 to 15 dollars a month (£1 to £3) and perhaps more."

Portage la Prairie. Mrs. B. Franklin: — "1. Yes, if they are willing to work. There is a great scarcity of girls because none here like to go to work on a farm, because they have to assist with the milking (a good healthy exercise). My advice would be: 'Don't be afraid of good honest work, even if it is sometimes hard.' 2. From 8 to 12 dollars (36s. to £2 8s.) per month, in towns to general servants. I do not know about the country." Mrs. A. Scott: — "1. A large number of honest girls, such as a farmer's wife could take into her family without fear, would find good homes and good wages. We will willingly teach them the customs of the country."

Rapid City. Mrs. J.N. Davidson: — "1. There is a great demand for working girls here. The only trouble is they get married before they have been here six months or a year at most. There are only two single girls in this township, and I could not say how many bachelors. 2. Cooks in hotels get from 15 to 25 dollars a month (£3 to £5); farm girls get from 7 to 20 dollars (£1 8s. to £4), according to what they can do." Mrs. M.M. Drury: — "1. Yes, in certain localities. Let them apply to the minister of whatever denomination they belong to as a precautionary measure. Bring plain, comfortable clothing, and sufficient good sense to avoid all romantic ideas of accepting the first offer of marriage on arriving here; also frivolous notions about dress, reading novels, and the like. Set themselves to work steadily to learn the ways of housekeeping in this country, after which they prove bright ornaments to the bachelor-farmers' homes."

Rat Portage. Mrs. M. Grelboja: — "1. Yes, get acquainted with the country before getting too independent in their own minds. 2. From 8 to 15 dollars (32s. to £3) per month."

Readurn. Mrs. J.K. Champion: — "1. Hard working, honest girls are in demand at reasonable wages. 2. Farm helps get from 8 to 10 dollars (32s. to £2) a month."

Regina. Mrs. G.E. Boulding: — "1. I think there is plenty of work for good girls, at good wages. 2. Good cooks get 20 dollars (£4) or more a month; others from 7 to 15 dollars (28s. to £3) a month, according to work."

Richmond. Mrs. W. Copeland: — "1. All who are willing to work will soon get a place at good wages according to what she can do. 2. From 10 to 20 dollars (£2 to £4)."

Rossburn. Miss E. Lawford: — "Yes, there is great demand for servants on farms and in households, at £1 per month on farms, and £2 in households. If a girl is willing to learn, and respects her character she is such a prize. The trouble is, we cannot keep them, as there are so many in want of wives, but it is better to learn the ways of the country and the character of the man before settling down. There are many foolish girls who come out here and get married in haste and repent at leisure. 2. A good cook 12 dollars (£2 8s.), housemaids 10 dollars (£2), girls on farms 5 to 8 dollars (£1 to £1 12s.)."

Rounthwaite. Mrs. W. Henderson: — "1. They can. If girls are steady and well behaved they will have no trouble in getting work. 2. Farms girls get from 6 to 10 dollars (24s. to £2) a month."

Selkirk. Mrs. A.H. Vaughan: — "1. A good country for working girls. No difficulty in getting good situations, at high wages as compared with other countries. Get a good situation and remain steady. 2. Cooks get high wages according to their ability. Housemaids and farm helps about 10 dollars (£2) per month."

Shell River. Mrs. G. Butcher: — "1. Most of the people hereabouts are not in a position to keep servants at regular wages. There seems at present but slight prospects for servants in rural districts. The country is as yet too young. I have heard it is different in town."

Souris. Mrs. J.A. Moir: — "1. Yes; good girls are very scarce and command good wages. I would advise all girls coming to the country to hire on a farm at first. 2. Cooks get from 20 to 35 dollars (£4 to £5) per month; housemaids and farm helps, from 10 to 20 dollars (£3 to £4) per month."

Sourisford. Mrs. R.H. Little: — —"1. They can easily obtain situations at good wages, but I would not advise them to try for country situations. 2. From 8 to 12 dollars (£1 12s. to £2 8s.)."

Springfield. Mrs. M. Corbett: — "1. I think they can get good wages and good homes. 2. Farm helps, from 8 to 12 dollars (£1 12s. to £2 8s.) per month."

Stonewall. Mrs. W. Eagles: — "1. Any industrious girl can get a situation and good wages if she knows how to do housework. I would advise girls who have to earn their own living to come here. 2. From 8 to 15 dollars (£1 12s. to £3) per month."

Swan Lake. Mrs. G.B. Gordon: — "1. Yes. The Girls' Friendly Society, Winnipeg, affords perhaps the best medium for obtaining good suitable situations. 2. From 8 to 15 dollars (£1 12s. to £3) per month."

Turtle Mountain. Mrs. J.D. Hanson: — "1. In many places hard-working girls are in great demand, and can command good wages when they can work, bake, churn, milk and cook. People are willing to show those who are willing to learn. Let a girl come with a good character and go to a minister, and he will recommend her where to apply. Nurses would do well out here. 2. Capable general girls' wages vary from 6 to 15 dollars (£1 5s. to £3); farm helps, 20 to 30 dollars (£4 to £6) per month, according to seasons; harvest hands, 30 dollars (£6) per month."

Virden. Mrs. J.M. Sutherland: — "1. Good girls are in great demand for household servants; the wages given are about 10 dollars a month (£2).

Warella. Mrs. C.B. Slater: — "1. Good domestics always in demand, at from 10 to 20 dollars (£2 to £4) a month. Come along all who are willing to work. Lots of bachelors needing wives. 2. Hotel cooks 20 to 30 dollars (£4 to £6), for housemaids 15 to 20 dollars (£3 to £4), and 10 to 20 dollars (£2 to £4) for farm helps."

Wattstien. Mrs. N. Bartley: — "1. Plenty of work for good girls at fair wages. 2. Towns, from 10 to 20 dollars (£2 to £3 12s.), farm helps 6 to 10 dollars (£1 5s. to £2 8s.) a month."

Westbourne. Susan Rhind: — "1. Very easily. Take advice from Government Emigration agents or clergymen. 2. Girls in the country get 8 to 12 dollars (£1 12s. to £2 8s.) a month."

Whitemouth. Mrs. S.J. Carrigan: — "1. Yes, they can, as girls are scarce and wages high. They are getting 6 to 20 dollars (£1 4s. to £4) per month. In Ontario I have had girls for 4 dollars (12s.) per month. This is a good place for girls. 2. Cooks get from 20 to 25 dollars (£4 to £5) per month, and on the farms and in private houses they get from 6 to 15 dollars (£1 4s. to £3) per month."

Winnipeg. Mrs. E.O. Conklin: — "1. Bring all the girls possible to this country. Servants get good wages, and are in good demand. 2. General servants in the city, 12 to 15 dollars (£2 8s. to £3) per month. Cooks extra." Mrs. V. Lawren: — "1. As a general rule good experienced girls can obtain good situations in towns at fair wages. About from 8 to 12 dollars (£1 12s. to £2 8s.) a month."

Wolseley. Mrs. A.W. Haney: — "1. As far as I am aware girls get from 10 to 12 dollars (£2 to £2 8s.) a month."

Woodlands. Mrs. H. Proctor: — "1. A number of steady girls, who have been used to farms and dairies in England, will do well at reasonable wages, and doubtless would marry well to this country. Other branches are fairly supplied. 2. Farm servants, about 10 dollars (£2) per month with board; cooks, 20 dollars (£4) or more, according to ability."

OPENINGS FOR GIRLS IN TRADES

Question: Are there openings for girls in trades, such as milliners, dress-makers, &c., and can you state general wages?

Alexandria. Mrs. T.D. Elliott: — "Plenty of these girls needed. I cannot say what wages they would get."

Asessippi. Mrs. B.J. Brooks: — "Good openings. Milliners, dressmakers &c, are scarce."

Assiniboine. Mrs. A. Gowler: — "Yes, a great deal of work and good pay."

Austin. Mrs. M. McGregor: — "For plain sewing girls get from 4s. to 5s. per day."

Beaconsfield. Mrs. Wright: — "Dressmakers find plenty to do."

Beautiful Plains. Mrs. E.J. Gardiner: — "There is a good chance for milliners and dressmakers, and good wages."

Bird's Hill. Mrs. C.C. Clitten: — "Good openings in these lines. Sewing girls get 5s. and 6s. per day." Mrs. A.G. McDonald says: — "I think times are pretty dull in that line of business at present."

Birtle. Mrs. S. Chambers: — "Yes, sewing girls here get 3s. a day and board." On the other hand, Mrs. F. Robbie says: — "At present there is no demand for this class in this part of Manitoba."

Blithfield. Mrs. R. Griffith: — "Dressmakers get 4s. per day and board, sewing at a person's own residence." Mrs. J.W. Parker says: — "Dressmakers could find employment around and amongst farms at good wages anywhere."

Bradwardine. Mrs. J. Parr: — "Yes, any number, they could make from £4 to £10 per month."

Brandon. Mrs. J. Leech: — "The demand for milliners and dressmakers in our town is rather small as it is pretty well supplied with both." Mrs. C. Powers says: — "More demand for girls who can make boys' and men's clothing."

Broadview. Mrs. J.H.I. Joslyn (Rev.): — "I think not." Mrs. A.H. Tullock, however says: — "Milliners and dressmakers do well in this country."

Burnside. Mrs. H. Bell: — "Yes, they can get from 3s. to 4s. per day." Mrs. J. McKenzie: — "There may be a few openings for such, but like dudes, kid gloved gentry, &c., &c., there seems to be a plentiful crop in our cities and towns here, but they are of little or no value on a farm, either as servants or wives. But I have known several brought up town and city girls who have turned out first-class, both as helps on the farm and farmers' wives, when they set to work and learnt, but those who say 'I was never brought up to work,' are of no use here or elsewhere."

Calgary. Mrs. E. Robb: — "Very few openings here for trade girls."

Carberry. Mrs. L.J. Lowes: — "There are plenty of openings for milliners; average wages £3 per month."

Carman. Mrs. L. McKnight: — "Plenty of work for dressmakers, especially in towns or villages, but I cannot state wages. Do not know about other trades."

Cartwright. Mrs. J. Gimby: — "I don't know the wages, but there are openings for such lines of business."

Crystal City. Mrs. R. Downie: — "Yes, there is a demand for this class here."

Dalton. Mrs. E. Yeomans: — "Yes; wages from 2s. per day and board, and upwards."

Dominion City. Mrs. D.G. Dick: — "Cannot say what wages, but know there are openings."

Emerson. Mrs. E. Vesey Fitzgerald: — "About 12s. a week for milliners, etc."

Emerson. Mrs. A.M. Duensing: — "No openings just here, but no doubt there are in Winnipeg and other new starting towns. Sewing girls from 50 cents (2s.) to 1 dollar (4s.) per day. Dressmakers get from 1 dollar (4s.) to 2 dollars (8s.) per day."

Gladstone. Christina McDonald: — "Girls can get work of any description by applying to any agent in Winnipeg, on landing. Wages for situtations behind the counter 25 to 40 dollars (£5 to £8) a month."

Grenfell. Mrs. M.G. Anderson: — "There are openings for a limited number of milliners and dressmakers in the larger towns of N.W.T. at good wages, but am unable to state figures."

Headingley. Mrs. W.B. Hall: — "There seems a good general demand for girls in all these trades. Sempstresses get 1 dollar (4s.) per day."

High Bluff. Mrs. N. Brown (Rev.): — "First-class openings. They can make money fast. Sewing girls in private families get 1 dollar (4s.) per day and board."

Manitou. Mrs. R.D. Foley: — "The country here seems to be well supplied with such."

Medicine Hat. Mrs. A.J. Bridgman: — "There are openings; I can't state wages."

Miami. Mrs. R.P. Thompson: — "There are openings for all such just here; tailoresses are mostly in demand. Dressmakers get 6 dollars (£1 4s.) per week, and board themselves in Winnipeg."

Millford. Mrs. J.B.K. Wilson: — "There is room for milliners' shops, and dressmakers can earn 75 cents (3s.) a day to go out through the country."

Minnedosa. Mrs. H. Sanderson: — "There is a fair supply here, they seem to get plenty to do; their charges are high."

Neepawa. Mrs. J. Hunter: — "There is not much for milliners and dressmakers to do here in this part, for the shopkeepers get all the hats trimmed, and everyone makes her own dress."

Nelson. Mrs. T.N. Wilson: — "Sewing girls are much needed in the country and towns. Wages from 2s. to 3s. per day, with board."

Ossowo. Mrs. Emma Cowlord: — "Yes. Wages from 1 dollar 25 cents to 1 dollar 50 cents (5s. to 6s.) a day." Mrs. C.F. Newman: — "There are none in the country."

Portage la Prairie. Mrs. M. Whimster: — "Girls going out to work by the day sewing, get from 75 cents to 1 dollar (3s. to 4s.), and dressmaking from 4 dollars to 6 dollars (16s. to 24s.), according to the amount put on them." Mrs. P. McKay: — "These trades are well supplied." Mrs. A. Bell: — "Not a great demand. Better for sewing girls going from house to house; wages 75 cents (3s.) a day and board, except Sundays."

Rapid City. Mrs. J.W. Davisdon: — "Girls of this description are plentiful. Wages are from 50 cents to 1 dollar 50 cents (2s. to 6s.) per day. I believe they can do well at piece work." Mrs. Turnbull: — "No such openings in Rapid City; those who were here in the business had to give it up."

Regina. Mrs. J. McIntyre: — "We want milliners and good dressmakers in Regina. Please send them along." Mrs. G.T. Boulding: — "Yes, there is. We have to pay high prices for such kinds of work." Mrs. W. Copeland: — "I know a girl in Winnipeg who gets 100 dollars (£20) a month as head dressmaker."

Ste. Agathe. Mrs. M. Lowe: — "This line has much adopted by the housemaids. It seems to be a fair line of business for a smart girl."

Shell River. Mrs. G. Butcher: — "There appears to be a demand for milliners and dressmakers. The charge for making a trimmed dress here is 5 dollars (£1)."

Smiths Hill. Mrs. J. Armstrong: — "In this country chances for such are very small, but sewing girls get 50 cents and 75 cents (2s. and 3s.) a day."

Souris. Mrs. A.B. Wenman: — "I believe milliners and dressmakers get plenty to do here, and are well paid, but I cannot say what they pay assistants."

Treherne. Mrs.T.C. Forbes: — "The supply equals the demand at present."

Turtle Mountain. Mrs. A. Gregory: — "Not many in the country; dressmaking, etc., is generally done at home. Have no experience of towns."

Two Rivers. Mrs. F. Clark: — "Yes, very good in towns of any size; but they can do better as farm help."

Virden. Mrs. J.M. Sutherland. — "Girls here set up on their own account, and have the profit all to themselves. I pay 5 dollars (£1) for getting a dress made."

Wattsview. Mrs. N. Bartley: — "I should think so; in villages or towns. Dressmakers, from 5 dollars to 10 (£1 to £2) and upwards, according to amount of labour."

Whitemouth. Mrs. J.S. Carrigan: — "Yes, we have lots of that work to do, and they have, I think, been getting about 1 dollar (4s.) per day."

Winnipeg. Mrs. E. Lawrence: — "Very few openings in these lines at present."

Wolseley. Mrs. E. Kenny: — "Good openings, but I cannot state wages, that depends on themselves."

1. These questionnaires, now in the Public Archives of British Columbia, were sent out by Alexander Begg, who then compiled the pamphlet for the C.P.R. (PABC, Additional *Ms.,* File No. 467, vol. 3). The originals give the respondents' place of birth and are indexed according to nationality, and so are immediately usable by researchers interested in pursuing the question of the national origins of women settlers in the west in the mid-1880's. This information has come to me in the page-proof stage of this book from Dr. Patrick Dunae, and I am grateful to him for passing it on.

3

Women Wanted
Commentary

As the 1880's wore on it became increasingly clear that the Northwest had indeed too many bachelors: too many for the ease and comfort of the Manitoba house-wife, whose desperately needed domestic servants were invariably married and installed in households of their own within months, sometimes weeks, of their arrival; too many also for the stability of western society as a whole, looked on as a long-range venture. For as the number of homestead entries rose, so too did the number of cancellations, especially during the 1880's, and worried government officials gradually came to realize that one of the principal causes was the loneliness and discomfort of homestead life for the single man.

The seriousness of the situation was emphasized by a pamphlet issued in 1889 by the Manitoba government entitled *Manitoba and Its Resources.* Defining "Who Should Come," the pamphlet extended the usual invitation to four customary groups of intending emigrants — "capitalists" [that is, investors], "prosperous heads of families," "farmers' sons," and "working men" — but it then added a fifth group, a class identified under the simple heading "Women." This section of the pamphlet reads:

> Of all classes, those for whom there is the greatest demand are women. The demand for women is practically unlimited. There are hundreds of comfortable homes for respectable young women, as waitresses in boarding houses, as helps in farm houses, and as domestic servants. The Women's Christian Temperance Union in a resolution passed in September, 1887, said: "There is a great demand for respectable young women as domestic servants. . . . There will be no difficulty in securing comfortable homes for large numbers of respectable girls and young women." Remuneration ranges from $8 to $20 per month. The principal reason for the continuous demand is this: That young women scarcely get settled in a situation, when they leave it to take charge of a home of their own, in other words, *get married* [italics in the original].

Another sign of the times was a pamphlet printed at the office of the Qu'Appelle *Progress* in 1889, not in this instance by a government or railway propagandist, but by a private individual, one C. T. Lewis. Entitled *The World's Return Rebate Marriage Certificate; or, The Want of the West,* this eighty-four-page pamphlet outlined Lewis's scheme to redress the balance between the sexes in the Northwest. His proposal was simplicity itself: any single man who travelled eastwards from the territories in search of a wife, Lewis said, should get a rebate on his railway ticket if he brought a bride back with him. (What came of this scheme is not presently known, although research in contemporary Northwest newspapers would probably turn up some comment.)

Something of the same sense of urgency lies behind the third major selection in this survey of the Northwest of the 1880's from a woman's standpoint. It comes from a book published in London in 1890 by James Nisbet & Co.; the title is *West Nor'-West,* and the author was Jessie M. Saxby.

In her personal circumstances Jessie Saxby well represented the hazards of middle-class womanhood in late nineteenth-century Britain. Born in the Shetland Islands in 1842, she was the daughter of Laurence Edmonston, M.D., and Eliza Macbrair Edmonston. She received no formal education, but from "much reading and a close study of Nature, and the society of literary and scientific parents" (*Who Was Who,* 1941-50), she acquired better intellectual training than most women of her time. At the age of seventeen, she married Henry Saxby, also a doctor and an authority on the natural history of Shetland. In 1873 her husband died, leaving her the sole support of five young sons; whereupon she turned her literary and scientific interests to useful account, contributing numerous articles to newspapers and magazines and then branching out into the writing of books. By her death in 1940, aged ninety-eight, Jessie Saxby was the author of more than thirty volumes of boys' adventure stories, poems, travels, natural history, folklore, and personal musings.

In the summer of 1888 Jessie Saxby travelled alone by steamship and the recently completed C.P.R. to visit two of her sons, who were homesteading in the Qu'Appelle Valley. In an early chapter of her book, entitled "Prairie Homes," Mrs. Saxby set out at some length her belief that colonial settlement was very much an Imperial affair, with quite explicitly moral, religious, and racial overtones. "Overcrowding is poisoning and killing the life of Britain, its social, happy, prosperous life as a whole," she wrote, and she continued:

> When Britain fully comprehends her mission on earth ["that of a dominating race"] she will undertake this noble business of emigration in a very different spirit from heretofore, and the world as well as Britain herself will go forward on broader lines, and on the more enduring basis of religious duty.
>
> Such were my thoughts as I gazed on rich lands with here and there a sign of man's presence, and scarcely anything to tell that *woman* was in the territory at all! I wished with all my heart that I could have shipped off a dozen cargoes of well-assorted damsels from Scotland to Canada, where women and women's work are so much required (pp. 32-33).

Mrs. Saxby did not go so far as personally to ship off cargoes of damsels, but she did include in *West Nor'West* this chapter, entitled "Women Wanted."

Jessie M. Saxby

Women Wanted

In Britain one of the most urgent social difficulties is what to do with our surplus women — how to provide for them, how to find remunerative employment for them. In Canada one of the most urgent social difficulties is how to persuade women to come there, how to get along without them. In Quebec, in Winnipeg, in Regina, everywhere, I was told the same thing. "Oh, if respectable women from the old country would come out West!" "Do persuade girls accustomed to domestic service to emigrate." "We can take them by shiploads, and find good homes for every one at once." At Quebec, Mrs. Corneil, of the Women's Protective Immigration Society, and the agent for the Women's Christian Association, told me the same thing. "Girls needn't go West; we can employ numbers *here*." "I have at this moment application for over seventy servants (British)." Wages in Quebec, Montreal, &c., range from seven to ten dollars a month. Trained cooks may command over twelve dollars (that is, about £2, 10s.). It should, however, be borne in mind that the conditions of "life" in the older and eastern provinces are very much the same as those which rule social life in Britain. Many girls who cannot pay their way further take service in Quebec and the neighbouring cities, for six months or a year, until they have saved enough to carry them westward ho! When they reach the prairie lands of promise they are in a woman's paradise. They may ask any wages they please, and will get them if they are efficient workers and of respectable character. Girls I conversed with in some of the western towns told me they got from twenty to thirty dollars. "But that's not so much. A good cook gets over forty dollars a month." The women's duties are light compared with those of servants in Britain. Generally the men do all the heavy and dirty work, scrub the floors, fill the watercans, carry wood for the stoves, wash the dishes, and so on. Servants on farms are admitted as equals into the family life. It is by her own choice that a "nice little woman" remains single out there — not for want of good "offers." She may choose her mate from a race of able, prosperous, handsome men. It is refreshing to eyes accustomed to the tired, anxious faces, and listless or stilted gait of the average Briton, to look on those manly Titans of the West. *They* are Britons; yes, but Britons of larger body and larger heart than those at home. There is a freedom of gait, a heartiness of manner, a hopefulness of expression, a frank courtesy, a liberal-mindedness which impressed me very profoundly. You feel that here is a race of men who *must* be winners in life's battle, and who can keep what they win "by the might of a good strong hand." The few women one meets look happy as can be. Little wonder! They are cared for with a chivalry and tenderness which cannot fail to bind the feeble sex in willing chains.

The want of home life is keenly felt as a very great calamity by those western settlers. They envy such of their number as have been fortunate enough to induce sister, wife, or mother to come and "keep house." All would gladly do likewise. There seems about one woman to every fifty men, and I believe the old country could confer no greater boon upon this fine young nation than by sending it thousands of our girls to soften and sweeten life in the Wild West. The want of feminine influence tends to make the men (so they acknowledged) restless, dissatisfied, reckless, and godless. A Canadian gentleman of influence and education said: "Better even than money — and, goodness knows, we need capital badly — should be a cargo of home-loving girls." Mr. Fowler, agent for the "C.P.R." at Regina, told me that if some women — "any number" — will come out West, he can promise they shall be looked after well, and shall find employment at once. Mr. Davin, M.P., said much the same thing. I may mention here that I had a very pleasant and interesting interview with Mr. Davin. He had just returned from a meeting of Parliament at Ottawa, and had his hands full of business, but was none the less ready to give me full information and a "patient hearing." He was at much pains to explain the reason why Regina must become one of the great centres of western commerce ere long. It is growing with that wonderful speed which is so characteristic of all forms of life — vegetable, animal, national, social — in the glorious West. Mr. Davin is cultured and far-seeing, and I do not doubt he "speaks as wise men speak, knowing that which shall be." He told me of girls who had come out as servants, and who are now married to wealthy leading men, and who are taking their place at Ottawa among those assembled to do honour to our Queen's representative! I asked him if another class than servant girls could find employment in Canada — educated girls who at home go out as lady-helps, nursery-governesses, telegraph clerks, shop girls? "If they can perform *domestic* duties, yes," was the answer; "*these* would probably find 'permanent employment' very soon!" "Permanent employment" of course meant matrimony, and I was very glad to find that the West-nor'-West does not look upon marriage as a failure. I am old-fashioned enough to believe somewhat in the simple plan which satisfied our fathers and mothers — the loving clasp of man and wife, joined till death part, for the benefit of posterity, and because mutual love and mutual necessity require their union; therefore I was glad to learn that those "Prairie-dogs" fervently desire to wear the bonds of wedlock. The difficulty, however, is the want of women — as I have already said — and I should like to add a few words on the subject of female emigration.

When a new country is being opened out we send our men only to do it; feeling, and perhaps rightly, that women are not able to meet the hardships of pioneer-life. But we go further than that; we don't let our women join the men even when the *first* difficulties are overcome. We are content that the stronger sex should toil on in their new settlements, uncheered by feminine society and feminine ministrations, while the women are supported at home by the proceeds of the emigrant's toil. For why? Certainly *not* because sister, wife, and mother in the old country prefer old country luxury to the society of their men, but because an entirely exaggerated belief regarding the trials and dangers and hardships of colonial life has been propagated among us; and yet more because we have fixed and erroneous ideas regarding the nature of those trials, dangers, and hardships to which our women would be subjected if they shared the life of the prairie and backwoods man.

It seems terrible to us that our girls should have to cook the food, knead the loaves, mend and make garments — be, in short, their own domestic servants and tradespeople! Such hard work! Our girls are not strong enough for it! Yet our girls are able to climb mighty Alps, and play lawn tennis for half a day. They can dance, and skate, and ride, and row with tireless energy. They can spend hours on hours stitching fancy work. It spoils their hands to do a little kitchen work at home, but they never mind scrubbing church brasses, and kneeling on cold stones at the bidding of a parson.

Oh! it is more than time we fling those shams on one side, and declare selfishness to be at the root of the matter. It is absolute selfishness that prevents a proper proportion of our women from going out bravely to work with the men in building up those grand young nations of which Britain is so justly proud.

But the selfishness reacts upon ourselves. We have far too many women in the old country, and the result to them is trials, dangers, and hardships of a kind more pitiful, more appalling, than if we exposed them to the worst inconveniences of pioneer-life in a colony.

I am speaking, of course, of the educated middle class, the women who cannot hire themselves as domestic servants at home because of losing caste, therefore have to go out into the world (if they wish to live honest, independent lives), and struggle for a living in less safe ways than that of domestic servants. How many fail, God only knows. One thing *we* know, and it should make us cry out, "Any toil, any simple country life in far lands, rather than that;" we know that the lost, forlorn women who throng our cities are recruited from our educated middle class far more than from the lower orders.

It is not the domestic servants who have the hard lot in our land. It is the domestic servants we need, and have not enough of. Yet it is *they* we are sending to the colonies by thousands; and it is they who become the wives of our sons and brothers there. The men "out there" must, and will, marry if they get a chance, and since we do not encourage our educated, refined girls to go to those lands where men need helpmeets, of course the men take what they can get.

Thus a settler, born and educated a gentlemen, has to marry "beneath him," or continue the "batching" (bachelor life) which is so hateful and demoralising to him.

I don't want our girls to be sent out to the colonies in search of husbands. Certainly not! But I want them to believe that the home duties, the domestic service, which they cannot, or will not, do at home are neither degrading nor exhausting; and that if they will but fling the prejudices of caste aside, and say honestly and bravely, "I want to earn my own living," they will find happy homes glad to receive them in Canada, North-West.

One lady said to me: "We *must* treat our servants as our equals, or they won't stay; and it is not agreeable, as you may suppose, to live on such terms with an ignorant, coarse-minded woman of the lower orders. How thankful I would be if a girl in my own position would come and be my help. There are scores of ladies in my position who would thankfully receive such girls." I ask any young woman who has been snubbed and cuffed about as our nursery governesses, our mothers'-helps, our female clerks, are, if her lot would not be a happier one, in the farm of a Canadian settler, doing the duties of a daughter, and eventually finding a "man of her mind" among her neighbours there?

The point I should wish above all others to make clear is this matter of *hard work — degrading service.*

We are shocked to think of a gently-nurtured woman riding over the ranche at the tail of a herd, doing the work of a cowboy; but we are rather proud to claim acquaintance with a lady who follows the hounds, and has even ridden with troops, as newspaper correspondent. In the towns — as I said — women's duties are light, but on the farms of course they have to work harder.

"How dreadful!" one exclaims, on learning that a prairie farmer expects his wife to wash his clothes — even to make them. "How good of her! how noble!" the same individual says of a lady who takes to "slumming" in our foul city dens. "Think I'd let my girl go where she would have to carry milk pails!" Yet the watchful mother who utters such words does not consider the other mother's daughter who stands all day long behind a counter, lifting heavy bales, and breathing a poison-atmosphere, whose duties are far harder physically than those she would be called to do upon a Western farm. I wish our women would consider more the absolute duty laid upon them in this matter. We have no right (we women) to encourage our sons and brothers to go away in quest of fortune, if we are not willing to follow them and share their life — whatever it may be. We have no business to let them go from all the sweet, ennobling influences of home life.

Emigration must languish and not work on satisfactory lines, while men go by fifties and women by units. If the mother, sister, daughter, sweetheart, wife, cannot go *with* the men, they should certainly follow at an early date, should never contemplate retaining the old home when its best element is withdrawn; their first duty should be to follow the men! Somebody has said, by way of satire, "Woman came after man at the beginning, and she has been after him ever since!" Perhaps if we looked into things more than we do, and insisted upon calling a spade a spade, we should acknowledge that a profound and wholesome truth is in that little joke.

I believe that not only has woman been after man since the beginning, but that she was created for that very purpose, and it is her duty to follow where he goes!

It may be useful to append *here* a letter I sent to *The Scotsman* after my return home, also communications from the *Canadian Gazette, Manchester City News,* and *Regina Leader* on this subject of female emigration:—

"Sir, — I have received a great many letters and visits of inquiry on the subject of female emigration to Canada, and although very glad to help in this matter, I find it quite impossible to attend to all those inquirers; therefore give here the addresses of such persons as, I doubt not, will answer full all questions:—

"The Women's Protective Immigration Society, 141 Mansfield Street, Montreal.

"Mrs Corneil (agent for above Society), Quebec.

"Women's Christian Association, 120 St. Ann Street, Quebec.

"Mr. W. C. Van Horne, Vice-President C.P.R., Montreal.

"Mr. L. A. Hamilton, Land Commissioner, Winnipeg.

"Mr. W. C. Fowler, Agent C.P.R., Regina.

"My brief visit to the Far West conclusively proved how easily women may make the journey there; and I hope that though I, as a private individual, with little leisure time at her disposal, cannot undertake to direct all those anxious to emigrate who apply to me, they will yet believe that I am profoundly interested in their doing so, and am sure success depends upon themselves. The secret of 'getting on' in a new country lies in casting off the trammels of old-world habits, and in learning quickly to be 'in touch' with novel surroundings.

"There are rough places to be gone over in Canada as well as in Britain; but there is elbow-room in the new world, and no danger of being trampled under foot by jostling crowds. But let it be well remembered that earnest endeavour, ready hand, and quick wit are necessary to all success. Folks must *work* abroad as well as at home, but I apprehend individuals will have themselves to blame if they are left behind on Canadian life-roads. —I am, &c.,

"Jessie M. E. Saxby."

The *Canadian Gazette* says:— "Mrs. Saxby's remarks on the subject of female emigration to Canada have called forth a valuable suggestion from a correspondent of the *Manchester City News*. There is no doubt of the superabundance of women in the United Kingdom, and the great need of them in Canada. Could not a few friends of the female emigrant do something in the way here suggested? — A 'Canadian Registry Office,' on similar lines to those in use at home, would, I think, supply the need, and that without the much-talked-of State aid or public subscription, as it would be a self-supporting institution in constant work. We will suppose a servant pays a small fee to be placed on the list of applicants which is despatched weekly to the Agent's Registry Offices in Canada (say at Quebec, Montreal, and Ontario), with a full description of age and experience, and a photograph where possible. This would at once provide Canadians with an extensive list from which to select a servant when they needed assistance, and would be a boon to them as well as to the servant. Care could be taken to include only respectable persons, and judgment used in selecting good homes for them, whilst the cost of passage would be in most cases secured, or a deposit obtained for the emigrant. They would always have the office to go to for information, and they could learn there when ships were sailing with suitable company for the voyage out. If a few ladies, interested in philanthropic work, could devote a few hours each week, a useful, inexpensive work would be the the result."

As will be seen by the following announcement, the *Regina Leader* is ready, free of charge, to help in the solution of the problem for the Territories:—

The "Leader" registry office for the Territories.

"We have made arrangements in England whereby we shall get the names of good female servants wanting places. Any lady in the North-West who wants a servant can write to *Leader* Office, Regina, giving names, wages, &c. This will be registered by us free of charge. In the same way any young woman in England, Scotland, Ireland, or any part of the Continent, can send us her name, which we will register. Those desiring places and those wanting help can thus be brought into communication. This will all be done free of charge.

"The central position of Regina will make it a convenient place of registration. We will, without giving names (unless desired), advertise the places vacant and applicants free of charge.

"Farmers and families who would like to have a young woman as a member of their family will please say so.

"It is desirable that young English, Scotch, or Irish girls should send photographs. This is not an absolute necessity, but copies of their 'characters' from former places, or from their clergymen, must in all cases be sent.

"Old country papers will please give prominence to this offer on our part. Old country girls can address us in English, French, German, Italian, or Scandinavian. Address — Registry Department, *Leader,* Regina, N.W.T., Canada."

A correspondent in *The Lady* writes:— "The positions of comfort and independence which many of our *servants* obtain in colonies are to be envied, and should — as they would be better graced by them — be secured for our *daughters.* I also hold that, progress being the law of nature, we are inverting that law by trying to force our daughters into positions to which they were not born, and which they cannot occupy *here* without losing caste; and allowing positions which they could hold with credit in the colonies to be secured by their inferiors both as to birth and education.

"Many parents should be glad to send their girls, shivering on the brink of want and its inevitable consequences, to the colonies, where their services would be amply repaid, and where a new, bright, happy life would await them."

PART TWO

The Doldrums:
The 1890's

Plate 10. The Shaw ranch in Midnapore, Alberta in the 1880's. Samuel Shaw operated a woollen mill as well.

Plate 11. The stark interior of an unidentified log house shows the variety of uses to which a single room might be put.

Plates 12 Hugh and Margaret Robinson of Jumping Pound, Alberta, c. 1902, the year of their marriage. Hugh Lorraine
and 13. Robinson and Margaret Hattam came separately to Canada in 1898 from Liverpool and London, respectively,
Hugh to homestead in Alberta, Margaret to enter service as governess with the Duke family. Margaret said "she
never wanted to go back and never did."

Plate 14. Women haying at Kandahar, Saskatchewan, c. 1909. Emigrant gentlewomen evidently preferred to pose for more
formal portraits, and few photographs of any quality seem to survive of women working in the fields.

Plate 15. Louisa Blake (inset with her husband George) came to Canada as a governess. Their DB Ranch at Beaver Creek, Alberta, in the foothills region, closely resembles that described by Moira O'Neill.

Plate 16. Polo at Millarville, Alberta, c. 1910. Polo teams were established by the British settlers in the district before 1897, and the sport continued to be played until the 1930's.

Plate 17. Main Street, Winnipeg, in 1876. The Gateway City to the West had less than 2,000 residents when it was incorporated in 1874; within a decade, its population had increased tenfold.

Plate 18. By 1912, when this picture was taken, Calgary had grown to a city of 74,000.

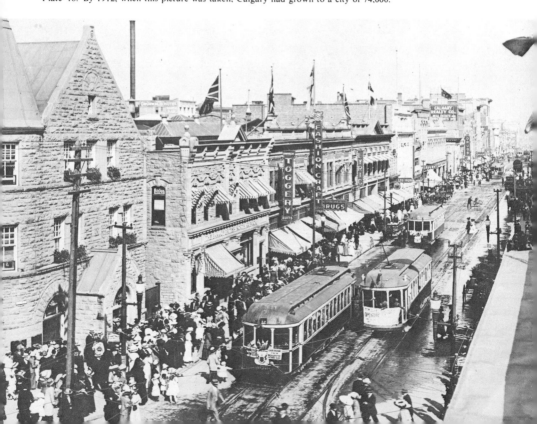

Three brief pieces from the British periodical press have been chosen to represent the 1890's, which was a slow time in prairie settlement, a kind of lull before the storm. Politicians chafed and railway promoters grew glum, but the respite allowed the survey crews to continue their gradual orderly spread westward from Manitoba. When the surveyors and the homesteaders who followed them reached southwestern Saskatchewan and Alberta, they encountered the established ranchers, among whom were a strong contingent of adventurous young Englishmen of good family and education. The life of the English ranchwoman, actual or prospective, became a favourite topic among contributors to the "better" English magazines, which formed a staple of reading not only in well-read families in Britain but in the homes of many Alberta ranchers as well.

The inclusion in this collection of "The English Ranchwoman" requires some explanation. In it are given the views of an Englishman, identified only by the initials "J.R.E.S.," who ranched for some fifteen years or more in the western United States.[1] The ranching frontier he describes is thus the American, not the Canadian one. Nor, for obvious reasons, can he be said to view the country from a woman's standpoint. Nevertheless, his article has been selected for reprint for two reasons. In the first place, the conditions he describes and the analysis he offers suggest that for the educated Englishwoman there was little to choose between the two ranching frontiers, the maintenance of the British connection aside. Secondly, this very article, published in *Longman's Magazine* in 1896, soon reached the eyes of Agnes Skrine of the Bar S Ranch near High River, Alberta. It is hardly surprising that Mrs. Skrine should have compared J.R.E.S.'s hypothetical English ranchwoman to her personal circumstances. Born to an Anglo-Irish family in County Antrim, Ireland, in 1864, Agnes Higginson had married Walter Skrine during one of his visits to England in 1895, ten years after he had launched his Alberta ranching career. The Skrines thus fitted in many respects the pattern set out by the writer of "The English Ranchwoman." From her own experience, however, Agnes Skrine did not think the ranchwoman's fate was as bleak as the article made out, and using the pen name "Moira O'Neill," under which she had already made something of a reputation in Britain as a writer, she composed her reply to J.R.E.S. Her article, "A Lady's Life on a Ranche," was published in the January 1898 issue of *Blackwood's Magazine*.

Parts of this article seem bent on convincing the readers of *Blackwood's* that its author has not forgotten how cultivated men and women converse with one another in print. The display of graceful, witty, spirited prose may or may not appeal to readers in this age of utilitarian composition. The projection of a charming and literate persona was not Agnes Skrine's chief object in writing, however. In addition, she depicts life in the Northwest as a kind of testing-ground of standards of behaviour too easily taken for granted where servants abound. "This is the country in which to find out how deep one's own personal refinement goes, how many dainty habits and tastes will survive when all the trouble of them had devolved upon oneself," she writes. "At home they are a form of unconscious self-indulgence; here they involve a principle, and an active one." (Incidentally, the "at home and here" formula of comparative social comment is the standard analytical structure for virtually all the pieces reprinted in this collection.)

The Skrines left Canada in 1902, returning to country-house life in Ireland. Soon after her return, "Moira O'Neill" published a much-admired book of poetry in which Northwest life and landscape took a prominent role. She died on 22 January 1955.

Finally, bringing to a conclusion this brief sampling of publications describing western life in the nineties is an article from the October 1901 issue of the *Fortnightly Review*, "Women's Work in Western Canada." The writer was Elizabeth Lewthwaite, who at the century's turn contributed articles on female middle-class emigration to a number of British periodicals, notably the *Imperial Colonist,* the monthly organ of the British Women's Emigration Association. When she left England in the summer of 1896 Lewthwaite planned to be absent only a few months. Her five brothers were variously established in Assiniboia (present-day Saskatchewan) and British Columbia, and her original intention was simply to visit them all in turn and then return home. In the end, after touring the country, she went back and settled on the prairie farm where three of her brothers lived.

"Women's Work in Western Canada" is more pedestrian in tone than Agnes Skrine's article, but it is also somewhat closer to the practical concerns of emigrating British gentlewomen. Lewthwaite bases her advice on four years' experience as housekeeper for her three brothers on their wheat farm near Indian Head. Like Mrs. Saxby, she sees the greatest difficulties of genteel female emigration not in the actual conditions of a settler's life, but in the problem of "bringing both employer and employee into direct communication." Here lay the main motive for her article, for she saw clearly that the press had an indispensable part to play in publicizing the existing means of assisting British women to "a fuller, freer life than could ever be their lot in the over-crowded Motherland."

1. All efforts to identify the author of this article have so far failed, *Longman's Magazine* not yet having been included in the *Wellesley Index.*

J.R.E.S.

The English Ranchwoman

If, as was pointed out in a former article,[1] the English ranchman's career is not as a general thing a triumphant success, how fares it with the English lady who has undertaken to share his Western home? Her husband most likely has had some experience of ranching, and is, presumably, here because an active life suits him. He has probably tried it for a few years, and has gone to the bottom. His friends at home have come to the rescue and set him on his legs again. He has had his experience, and has once more a little money to start again with. He has tried it as a bachelor, and believes that his failure was partly due to this very thing — the household duties taking so much of his time. During these first years of his ranching career he has heard repeatedly from his neighbours that "a bachelor has no business on a ranch." "You want a wife," he has been told by someone who has dropped in about dinner-time, and is watching with contemptuous pity his host's endeavours to prepare the meal. "I wouldn't live this way," says another on another occasion, with the refreshing frankness customary in the West, "as long as there was an unmarried woman in Missouri." "Darn this thing of baching," says yet another, taking in with comprehensive eye the disorder and confusion in which our friend luxuriates. "What a man lives for is for what little comfort he gets; and if he don't get that, he don't get nawthin'." And to each and all of these and similar remarks is appended the assurance that if he will only get married he will "make two dollars where, single, he can't make one."

Contrasting his own surroundings with those of his married neighbours, there is small cause for surprise if our Englishman begins to believe there may be some truth in it. The loneliness of his house, the time he loses getting his meals, the desolation which greets him if he gets home late on a winter evening and has still his outside "chores" to do before he can begin to prepare his own supper — all these are arguments which urge him to the belief that on a ranch, if anywhere, a man needs a wife. "How much which is almost unendurable," he thinks as he smokes a meditative pipe, "would disappear if the right person were here to take the house off my hands, and what a different thing this life would be. However, there's no use thinking of that in the shape I'm in. If I can't keep myself going, I don't want to bring a family to grief." And so with a grunt of disgust, and perhaps a glance at a photograph, he turns to his unmade bed, shakes up his blankets a little, and for a while forgets his troubles.

But the oft-repeated advice is fermenting in his head, and his heart quite possibly is urging him in the same direction; and when, a year or two afterwards, the first act of his ranching life has come to its inevitable end, and a visit to the old country has resulted in his being started again with fresh funds, he is accompanied on his return by a young lady whom he is proud to present to his friends and acquaintances as "My wife."

The neighbours had given him good advice from their point of view. Unfortunately, the wife they had in their minds and his new acquisition are as far asunder as their respective birthplaces. They were thinking of a daughter of the soil; one born and raised on a farm, used to hard work from childhood; one who would keep his house in such order and neatness as would make his home seem a veritable Paradise when he contrasts it with the wretched way in which he was living; one who would wash, sweep, bake, care for the poultry and young calves; milk, it may be; do up his "chores" at a pinch when he was away, and who would supplement his little capital with an experience far greater than his own; who would advise him in cases of doubt and difficulty with the keenness and zest of an identical interest; and one to whom these multifarious duties, though trying even to her, would not prove overwhelming. This is the kind of wife they had in their mind's eye, and this is the kind of wife to whom the prosaic argument they all used would apply.

But all this does not satisfy our Englishman. Rightly or wrongly, he refuses to let the business idea dominate the sanctuary of home. Here at least, he thinks, shall be some refinement and elegance, some escape from the coarse, rough natures with which he is in daily contact. Here shall be someone with whom he can interchange ideas other than those concerning the ranch and stock, someone, in fine, whose sympathies and feelings are those of his own class. He has never given up the hope that some day his term of exile will be over, and that he may be able to go back to the old country to live, and consequently refuses to take a step which must make the severance final, which would indeed be a burning of his boats. And so he has wooed and won in England, and brought his prize across the Atlantic to keep house for him in some cañon of the Rockies, or, more lonely still, somewhere on the wind-swept plain, where, with her middle-class English ideas, education, and accomplishments, her grace of manner and refined soft voice, she will, for a while, at all events, be regarded by her homely neighbours with as much suspicious surprise as would be a canary among a cage full of sparrows.

The lady ranchwoman may practically be considered exclusively an English product. No other nationality contributes an appreciable quota of the ladies of gentle birth and education who are to be found scattered over the Western States of America, and this fact may be cited as additional proof of the enterprise of the English race. The number even of English ladies may not be actually very large, but every Englishman who has spent a few years on a ranch will have known several, while he can probably count on the fingers of one hand the female representatives of the same class of all other nationalities put together whom he has met or even heard of. This state of affairs is largely accounted for by the fact that among educated ranchmen Englishmen have an immense preponderance in numbers; but the English ladies must themselves be accredited with a greater daring and readiness to undergo hardship than their sisters of other countries display. Possibly, too, the unsympathising foreigner would suggest that this fact may be taken as additional proof that English people are all more or less crazy; and assuredly, if one considers what the English lady leaves, and what in many instances she comes to, there would seem to be, as the Westerners say, more truth than poetry in this particular application of the assertion.

It is almost certain that the English lady herself has not been able to form an accurate, nay, even an approximate, idea of what her life and surroundings will be. Everything has been looked at through rose-coloured spectacles, or rather, considering the distance, through a rose-coloured telescope, and she has not been able to take the harshness and loneliness of the life into close account under the excitement of her engagement and marriage. Nor, for the matter of that, if she had had days where she had not had hours to ponder the matter, could she gauge her own capacity for a steady unending struggle with a side of life of which she has had no experience. All she can tell on this score is, that she has the courage to face it. Her husband has explained to her that the surroundings are somewhat rough and unfinished at present, but he has also added, and no doubt believed, that they can and shall be ameliorated. The house shall be added to, the little enclosure in which it stands shall be laid down in grass, and the present rough board fence shall be taken down and a neat picket fence substituted. There shall be a milk-house on the most approved principle, and just as soon as time will allow a well shall be dug and a pump provided, coming up through the kitchen floor, so that she won't have to go outside for water, as must be done at present. There is a horse there which will carry a lady nicely, and she shall accompany him on his rides after stock. There is a nice lot of poultry on the place, which helps to make it look cheerful and homelike — and, in fact, it only wants a woman's presence and a woman's touch to render it "highly desirable," as the auctioneer's advertisements read.

Listening with great interest to these very hopeful accounts, she draws a mental picture of the place as it is to be rather than as it actually is. She sees a cosy cottage with a small lawn and garden, surrounded by a gaily painted fence and all trim and neat. Inside the house is as fresh and clean as a new pin, and the kitchen is to look so cheery and inviting that it will be a pleasure — great fun, in fact — to have her husband's meals ready for him when he comes from work, for a few years at least, till the business increases and a larger income brings more leisure. She has learnt to make butter, and has taken some lessons at a cookery class, and has perhaps made some trial of her newly acquired knowledge at home in the shape of some fancy dishes, and been loudly applauded. So she feels confident of her ability to manage the cooking, if she is a little uncertain about the bread-making; and the rest of the housework — the sweeping, dusting, scrubbing, washing, and ironing — she dismisses from her mind for the present, reflecting that other people have done it, and why not she? Perhaps, after all, she thinks, some way will be found by which it will be taken off her hands.

She has numbers of ornaments, pictures, and photographs to make her sitting-room look bright and cheerful; "just as well," she argues, "have a pretty room as an ugly one, and it makes such a difference to one's daily life." She is fully determined to have things nice about her, and brings out her wedding presents, including, no doubt, a good deal of silver plate and a five o'clock tea service.

A stock of clothes, comprehensive enough to include every emergency, from scrubbing the floor to a possible party, completes her equipment.

It is to be hoped that her modest castle in the air will not tumble about her ears when she finally arrives, after her long and dusty journey, and first catches sight of her new home. On very few ranches has much been done for the sake of neatness and effect, and her husband not having been, as we know, very successful so far, has had no money to spare for anything but what has been strictly necessary. The bare and desolate appearance of everything is almost sure to give her English ideas a painful shock, accompanied, if she be of a susceptible nature, by a reaction which may startle her in its intensity.

Well does the writer remember the revulsion of feeling he experienced when he first caught sight of the ranche he came to, fourteen years ago, fresh from the old country. The bareness and apparent desolation have an indescribably depressing effect on a person wearied with days of travel; and though he may have thought himself prepared for some such scene, the actually being there and seeing it, and recognising that here or in some similar place is a good share of his life to be passed, bring home to him the length and depth of the step he has taken, as no account of description or imagination has been able to do. In a few weeks he will wonder how he could have been so affected, so easily do most people grow accustomed to their surroundings, but the memory of the impression will abide with him.

The lady, as soon as she gets out of sight, will perhaps indulge in what we are told is the luxury of a good cry, after which she will feel better. The necessity of getting things into some kind of order is immediate, and will take her thoughts off herself. A good night's rest will work wonders, and after breakfast, which her husband gets ready, she feels fit for anything.

For several days the "straightening things out" and "fixing up" will occupy her fully. Her husband will be round all the time helping her, so that she will not be lonely; and if she is of a contriving turn, she will find plenty of chance to exercise her ingenuity in the matter of shelves and cupboards, curtains, and portières. At last, however, the household arrangements are complete — the carpets down, the stoves set up, the pictures and bookshelves hung, the modest furniture in place. Very neat the house looks inside, and if only the yard in which it stands were not so wofully bare, her mental picture would be approaching realisation. So far things have gone well enough. The getting things in order has been interesting, and the preparing the meals herself, with the assistance of her husband, has been a novel and amusing experience, a kind of picnic as it were. She is surprised to find him as handy as he is, thanks to his "baching" experiences, and has already discovered that he can give her a good many wrinkles about ranch housekeeping, if his methods may be rather too rough and ready for civilisation. She has had his society and help all day, and her life has been too full of movement for her to feel lonely. Now, however, the house is in order, and her husband must be getting to his work outside, which he has rather neglected during these first few days. She has had some little chance to learn how things are done, and it is time to shake down to business and rely principally upon herself.

To the credit of Englishmen, who bring English wives to Western ranches, be it said, that for the most part they appreciate the sacrifice the ladies have made, consider them and spare them all they can of the disagreeables that must be encountered. The English ranchwoman gets far more help from her husband than does the native. On most English ranches where no "indoor help" is kept, it is the practice for the husband to get up and make a fire in the kitchen stove, and start the breakfast preparations, putting on the kettle and the coffee-pot, the oatmeal — which is a standing breakfast dish on nine out of ten ranches throughout the country — and, perhaps, especially in cold weather, cutting a beefsteak ready for the frying-pan. Then he goes down to the barn and does his chores; that is to say, feeds his horses and usually milks. By the time he has got through these duties the lady of the house has got breakfast ready without very much trouble to herself. Often, where a hired man is kept, the master of the house will get breakfast entirely himself, leaving the chores to the man.

The born and bred ranchwoman is not so fortunate. The first one up in the house will make a fire, but it is not very often that any of the men folk will put a hand to a dish or cooking utensil, not from laziness or want of consideration, but because such matters are outside their sphere, are the woman's business, and what she is there for. No native ranchwoman expects anything else — not if it should rain for a week at a time, and her husband be about the house all day weather-bound.

After breakfast, which, during the greater part of the year, should be over by half-past six or a quarter to seven, the men folk start on their day's work, and the breakfast-dishes will be her first care. These disposed of, and the chickens fed with the scraps, there are the duties for the particular day to attend to. In most house-holds the routine runs — one day wash, next day iron, next day scrub, next day odd jobs, Friday sweep, Saturday bake and do most of Sunday's cooking. Besides this, there are the meals, of course — dinner at twelve and supper at six, and, most distasteful task of all, after each meal the inevitable dishes.

There is the milk to strain and skim, and once, if not twice, a week a churning. There is her own and her husband's mending, and job after job crops up which must be attended to sooner or later. Though there is a special day laid off in each week for the thorough sweeping of the house, a certain amount of it must, of course, be done each day. Here, my dear lady, you will find one reason why the native ranchwomen, even those who can afford it, have not been at much pains to beautify their houses, but content themselves on the most part with a bare neatness.

Not in the log cabins and board shanties of the West, neat and clean inside though they be, will be found "the best parlour" of a New England farmhouse, which has been in the possession of one family for several generations. The magnificence of this room deserves a word of description. The furniture usually consists of a black hair-cloth lounge and chairs, and a rocking-chair or two, with plenty of crocheted tidies sprinkled about. In the centre of the room stands a heavy mahogany table, and on it a wreath of wax flowers, the salvage from some funeral from the house. Sometimes the flowers are made from the hair of deceased relatives, and whether of wax or hair are duly protected by a glass shade. A photograph album and one or two Annuals complete the adornment of the table. In some of these houses silver coffin-plates, bearing the name, and date of birth, and death of the deceased, are tastefully grouped on the mantelpiece. The windows of this sanctuary are carefully darkened, and the room feels damp and chill as a vault.

But in the Far West one rarely sees much superfluity of furniture and ornament in ranch houses. It looks as though the inhabitants kept in mind the chance of "taking a notion to move," and confine their aesthetic aspirations to such few sticks of furniture as can be picked up and loaded on a waggon without much trouble, and without much possibility of damage. Hence, though the interiors of these houses are not specially picturesque or attractive, yet the amount of work necessary to keep them clean and neat is reduced to a minimum.

No need to say that neither the New England parlour nor the Western living room meets the requirements of the English lady. Her sitting-room must, of course, be meant for use, and at the same time be pretty, and she makes it so. But these same pictures and ornaments, photograph frames, and vases, and nick-nacks will make her a terrible amount of work which the native ranchwoman is spared. They will catch no end of dust, which, on the plains, at all events, driven by the constant wind, penetrates and accumulates in a way to break a housewife's heart. The silverware will look dingy and unattractive, unless she devotes lots of time to it, as at first most likely she will. She will start with the intention of keeping things up to the high standard she has been accustomed to. She cannot bear to think of anything she has left undone that ought to be done, or which seems like slovenliness. The stoves must be blacked and polished, the window-panes kept bright, though the dust will obscure them almost as soon as you turn your back. Where the work devolves on one single pair of hands you can, if you choose, give every hour, nay, every moment, to some detail of housekeeping, and still could if the days were twice as long. "A man's work is from sun to sun: a woman's work is never done," was surely said of a ranchwoman. These duties sound somewhat formidable for a young lady who has never even taken care of her own room. Though a girl raised on a ranch would laugh at the idea of there being any considerable amount of work in keeping house for two people, the newcomer's unaccustomed muscles will ache at first as she slowly attacks one task after another. Of course, as yet, she knows nothing about economy of time, and has yet to acquire a system and method. She has the conscientiousness together with the uncertain notions of the amateur. She does not know yet what *must* be done and what can be let go, and gives herself twice the trouble a professional ranchwoman would take, with no better result after all her pains that anyone but herself can or would notice. No doubt her mind misgives her if, looking into the future, she can discern only a long vista of days of similar toil. She will, if she is wise, refrain from indulging in this practice, and learn, as the diplomatists urge, to "take short views."

"Practice commonly makes perfect," say the old-fashioned copy-books. By degrees she gets things to a focus, as the Western expression is, and manages to do in half a day what her native neighbour has done by ten o'clock. Some one has been found not too proud and independent to do the family washing, the charge for which accommodation is a heavy drain on a very slender income, and with what help her husband can give her she manages pretty well, though, if haply her lot is cast on the plains, she is greatly tried by the fiery sun blazing down on the sandy and treeless expanse, and sending a furnace-like heat through the thin walls. Most ranch houses on the plains have a kind of lean-to on their north side open at either end, so as to allow the air to circulate, into which the kitchen stove is moved in the summer. Let us hope one has been provided for the lady whose case we are considering.

So passes her novice's year. In the second year of her stay, when a greater familiarity with her routine enables her to get through it with greater ease to herself, the situation is usually complicated by the arrival of a tiny third party on the scene, and now, to use a homely expression, the fat is in the fire with a vengeance. If her duties had been all, and more than all, she could accomplish when there were but two of them, what must be the state of affairs now? For a while, of course, there can be no question help must be and is procured, but when the mistress of the house is on her feet again, how is she to manage with these new claims on her time and attention? Her hands were more than full before; help of some kind she must have, and as female help is excessively hard to procure and very high-priced, the only way out is for her husband to give up some of his time to such household duties as he is capable of performing. But if it takes him all his time, doing the best he knows how, to make ends meet, working at his own proper avocations, how is it to be done when he has to leave the work — which pays grudgingly and sparingly, it is true, but still which brings in all the income they have — to do the household chores, vastly more in number too, these, be it remembered, than in the days when he was a bachelor? Is this the "two dollars married where, single, he couldn't make one?" He is face to face with an *impasse* which may well make the good man scratch his head and wonder what the devil must be done. After all, matters seem worse than they are. They are both young and strong, and able to endure, and somehow or other they "tough it through." Perhaps a neighbour has a sister-in-law staying with her who can come in twice or three times a week and take the hardest of the work off her hands. Perhaps there comes a cheque from the old country about this time in view of the extra expenses of the year. The infant is pretty sure to be sound and healthy, and before long matters go on much the same as before, brightened by a new interest.

No bed of roses this so far, however. She has to work each day far harder than any of the servants in her father's house, and feels regretfully that she has next to no time to herself for reading or keeping up any of her accomplishments. She is sinking into the *haus frau* she fears, with no thought or aim beyond having a good dinner for her husband, her house and its belongings in apple-pie order, and her children well fed and decently dressed. Her love of culture may not have been more than skin deep, but once on a time she had not proposed to herself to satisfy her leanings towards sweetness and light over the cook stove and wash-tub. Then, too, she wonders and fears that a greater familiarity with the coarser and more sordid side of life may not, ever so slightly, but still appreciably, mar the bloom of the surface delicacy of her nature. This acquaintance with unlovely sights and sounds, the rough talk that occasionally penetrates to her ears, will they not make some difference in her that her friends may notice if ever she returns to civilisation? The men that have come out young and stayed long, have they not deteriorated somewhat from the standard they were very fair representatives of once; lost a little of their polish, indefinably gone off a little? And if they, why not she?

If ever she returns to civilisation! But will she, she wonders. Is her husband doing any good, poor fellow, with all his endeavours? Hard as he works, the daily struggle gets no easier; it even seems to her as if there were less money for expenses than a year ago, though he says little about it. He should have married one of these women out here, she thinks, half resentfully and half sorrowfully, who would have been a help to him instead of an expense. But the baby is crying and supper is to get. Action dispels gloomy thoughts, and if some traces of perturbation are still noticeable when her husband comes home from work, we will hope he is sensitive and sensible enough to throw a little extra kindness and cheeriness into his manner. So far it has been supposed that our young couple are not well enough off to hire much, if any, help; and an attempt has been made to portray in the above sketch what the lady's life must be where this is the case, as it is perhaps in the majority of English ranch households. But where the income, from whatever source — almost certainly it will not proceed from the ranch — is of sufficient size to allow of a girl being kept, the English ranchwoman's life will not be the incessant round of drudgery that it must be where she has all the work to do herself and a family to look after into the bargain. Lonely it will still be and monotonous, but at least there will be some leisure to read or follow her favourite indoor pursuits. The great brunt of the household duties will be off her hands, and this makes all the difference in the world, or would, if it were not that for weariness of body she has substituted vexation of spirit when she undertakes a Western hired girl, unless she is rarely fortunate. If she gets one of the neighbour's daughters, she must treat her on a footing of absolute equality if she wants her to stay more than a day. Her employer and his wife are ranch people, and so are her parents, and in the girl's eyes there is no difference whatever in station. She has been brought up not only in the belief that she is as good as anybody, but to be ready at all times and all seasons fiercely to assert it, and most of all, perhaps, when she has hired to an "English outfit." Very little fault-finding will she stand, and she expects to be treated as one of the family; that is to say, to take her meals at the same table, and when the dishes are washed after the evening meal to sit with them. If any visitors come to the house she expects an introduction. It is within the writer's knowledge that, where a lady of his acquaintance, not an Englishwoman as it happens, had neglected to do this in the case of a girl she had hired, whose parents lived in the neighbourhood, the girl's mother came to the house and made quite a scene, using this omission as her text, and winding up a long harangue with the *argumentum ad hominem,* "How would you like it for one of your own daughters? My girl is no nigger, I want you to know." Then she left the house and took her daughter with her. Nor was the mother at all the virago one might expect from this story. On the contrary, in appearance and on ordinary occasions, in manner, she was exceptionally nice, and a good deal above the average Westerner.

If the bumps of pride and self-esteem are not to be found in a high state of development on every Westerner's head, there is nothing in phrenology. English people are not supposed to be deficient in these qualities, but the average Englishman is not within measurable distance of the frontiers' man. This it is which makes it so hard for English people at first to keep in touch with their American employés. They are "helps," not servants — you are employer, not master or mistress. They will take orders from you but not peremptory orders; and if there is one thing that will rouse them quicker than another, it is the frigid and distant tone usually employed by English people in addressing their inferiors.

They detect, or fancy they detect, a shade of contempt in it, and this is as a lighted match to tow steeped in turpentine. If you can treat them in a friendly way you will get along with them all right, but your manner must be natural and spontaneous, not merely affable and gracious.

This young lady, then, who has consented to accommodate our English friends for a while will have the faults of her class more or less developed, and certainly she will have her full share of independence. Very likely she will do her work well and quickly, but after hours her time is her own, and she employs it as suits her best. Her young men, or "fellows", as she calls them, will come to the house and escort her to every dance in the neighbourhood, nor will she think it in the least incumbent on her to ask her employers' leave to attend them. She is much more likely to announce that supper must be an hour earlier as Sile Reed is coming to take her to the dance at Hills', and he won't want to be kept waiting. She is not very likely to stay long. Even if there is no actual rupture, she and the English lady find a good many causes of friction, and they soon part company. Even though things may have gone smoothly, she will soon want to go home. She wants some money for some purpose, twenty or thirty dollars, perhaps, and when a month or six weeks' work has put this sum in her pocket she takes her leave.

There is this disadvantage in having a girl from the neighbourhood that, if there should have been a regular quarrel, and the girl has been discharged, or taken herself off in a huff, one family at least in the immediate circle has become hostile, and may, by talking and circulating reports, do a good deal to rouse the prejudice always lurking in the Western mind against the English. The lady, in spite of her husband's repeated warnings, is exceedingly likely to have dropped some careless remark about Western ways in the girl's hearing, or to have jested about some peculiarity in the appearance or speech of some one who has come to the house, and this will be repeated and added to. The utmost care should be taken by English people settled in the West to say as little as possible about their neighbours in the hearing of any of them. The most innocent remark will be distorted, and meanings violently twisted as the story proceeds from mouth to mouth, losing nothing in the telling each time. There are so many chances in ranch life for an ill-disposed neighbour to do an injury where he thinks he has a grudge, that it is well to take all reasonable pains to avoid giving offence.

In spite of these drawbacks there is more chance of getting satisfactory help out of a girl used to ranching than there is by taking one of the professional "hired girls" of a Western town. To begin with, it is next to impossible to do this. Hardly any wages will induce them to leave town, and no wages will induce them to stay longer than a month or six weeks. They have been used to town conveniences, water in the house, hot and cold, a sink, everything brought to the door by tradesmen, and their night or two out in the week. If one of these should have consented to ruralise for a while for some private reason, such as a lovers' quarrel, the chances are she will begin to grumble the instant she enters the house, and never leave off till, driven to desperation, her employers pay her off, sacrificing her fare, which she was to pay herself if she went of her own accord.

Perhaps their next experiment will be a man and wife, and this would seem to be the likeliest chance for a satisfactory arrangement were it not that in this perverse world the best women seem to get the worst husbands and *vice versa*. It is surprisingly difficult to find a couple of anything like equal value, though when you do, an arrangement of this kind is far more likely to have some element of permanency than any other that can be made. They will get their board and from forty to fifty dollars a month between them, and this is too good a thing for them to lightly throw up.

Or they may try an Englishman and his wife, or a girl from the old country. This is costly and dangerous. The journey has to be paid by the employer, to be repaid by instalments out of wages, and if the new arrival don't suit or gets discontented, as often happens, what is to be done? The truth is that the question of help in the house, difficult of solution anywhere in America, is doubly so on a ranch, and the mistress of the house is often tempted to exclaim she would rather do the work herself than be so harassed and tormented. Perhaps she finds her solution by alternating between the methods, according as exhaustion of mind or body prevails.

There is not much time for amusement for its own sake on a ranch, nor much chance to find it if there were. In the man's case, though the life as a whole is monotonous, that is, it is uneventful, and one year is pretty much like another, yet there is much variety in his days. He is seldom doing the same kind of work for many days together, and he is in constant communication with his fellows. Here his wife, however, is not so fortunate. Each day when she gets up she can tell exactly what there will be to do, and that is what she did yesterday, and what she will do to-morrow. Minor variations there will be, of course, but the kind of work will not vary, and the English lady will pass day after day occupied in housework without seeing a soul beyond the members of the household, and these only at meal-time, being in respect of society much worse off than her native neighbours, who are in and out of each other's houses tolerably often, and who, it is presumed, enjoy each other's visits. Without ostracising her they let her alone, recognising, of course, that a difference exists, resenting it a little, and for the most part keeping away. Some of them will have paid her a visit when she first arrived, and she has returned it, and there it has stopped. The people are not in the least like those she has been accustomed to go and see in her father's parish, and she is quite ready to acquiesce in the neighbours' opinion that she is better left to herself. Her life therefore is duller than theirs — much duller, as they are leading their natural lives, have their dances, and picnics, and social gatherings, and take a most enormous interest in each other's sayings and doings.

There may be, almost certainly will be, some English family within reach, or at all events some English bachelors, and from time to time a meeting will be contrived and much enjoyed. The young Englishmen will perhaps make a practice of riding over on Sundays, and these will be the pleasantest days. If there are young children, and a distance of, say, ten or twelve miles divide the two families, the ladies will not meet very often, in spite of promises and intentions, not nearly as often as in their mutual interest they should. For unless the ranch is big enough to justify help being kept, it is not easy for the owners to be away one night. Stock has to be attended to, milking cannot be neglected, and if there are no quite near neighbours it will be difficult to find anyone to attend to these duties. The "chore" question is an obstacle which stands in the way of any sudden resolve to go over and see one's friends, and where a visit has to be planned and provided for, it is very apt to be indefinitely postponed.

Social diversion, then, of a kind she will care about, being only attainable at rare intervals, is there any chance for her to get any variety into her life out of her own immediate resources? How about that horse her husband promised her, for instance? How many times has she been on its back since she came out? Regard for truth compels the statement that the side saddle is hanging up by the stirrup with perhaps six months' dust on it. Since the babies began to come she has hardly ridden at all, though in the first months of her stay she used to accompany her husband tolerably often. If her lot is cast on the plains, which, for her sake, it is to be hoped is not the case, there is not much to tempt her out. There is little scenery and no shade, but instead a glaring sun and abundance of alkali dust. A ride for pleasure under these conditions seems rather a misnomer. At first, of course, when the whole country was new to her, and before she had got into that half-tired state which seems to be her normal condition now, what with heat and work together, she used to take a good deal of pleasure in accompanying her husband. The common sights of the prairie were novel and interesting. The cactuses when in bloom are brilliant and striking, and prairie dogs, lizards, an occasional rattlesnake, and sometimes a coyote, are at first looked at with curiosity. But even of these attractions there cometh satiety, and before long she will let her husband go by himself.

But if her husband is "running a bunch of stock" somewhere in the mountains, and they are living at an altitude, say, of about 8,000 feet, life will lose many of the disagreeables which plain people have to put up with. As far as comfort in living is concerned there is, in the writer's judgment, no comparison between the plains and the mountains as places of residence. It is true that the "big money" in cattle was made on the plains and not in the mountains, but that was years ago, when the ranches were virgin and covered with the nutritious gramma-grass on which stock flourished and multiplied exceedingly, needing next to no care. No provision for wintering them had to be made, and all the cattle owners had to do was to keep a man or two on the ranch to "keep track" of their whereabouts, attend to the branding of his calves in the spring, and the rounding up of his beef in the fall, and spend his winters where he pleased. If his wife ever visited the ranch, it was only for a few weeks at a time. The years between '60 and '75 were halcyon days for stockmen. But the day of big herds is almost gone, the ranges are eaten out, and the small occupier has settled wherever water for irrigating can be brought from river or creek, to the additional injury of the range industry. These men have their few cows and horses, and devote themselves principally to farming, and this is what ranching on a small capital means. There is no "big money," or hope of "big money," in it, and this being so, if ranching is your business, as well make yourself as comfortable in your daily life as circumstances will permit, and if life seems more attractive in the mountains, pitch your camp there.

There you will escape the great heat and dust and alkali water. The mountain water is nearly always as good as the water on the plains is bad. This is quite an item when it is a question of choosing a home. There you have scenery and shade, and the sigh of the wind in the pine trees, and babbling brooks in the spring, and in early summer wild flowers without end. In some parts of the mountains there are still elk and deer, and there are trout in nearly all the streams. The climate during the summer and fall is probably as near perfection as can be found on this planet, and the winters, though long, are not unduly vigorous. The struggle is no less anxious than on the plains, but it is carried on under pleasanter conditions.

Here, if the English lady takes a ride, she can get some pleasure out of it. And if she will get her husband some summer's day to keep up a saddle horse for her over night as well as his own, and next morning get up about five o'clock and go with him to run in the horses before breakfast, if perchance some extra ones may be wanted for some purpose, she will get a taste of the full glory of mountain air and scene which will be a memory to her, it may be, for years. The air has an indescribable freshness and invigorating quality, with nothing of the rawness which it has in England at that early hour, and it comes to them laden with the balmy scent of the pines and spruces as they ride through the timber listening to the tinkle of the house bell. Following a trail which leads through a spruce thicket, they come out on a knoll overlooking a "little park" in which they see the horses grazing. Perhaps they stay a few minutes drinking in the beauty of the scene — the pale green of the mountain aspens — quaking, as its local name is — against the darker background of the pine woods, while in the far distance the sun strikes on some snow-clad peak and tinges it with a rosy glow. Now one of the saddle horses "nickers" to a friend he recognizes in the "bunch" below him, and reminds the riders of the motive that brought them out.

That old buckskin mare has had too good a thing lately, and is fat and sassy — she doesn't mean to be corralled this morning without some frolic. So as our friends pick their way down the hill side she starts at a run out of pure mischief and devilment, and the rest follow madly, snatching at each other and throwing up their heels. They are soon lost to sight in the timber, but the bell rings wildly and "gives them away," and after an exhilarating chase they are headed off and "hit the trail for home." The bars of the corral are down, and pulling their horses to a walk, they watch them file in. The bars are put up and our couple begin to think that breakfast will be a desirable move.

In the mountains, too, here and there are to be found wild raspberries of a delicious flavour and remarkable size. These grow "in patches" of from one to three acres in extent, and to these patches, when the raspberries are ripe, the neighbours repair with buckets and kegs to pick them for preserving. This is a great outing for the women-folk, as it means camping out for a day or two, and a break in the sameness of their existence. Perhaps the English lady will like to try it, if only for the sake of the variety it affords. Yet quite likely once will be enough. Camping is very nice for an experience, but most people decide after trying it that a house is good enough for them. Perhaps a pithy remark heard at one of these raspberry patches includes most of the ladies' objection to it. The writer was in conversation with an old lady who, by the way, could pick more berries in a day than he could in two if not three, and do it easier. She was asking him how it was he had not brought the folks along, meaning thereby two sisters of his whom she knew were staying with him. "But then," she added before he could speak, as one who saw the absurdity of the question, "it's rough work climbing over these logs unless you're used to it. Their hides is tender, and there's so much wallering round in camping."

Few people are strong enough to offer a steady resistance to circumstances. The life of most of us is an acquiescence, sometimes hearty, more often grudging, in the conditions in which we are placed, without much effort of our own to alter them if they do not suit us. By the pressure of circumstance the English lady will sooner or later cease the endeavour to bring variety and colour into her life, and content herself with discharging mechanically monotonous duties or overseeing their discharge. And with all her application what does she finally attain to? Just as the English ranchman seldom acquires the thorough knowledge and grip of all points of his business, which the native ranchman has unconsciously developed in himself by the infiltration of a lifetime's experience, not often does the English lady become the genuine practical hand that a ranchman's wife should be, but at the best a clever imitation of her. Her courage and will are undeniable, but submitted to the ordeal of steady work her muscle and endurance are not equal to the test. Nor do the native ranchwomen come out unscathed. The tremendous strain of rearing a family and performing their share of the daily operations of the ranch tells on them all. All bear traces of the conflict, and many of them are old women — in appearance at least — at thirty-five. Yet — and this goes to show that this sacrifice is necessary — hardly ever will a successful ranchman be found who does not owe his success to his wife's exertions in her own sphere, equally with his own in his.

Truth to say, it is no life to bring a lady to, unless at lest there are, actually and certainly, means sufficient to provide her with help. Emphatically, the means should not be in the future, to be provided by their joint efforts. If they are in the future, there they are exceedingly apt to remain. And in any case the lady's lot is far harder than her husband's. All the variety and movement fall to his share, and he sees twenty people to her one. Ask the English ranchmen how they like the life, and you will find the worst complaint they have to make is that there is nothing in it — too much work for exceedingly little money. If it paid better, a majority of them will tell you, they would be well enough suited. Some even would rather follow it than anything else, and of a truth there is a fascination in its independence and unconventionality which makes it hard to give up, in spite of its ruggedness and hardship. But not so with their wives. They get all the tedious part and very little of the good, and if you ask them, if they do not frankly tell you they detest it and long to get away from it, the most favourable answer that can be extracted is to the effect that it is not so bad; they don't mind it, and have got used to it by this time.

Even in the rare case where an English ranchman has been successful, having had perhaps large capital to start with and not having fooled it away, so that he is in an assured position with a thriving business so long as he is here to attend to it, and an income adequate for all comfort and some luxury, it is doubtful if his wife would not cheerfully sacrifice a good deal to get out of it all and return to her own country. Though she escapes the actual work which falls to the lot of her less fortunate sisters, so wearing is the question of household help, so trying the almost entire absence of society and amusement, so troublesome the question of educating children, especially the girls, that she would cheerfully accept a reduction of income and live in the old country among her friends and people of her own habit of mind. Better, she will think, the gleaning of the grapes of Ephraim than the vintage of Abiezer.

If what has been said in this article is chiefly gloomy, it must not be supposed that the English lady on a ranch passes her life in a state of despondency. Much praise and admiration are her due for the courage and cheerfulness with which she faces her hard conditions and makes the best of them. There is this in favour of her life, that, being hard as it is and simple as it is, small pleasures and small luxuries produce the same effect as greater ones in a more conventional way of living. Very likely they are more keenly enjoyed. Nowhere does a little money go so far; nowhere else would the arrival of a box containing some delicacies for the table, a carpet and curtains too worn for town use, and some books and magazines, mark an epoch in your life. More important yet is the absence of that Moloch of civilisation, the heart-breaking struggle to keep up appearances on an insufficient income. Here is no one to see, and no one to care. Among the blind the one-eyed is king, and you may even be an object of envy to your neighbours, though they would perish rather than betray it, as they gaze on the splendour of your sitting-room, your walls covered with wallpaper instead of newspaper, your carpeted floor, or your best dress of the fashion of five years ago. Nor is the unpleasing contrast between poverty and wealth forced upon you, unpleasing, that is, as long as the poverty is yours and the wealth some one else's. If any in the neighbourhood are better off than others, they are not much better off, and in any case in dress, manner, and appearance present no difference.

Yet when all is said, the recommendations of the life appear to be chiefly negative, and the intending ranchwoman will have a use for what patience and self-denial and fortitude and resignation she can find in her moral equipment. Eminently Christian virtues these, and their faithful practice will result in a noble character. None the less, having regard to the frailty of human nature, some sympathy may be accorded to those English ladies who look askance at the martyr's crown that is thrust upon them, and who sigh occasionally for a life where these qualities shall not be called into such active and constant exercise.

1. *Longman's Magazine,* May 1895.

Agnes Skrine

A Lady's Life on a Ranche

Living as we do about twenty miles from anywhere on a ranche in the North-West of Canada, we get our magazines rather late, and with more or less irregularity. But we read them attentively, and of course we read anything about ourselves with that absorbing interest which the subject naturally arouses. I was surprised to find myself rather a prominent person in the magazines of last year, and still more surprised to learn that I was a woman set apart, and an object of pity. I learned that "an English lady on a ranche" is a self-devoted being, a household drudge, to be regarded with respectful admiration and compassion. I learned that I had married a failure, for the young Englishman in the Colonies was set down as hopelessly incompetent, with the best of intentions indeed, but the worst of methods. This part of the history I particularly resented, for it is so weak to marry a failure. Then I learned what our future lives were to be. He was to struggle hard, and perhaps, if he were very good indeed, to win a bare subsistence. I was to struggle even harder, in a virtuous and heavy-hearted manner; and virtue would be its own reward — perhaps. We were to have no time for reading or amusement, no congenial society, and apparently no sport. We were to linger out an unenviable existence in the bare-handed struggle to make existence self-supporting, and that was all.

Now I cannot answer for all the English wives on all the ranches in Canada. I can only answer for one ranche which is flourishing, and for one small Irish-woman happily situated on it. There is perhaps a good deal of sympathy between Ireland and the North-West. In the old country we are accustomed to disregard appearances, to make all kinds of shifts and laugh at them, to neglect super-fluities, mind our manners, follow after sport, and love horses. All that is good training for the North-West. But on coming here one finds everybody engaged in making money, or trying to; and that is a new and bracing atmosphere to an Irish constitution. No one is rich here. On the other hand, hardly any one is distressingly poor, of those at least who live on their ranches like ourselves, and make their money by horses and cattle. As to whether they make or lose most, and how they make or why they lose it, I know just enough to be silent on the subject for fear of making some "bad break." The Western tongue is expressive. This, however, I know, that it is a very novel and pleasant experience to belong to a community of which all the members are more or less equal in fortune; and also that it is the most refreshing thing in life never to look at or handle money from month's end to month's end. Wages and bills are paid by cheques. There is no expenditure of small sums when one lives twenty-four miles from a shop; and the diminution of wear and tear to the brain-tissue when one never has to do the sum of fifteen times sevenpence-halfpenny is considerable. After living here for eighteen months, I realised one day that I did not know the currency of the country by sight. Who ever enjoyed such a blessed ignorance in England for a week?

As to the want of congenial society, that complaint may be preferred from many a corner of the British Isles with as much reason as from North-Western Canada. But one observes that those who are always complaining of the society round them are not, as a rule, its most useful or brilliant members. Here, besides our Canadian neighbours, who are unfailing in kindness and hospitality to new-comers, there live a fair number of Englishmen, ranchers and others; and some of the more adventurous have wives. What should hinder us from enjoying each other's society? It is true that we do not scatter cards upon each other or make many afternoon calls, for reasons connected with time and space and other large considerations. We do not give each other dinner-parties either; but we give each other dinner, generally at 1 P.M., and beds for the night. People usually come when they have some reason for passing this way; and in a ranching country, houses are so few and far between that hospitality of necessity becomes a matter of course. As a matter of course also, people do not expect to be amused. We have no means of formally entertaining each other, and it is not thought amusing to talk from morning till night. A visitor prefers to smoke his pipe in peace, to find his way out and wander round the corrals, inspect any bit of building that may be going on, or cast a critical eye on the stock. After which he saddles his *cayuse* for himself, and departs on his own affairs.

We are all a good deal taken up here with attending to our own business; consequently we do not see so much of each other as people do at home. Will that be thought unfavourable to friendliness? Personally I incline to the advice given in the Book of Proverbs: — "Withdraw thy foot from thy neighbour's house; lest he be weary of thee, and so hate thee."

But when people who have like aims and occupations do happen to meet, the converse is particularly interesting, at least to themselves. Of course they talk shop. Nearly all the conversation worth listening to is shop of one kind or another. Prairie shop has a fascination of its own — cattle, hay and horses, timber, grass and calves, weather, Indians and wolves, fencing, freights and the English beef-market. Wherever Englishmen abound — and this is emphatically a Land of the Younger Son — there the talk is on out-of-door subjects, and there is a sympathy with all that is doing in all the ends of the earth.

But to come home again, let us give heed to the household question — that question which is with us all, and always with us. I have seen women in England nearly worn out with their servant-worries, their kitchen-ranges, and their complicated household arrangements. I would not change places with them for any consideration, even to have dinner in six courses every evening. Here we enjoy the luxury of one servant in the house, an able-bodied cook, and I never heard him complain that his cooking-stove had "gone back on him"; nor if he did, should I lie awake at night thinking about it. I made the usual mistake of bringing out a maid from home; but when in course of time the mistake rectified itself, and she went the way of all womankind in the West, I took to the broom and duster, and was surprised to find what a calmness descended on my spirit with release from the task of supervision. An average of two hours' housework a-day, and the trouble of mending one's own clothes, is not much to pay for all the joys of liberty. I keep up a conscientious endeavour to find some substitute for the vanished maid; and still every failure to secure one brings a secret relief, a sense that the days of liberty are lengthened. I own to have been tempted once, when the fascinations of a certain elderly dame very nearly overcame me. She was of striking appearance, thin, and high-stepping, with short grey hair confined by a band of cherry-coloured velveteen, and she wore a profusion of blue beadwork. She told me that she was capable of doing all I could possibly require. Only one thing was beyond her, and that was a particular "kind of a hotel cake, one of these regular slap-up cakes, with icing." She took credit for this voluntary confession of her limitations, being, as she said, quite above deception; and then she explained that all she required of me was a candour equal to her own. She "liked that, and she liked her boss to come right in to the kitchen too, and pass a joke with her, and not be stiff." Nothing came of the interview, though I was well inclined to prolong our relations and do my best about the jokes, while the lady of the beads was sure that we should value each other. But it was not to be.

No doubt there is a certain difficulty about household service on a ranche. But then housekeeping is of a very simple kind. There are no elaborate meals, no superfluous furniture or plate to be cleaned; there is no attendance beyond what is necessary: in short, everything that may cause extra trouble is avoided. There is plenty of comfort on a ranche, but very little luxury; and every one must be ready to help himself, and to help others too, when the occasion arises. In case of sudden defection on the part of the cook, it is well to know how to prepare some simple things; though indeed almost any Western man can fill up the vacancy, so far as baking bread and cooking beef go. Then, in case of being weather-bound or otherwise cut off from a laundress, it is well to know a little of the gentle art of washing. No art is more useful, and none is easier to acquire, in a country like this, where "washboards," "wringers," and all kinds of conveniences minimise the labour.

When I first came here I did nothing at all, and enjoyed it very much. But now that I have a little — *a very* little — daily occupation, I enjoy it a great deal more. The fact is, that in a community where every one else is at work one does not feel quite at home in complete idleness — in riding over the prairie, gathering flowers, writing letters, and reading poetry-books all day long and every day. Abstraction is very pleasant; but it is pleasanter still to have a share in the general life, and by a very light experience of work, to gain some sympathy with those whose experience is of little else but work.

The winning of new sympathies is the chief interest of life. Here you may learn sympathy with lines of life so long and varied that they extend from the Patriarchs to Dick Swiveller's little Marchioness. One might go even farther back — namely, to Jabal, who was *"the father of such as dwell in tents, and of such as have cattle."* There is nothing like life in the North-West to give one an insight into patriarchal history. How plainly it makes one understand the strife that arose between the herdmen of Abram and the herdmen of Lot, when their cattle had increased *"so that they could not dwell together."* I suppose there is not a cow-hand in the West who could not furnish one with some instructive particulars of that strife, or who could not exactly appreciate Abram's generosity in allowing to Lot the first choice of a range, and Lot's very natural mistake in choosing the plain of Jordan because *"it was well watered everywhere,"* though far too thickly settled for a cattle-range.

Of course, when there was no central government that could "reserve springs" in the interests of stock-growers, one is not surprised to find that every watering-place was a source of strife between the herdmen of respective owners. The cowboy is not even yet the most peaceable of mankind, and to see his herd perishing of thirst would naturally exasperate him. Besides, to fill up the wells that other people had dug was "playing it very low down" — as the herdmen of Isaac seem to have thought at the time of the trouble with the men in Gerar.

Among all the worthies of the Old Testament, Jacob is that one who enjoys least popularity at home. His trickiness is invariably objected to, his trials go unpitied, and his talents are disparaged. Now here, having enjoyed the advantage of hearing an experienced cowboy explain the career of our father Israel, I see what injustice has been done to his memory. Jacob was, in fact, a herdman, or cowboy, "from away back," an undeniably smart hand. His guiding principle in life was to forego no advantage; and this is the essence of smartness. To outwit his simple brother was an easy matter to him in his youth; in later life his wily old uncle Laban was no match for him, though for twenty years the underhand struggle went on between the two. It is easy for the superficial to say that Jacob lacked a conscience. Nothing of the kind. Like a born herdman as he was, he put so much conscience into his herding that there was none left over for the less important affairs of life. The anxieties and hardships of a Western herdsman to-day were Jacob's too at the date B.C. *cir.* 1745: — *"Thus I was; in the day the drought consumed me, and the frost by night; and my sleep departed from mine eyes."* He was no ordinary hand who could say to Laban, *"It was little which thou hadst before I came, and it is now increased unto a multitude."* It may be observed, too, that Jacob made good all losses to his employer, even loss from wild animals; and this was pointed out with admiring reprobation by the man who imparted to me the true sense of the narrative. How, he asked, did Jacob make out to replace all losses from the herd of Laban at a time when he had no herd of his own, and was not worth a cent anyhow? The inference is plain. There were other herds on that range, and Jacob must have "rustled" what he wanted from them. You bet your life! our father Israel was a "rustler." Nothing is wanting to constitute him our patron saint of the West.

This excursion into the eighteenth century B.C. is no digression, of course. I have only been showing that we like to connect ourselves with the dignity of history. But I am glad the connection does not extend to living in tents. A Canadian winter under canvas would probably bring the history to an early close; and even in summer, except for the idea of the thing, a house has many advantages. English ladies are much pitied, I see, for the sad, rough houses they have to live in on these sad, rough ranches, "so different from their refined English homes." As to refinement, of course that is neither here nor there. It belongs to the person, and not to the house the person inhabits, or at least only by communication to the house. But why should there be all this sadness and roughness and pity at all? Of course, a house on a Western ranche is as different from a house at home as it can well be. Still, you cannot judge of the merits of anything by pronouncing it different from something else. A log or lumber house on a site determined by the existence of a spring and moderate shelter, is built in two or three months, then simply furnished, and that is all. It seems a little superfluous to draw the contrast between this and an English home. But on the other hand, why should one not enjoy all reasonable comfort in a lumber-house? If well built it is very warm and tight in wintertime, of course with the addition of double windows; and if warm in winter, it will be cool in summer. Besides, one can have a verandah on the eastern side, where the little flower-garden will be; and as soon as the sun is overhead, the verandah makes the pleasantest sitting-place with the scent of mignonette and the cucumber-vine about it. If the house is well finished inside, it can be made very pretty in a simple way. A friend once described our house as "ceiled with cedar and painted with vermilion." Having lived for some time now within cedar-panelled walls, I have come to the conclusion that no other walls are half so pretty. The warm brown-and-gold tints of the wood make a perfect background for water-colours, china, books, and anything else that may be conveniently disposed of upon them. Then at home ceilings are usually a trial to the eyes, but cedar-panelled ceilings add a joy of their own to life. I cannot think that the look of one's rooms is unimportant, for in winter one spends so many hours indoors; and the unbroken whiteness of snow without makes every feature of form and colour within more insistent.

For nearly half the year, however, we can lead a regular out-of-door life here, and that is what makes the real charm of the country. That is what gives the health and brightness and hardiness to a life that acts with a kind of slow fascination on us all. Englishmen who have lived here will abuse the country sometimes, go home for good, bidding a joyful last farewell to the prairie — and come back within the year. They profess not to know what has drawn them back to these world-forsaken wilds, and they abuse the country again. But they can't keep away from it. The logic of such proceedings is quite beyond my grasp; but speaking as a mere illogical female, I like the country so well myself that I think it is good to be here. I like the simplicity, the informality of the life, the long hours in the open air. I like the endless riding over the endless prairie, the winds sweeping the grass, the great silent sunshine, the vast skies, and the splendid line of the Rockies, guarding the west. I like the herds of cattle feeding among the foothills, moving slowly from water to water; and the bands of horses travelling their own way, free of the prairie. I like the clear rivers that come pouring out of the mountains, with their great rocky pools and the shining reaches of swift water where we fish in the summer-time; and the little lakes among the hills where the wild duck drop down to rest on their flight to the north in spring. When the grouse-shooting begins in the autumn, — or, as we say here, "when the chicken-shooting begins in the fall," — I like to ride with the guns to watch the sport, and mark down the birds in the long grass. I like both the work and the play here, the time out of doors and the time for coming home. I like the summer and the winter, the monotony and the change. Besides, I like a flannel shirt, and liberty.

I certainly never heard of any one who could not enjoy some part of the summer here; but most people are glad to get away in the winter. There seems to be a fixed idea that winter is nothing but snow and monotony and weariness of spirit. Well, I do not deny the snow, but there is even more sunshine than snow; nor the monotony — but then I adore monotony. For the weariness of spirit, that is another matter altogether; and I really think it must be the people who never spend their winters here that find a Western winter so trying. In some ways it is quite as pleasant as the summer; and when one can get coyote-hunting, summer is not to be named in the same breath with it. The fun we had coyote-hunting with our friends last Christmas-time passed all. But even when one can get no hunting, there is riding and sleighing; and always there is the lovely aspect of the hills under snow, white against the radiant blue, softened as a face is softened by a smile, every dimple and delicate depression of the ground marked by a transparent shadow on the snow, its sunlit whiteness set off by the dark of leafless willows that trace the windings of the frozen creek. "Fair as the snow of one night," was an old saying in Ireland: it often comes into my mind when I look out on a sunny morning here after a snowy night. Everything seems to be new-made, white and shining, and everywhere the wonderful blue shadows are resting or drifting over the stainless valleys. The sky is a clear forget-me-not blue. The far-off line of the plains is sea-blue against it. Each hollow is pure cobalt blue, and each cloud passing above sends a blue shadow gliding over the earth. Under the log walls of the sheds at the foot of the hill, the shadow thrown on the snow might be painted in ultramarine. Perhaps among the mysterious effects of colour, blue on white has the special property of making glad! — for all through the short, sunny winter day there is a light sparkle and exhilaration in the air which acts on the spirits like a charm. Then when the time of winter sunset comes, there is a half-hour of strange, delicate brilliancy, — a blush of colour across the snow like the flush on the leaves of the latest monthly rose, a dazzling whiteness along the ridges that catch the level rays of light, deepening into a hundred tones of blue and violet between dark stretches of the leafless willow and cottonwood trees, with here and there a gleam like the green light of an opal coming from the ice that spreads upon the overflow round the mouth of a frozen water-spring. In the beauty of these winter sunsets there is something curiously unearthly — partly by reason of the frozen stillness in the air, but even more, I think, because of the mystical purity of those colours shining on the snow. One can compare them only with the light of gems like the opal and the sapphire, or the bands of pure colour in the rainbow. Are there fountains of these colours springing in Paradise, that they always seem to give our eyes hints of a fairer life?

Such are the still days; but then we have wild weather here in winter, and enough of it too! — days when the north wind blows and the snow flies before it as nothing but snow before the wind can fly, in a blind white fury. All the months of winter are months of conflict between the north and the west winds. We watch the powers of the air fighting over us, and feel as if we lived in the heart of a myth of the winds. The north wind is the destroyer; when "He casteth forth his ice like morsels:/Who is able to abide his frost?" While the north wind blows, every breathing thing shrinks and cowers. The mere holding on to life is a struggle for poor unsheltered animals, and the longer it lasts the harder is the struggle, and the less their strength for it. But there comes a change in the air. Some night on looking out we see that the clouds have rolled upwards, as if a curtain were lifted in the west, leaving a well-defined arch of clear sky with stars shining in it. That arch means that the west wind, the preserver, is on his way; and sometimes we hear his voice beforehand in a long, distant roar among the mountains. When next morning breaks, the north wind has fled, overcome. You may go to the house door in a dressing-gown to look out on the snowy prairie, and the *chinook* blowing over you feels like a warm bath. It seems miraculous. All living things are revived and gladdened. Horses and cattle move slowly towards the sunny slopes, leaving long shining furrows behind them in the smooth snow, and there they stand or lie down, basking in the soft air. It is a kind of brief summer. Even those spiritless things the hens will come out of their house under the bank, where they have been sitting like so many motionless humps of feathers, and scratch about for a while in the sun, as though life had still something to offer in place of the toes they lost in the last frost. The snow-buntings will *whir* past your face in a cloud, with a flashing of little white wings. I am told that snow-buntings, if you get enough of them, are excellent in a pie; but I think they are more excellent in the sunlight. This may be a still *chinook* that has come, a soft warmth in which the snow melts away with extraordinary rapidity, while the sky wears all kinds of transparent lovely hues like an Irish sky; and if you take a ten-minutes' ride to the top of the nearest hill, you may see to the west a whole range of the Rockies, magnificient, exultant — based on earth and piled against the sky like mountain altars, the snow-smoke rising from their dazzling slopes and melting away in the blue, as if the reek of some mighty sacrifice purer than human were ascending on high.

But sometimes the *chinook* is far from still; it blows with soft, steady force, and then the snow, instead of melting, blows away. A most curious sight it is when first the wind sets it moving; it flies along the ground as fast as flowing water, with a kind of rippling motion, breaking into sudden eddies and puffs of white, the sunshine sifting through it and powdering the whole with sparks of light. Where all this snow blows to is a mystery to me still. I never see it blow *up* from the earth; I suppose it can hardly blow *out*, like the flame of a candle: all I know is, it blows *away*. And then the prairie lies bare, brown and tawny in colour, with stretches of pale sunlit gold; and all life is safe and warm and comforted till the north wind gets his turn again.

It is very reviving to have the tyranny of winter broken through every now and again by the *chinook*. But it is better still when spring comes — not the fleeting but the abiding spring. Some day you see duck flying up the creek, or you hear the weird cry of geese float down from very high overhead. Perhaps some one remarks that the creeks are running, and very soon not only the creeks are full of rushing dark-brown water, but every hill-top is a watershed sending streams of melted snow down into the valleys. Snow-birds vanish, and instead you may see "the hawk spread her wings to the south," whistling over the bare bluffs where by-and-bye a hawk's nest will be. Gophers wake up underground, and stick their smooth heads out of their holes again, with last year's familiar piping; and down by the water-side, where willows are covered with their silver-grey buds, you can watch little blue-tits feeding on them, generally upside down in their own fascinating manner. As soon as frosts cease to bind the earth at night, the longed-for grass begins to push up and grow; but before the first green blade has sprung, we are sure to have welcomed the earliest comer of all, the Pasque-flower, which is "merry spring-time's harbinger" in the North-West. They call it the "crocus" here, and *Anemone pulsatilla* is its name among the learned, I have heard; but somehow I cannot regard flowers as belonging to the Latin races, and this one is such a perfect herald of Easter that the Easter name seems to fit it best. Some time in March out of the cold, cold earth it comes up into the light, and you find its buds standing on the prairie, each wrapped up in a furry grey coat against the north blast. Perhaps for a week the shining fur coats are all that can be seen, tightly buttoned up; but one sunny day the furs open wide, and out slip the nestling flowers. Oh, how glad we are to see them! Hans Andersen would have made a pretty fairy tale about the opening of the Pasque-flowers. Their colours are beautiful and delicate — all the peculiar cloudy blues of the anemone, deepening almost to violet, and veined with lilac and grey. Leafless and unattended, they come in crowds, in millions; and gleaming all over the prairie among the withered, tangled grass, they show the fresh young year born out of the old one. Many richer flowers follow in their time, some lovelier; but I think none meet with quite the same welcome as the Pasque-flowers, which answer to more than the pleasure of the eyes.

One of the great charms of the prairie is, that the flowers grow in such masses and myriads over it. Until I came here I never knew what it was to see as many flowers as I could wish all at once. But here, — say it is the month of May; May with the fleecy blue and white skies, the light-hearted breezes blowing, the sad-voiced plovers calling, when for a short while pools of clear water shine here and there over the prairie, "as if," some one said, "the land had opened its eyes to look at the sky." Beautiful duck are resting on these pools very often, mallard, teal, pintail, and others; or cattle have come for a drink, and stand in groups that call for a Rosa Bonheur, making bright reflections of themselves on the water. This is the time when violets blow; blue and grey and golden, they come up by thousands in the short grass, and at the same time the "shooting-stars" make long flushes of crimson where they stand in their regiments, nodding side by side. Sometimes a pure white one bends like a bride among the rest. They are little winged flowers, reminding one of cyclamens, but "American cowslip" is their misleading name.

About the last week in May or the first in June it is worth taking a long ride to find the forget-me-nots which grow in certain high spots. One calls forget-me-nots blue at home, but the bluest would look as pale as skim-milk beside these. Enamel or the deepest turquoise would be dulled by them. They shine from the ground like gems, and you may see them quite a long way off, though they have none of the glisten and transparency of red and white flowers: they shine only from their pure, opaque intensity of blue. The place where we always go to find the first forget-me-nots is called "the Ridge," as though there were no other elevation of its kind in all this mountain country. It is a stony ridge, its top half covered with dwarf poplars and a little creeping plant with tasteless red berries, the leaves of which Indians smoke for tobacco and call *kinni-kinnick*. As you ride up and top this ridge, there bursts upon you quite suddenly the widest and most glorious view that can possibly be imagined. The ground at your feet falls away to a great distance, on your left by a steep slope covered with dark willows; there is a long, wide valley with stretches of willow and a gleam of water, then the ground rises and falls for miles in a succession of high, curving ridges, for all the world as if the earth had broken into billows like the sea. Some of these land-billows have exactly the curve and poise of a sea-wave before it breaks on the shore, but the cliffs they break against are the feet of the Rocky Mountains. Nothing could be more splendid than the immense chain of the Rockies seen from here. They rise and rise against the west, and from their very roots upwards to their shining crowns, you can follow the magnificent lines of their building, — their vast bases, against which the billowing foothills dwindle to far-seen ripples, their towering heights and depths, the clefts and ledges piled with mountainous weights of snow, the jutting cliffs that catch at passing clouds, the great hollows that one guesses at from clear-cut shadows on the snow, and then the final glory of their sun-lit crests. So high and shining they are, they seem like some rampart to the world. If you look for a long while from here, you are seized with a fancy that all the earth is rolling towards the west, and there is *nothing* beyond the Rockies; they end the world and meet the sky. You lose this idea when you are actually between the mountains, for then you can only see two or three at a time; but looking at them from this distance on "the Ridge," it possesses you for a while. Yet, great as they are, I do not think their size is nearly so amazing as their beauty. Some of these mighty heights are built on such mysterious laws of beauty that they compel the eye to follow and cling to their lines, just as the ear follows and strains after sweet sounds, with a kind of yearning. As to their colouring, it is seldom two days alike. I think it is more joyous than any other mountain colouring I have seen. Though the Rockies have their seasons of rage, tempest, and fury, they never seem to mourn or brood over the things between earth and sky, as some mountains will. Perhaps they are too far away, too near the sun. In full sunlight, when their great fields of pure snow are dazzling the air, shot with silver-gleams and crossed by those transparent blue shadows of the slow-sailing clouds, what a stainless splendour is on them! I have seen them scarcely less beautiful on a hot afternoon in midsummer, far, far withdrawn into a silvery haze, baseless, unsubstantial mountains, hanging like a picture in the sky, just made visible by the gleaming of their snows. Another wonderful aspect they wear in thundery weather, when the high-piled, motionless clouds seem resting in heavy, gold-rimmed curves against the very edges of the mountains, which grow every hour more deeply, mysteriously blue; and there is yet another effect, when mountains and sky grow faint and pale together in the noonday heat, till the sky is almost colourless, and the mountains are mere outlines of shining lilac and snow. But on the whole, I think the commonest aspect of the Rockies is also the most beautiful — that is, under fresh fallen snow and in full sunlight. It is no wonder that even living out of sight of them, as we do among the foothills here, we seem to be always conscious of the great mountains so close at hand; and the constant sight of them on one's ordinary rides and business lends a kind of splendour to our days. In the sightless hours, too, one sometimes wakes aware of them in their far-off places — "Oh, struggling with the darkness all the night,/ And visited all night by troops of stars."

But now it is time to ride down from "the Ridge": we were supposed to have ridden up there only to look for forget-me-nots in June. So many other lovely flowers follow the forget-me-nots that the chief difficulty is to name them; and that is no trifling task when you are without botanical knowledge of your own, and without books of reference. I think the flowers are especially puzzling here, because many of them are so very like some that we know in the old country, and yet not exactly the same. There is one like a white violet, but it grows half a foot high; and one with the smell of a bean-flower, but it seems to be a yellow lupin; and one that behaves like the little pimpernel, but it is as large as a buttercup, and pure coral colour. We call it the "coral-flower" for want of better knowledge. The "soldier-lily" was also christened at home — an upright lily of a splendid scarlet that flames through the long grass in June. Here, as everywhere, the month of June is the rose-month. Then, while prairie larks are piping their short, sweet tunes, the prairie roses blow in their myriads, white and pink, shell pink, blush rose, and deep carmine. The bushes are low and thick — they have no long sprays like the hedge roses at home; but these low rose-thickets spread and run wild over the prairie, and along the edges of the trail you may be driving on, till the horses' feet scatter scented rose-leaves as they pass. The scent is the most perfect thing in the world, very buoyant, very sweet, and just perceptibly aromatic. One little bowl of prairie roses will scent a whole room, and remain sweet after every leaf is withered. So the month of June is very sweet in the house. With July there generally arrives a flood of blue and gold. Lupins in every shade of blue stand thick up the sides of the *coulées*. Blue asters, short and daisy-like, cover the bare and half-grassed places. Golden gaillardias, dark-centred, with brilliant fringes, shine like miniature suns right and left, high and low, everywhere. Tortoiseshell and sulphur-coloured butterflies, and black and little tiny blue ones, flitter about. Then come the "harebells dim." Instead of being shy and solitary, as they often are at home, they come in their thousands — in their millions rather: acres of harebells and the delicate blue flax wave together in the faintest breeze, and when the low sun strikes over them, if you happen to be riding with your face to the west, you see them like countless drops of light transparently twinkling in the long grass. August withers the faint blue flowers, but brings instead the fireweed glowing on every hill and hollow, and slender sunflowers clustering in the loops of the creek. These dark-eyed single sunflowers are among the most uncertain of autumn's daughters. One year they are everywhere, the next year hardly to be seen. Then sooner or later comes the inevitable September snowstorm, and after that you may say goodbye to the wildflowers till next year, and turn your attention to shooting prairie chicken.

August and September are the best months for camping out, first to fish, then to shoot. We like to go up into the mountains then. But camping is such a varied delight, or else such a serious business, that it hardly fits into the space of this article. I mention it because it is one of the chief pleasures of our life here.

"What a primitive life!" some one will say; "all animals, flowers, and open air. No society, no luxury, and no art. It must be stagnation."

Or else —

"What an admirable life!" some one will say; "work without hardship; exercise, and leisure, a civilised yet unconventional life. It must be ideal."

There will always be some people who think that life can be made ideal by its circumstances, and some who think that it can be interesting only by its excitements. *De gustibus* — "the proverb is something musty." However, I am not concerned to prove that there is no life more enviable than this which we lead. I may think so, or I may not. But I am concerned to show that the common belief about a lady's life on a ranche — that it consists necessarily and entirely of self-sacrifice and manual labour — is a delusion. That it does consist of these in hundreds of cases is unfortunately true; and the reason why is not far to seek. Many people who would think it madness to allow a son or daughter of their own to marry in England without means sufficient to keep a single house-servant, are yet easily persuaded to allow it in the Colonies, because they are told it "doesn't really matter out there." Once convinced that there will be no loss of caste, they are satisfied. They are too inexperienced in the meaning of work, or else too unimaginative to realise that they are sending a son and daughter to live a life of much harder toil than a common labourer and his wife would lead in England, with none of the labourers' alleviations of familiarity and congenial surroundings, but probably under circumstances which cause them to think with envy of the labourer's lot at home, and perhaps in a climate which makes existence a struggle for six months out of the twelve. Every one who has visited an English colony has seen people of gentle birth in this position, and has wondered, more or less superficially, if their life were worth living. I cannot pretend to decide that question. Only those who have had the courage to try the life for themselves can say whether it is a natural and justifiable one or not. There is an obvious difficulty in putting the question to them. But suppose that surmounted, I imagine that their answers would vary in accordance with their conviction of the endurance of love and the dignity of mutual service. Some are but imperfectly convinced. And surely it requires no great exercise of common-sense to realise that life cannot be made easy for people without money anywhere on this globe; also, that however difficult it may appear for a lady to keep house without any servant in England, it must be ten times harder in a country where she cannot call in a charwoman to scrub the kitchen-floor, or get water by turning a tap.

But I want to make it plain that I am speaking of a lady's life on a ranche, without reference to those cases in which a pair of young people enter into matrimony with their bare hands and the labour thereof for sole support. Are there not plenty of people with small incomes, living busy lives and not desiring to live idle ones, yet released from drudgery or pressing anxiety, with health and leisure and capacity for enjoyment? These are the people who ought to be able to find happiness on a ranche in a good country; and if they cannot, they must be either strangely stupid or strangely unfortunate. I must be allowed to take it for granted that the ranche-owner is neither a duffer nor a "tender-foot," for the question of his methods and management does not enter into this article; yet a certain moderate amount of prosperity is necessary to happiness. Granted this, what is there to prevent a lady from enjoying her life on a ranche? In England, on a narrow income there is no such thing as freedom. You cannot go where you please, or live where you please, or have what you please; you cannot join in amusements that are really amusing, because every form of sport is expensive; you cannot accept pleasant invitations, because you cannot return them. And I think there would always be a wrangle with the cook, a railway journey, or a dinner-party lying heavy on your mind. But with the same income in a country like this, you can live on equal terms with your neighbours, and all your surroundings will be entirely in your favour; you have only to make the most of them. Shooting, fishing, and hunting, just the things which would bring you to the verge of bankruptcy at home, you can enjoy here practically for nothing. You can have all the horses you want to ride or drive. Your harness may show a certain dinginess for lack of the cleaning which no one has time to bestow on it; and the panels of your "democrat" will not be adorned with your worshipful crest and motto. But then — solacing thought! — neither will anybody else's be. Here all our appointments are the very simplest that will suffice. We are too utilitarian and labour-saving to accumulate more of the extras of life than we can help. It is not because we are all devoted to a high-thinking and low-living ideal; I never found, indeed, that our thoughts soared much higher than other people's, though we live so largely on stewed apples. It is because we lack "minions to do our bidding" — a much more credible reason. This is the country in which to find out exactly how deep one's own personal refinement goes, how many dainty habits and tastes will survive when all the trouble of them has devolved upon oneself. At home they are a form of unconscious self-indulgence; here they involve a principle, and an active one.

It may be thought that I am not describing a life that could possibly prove attractive to a woman. I can imagine some one saying —

"It's all very well for a man, riding and sport and waiting on himself — that kind of thing. But a woman can't live without some sort of social amusement, and maids to harry."

Can't she? Well, I suppose women are of different kinds, and in Ireland we like sport. I never went in for maiming rabbits and missing fish myself, but all the same I like an eight-hours' day in the open air; and whether it's afoot on the springy heather of an Antrim grouse-moor, or riding over the slippery long grass of the prairie, still I must be glad when I see the sun glinting off the barrels of a pretty brown gun, or see the point of a fishing-rod dip to the water in that supple-quivering bow which means a lively trout at the end of the line. I think even a woman with no instinctive love of sport might come to care for it if she lived in the West; but, of course, it is not in the least necessary that she should. Be she the most domestic creature that ever covered up her ears "when the gun went off," she would have here the finest field she could desire for the exercise of her special gifts. Nowhere else, I venture to say, do the domestic virtues shine with such peculiar lustre as on a ranche.

Of course the scrupulous housewife must look to receive some pretty severe shocks at the outset. She may chance to find, as I have done in, her best salad-bowl set down in the fowl-house with refreshment for the hens, or a white table-cloth flapping on a barbed-wire fence to dry. Breakfast may be late one morning because the Chinaman has taken a knife to one of the "boys," and the boy is holding him down on a chair in the kitchen. But this sort of thing only happens during the first week or month: after you have attained a strength of mind to disregard such trifles, they cease to occur. Then the notable woman begins her reign, and it is a glorious one. Praise and submission surround her; soap and water scour her path. Rich jams and many-coloured cakes own her hand, and the long-neglected socks her needle. Alas that that woman and I are twain!

Still, besides the idle wife in a riding-skirt, and the busy wife measuring out things in cups, there are other sorts. Some women are studious. If they can indulge their turn of mind at home, well for them; but perhaps it is lucky they do not know how much better they could indulge it here. Not only that the hours are longer and more free from interruption, while the solitude favours abstraction, but that there are so few competing interests, so few and simple duties, and no necessity at all for that daily division and subdivision of time which the making and breaking and rearranging of engagements entails on the members of society. It is not want of time so much as distraction which hinders half the would-be students; and distraction is far from the North-West!

Last winter I thought how easy it would be to take up a new language here, or a course of moral science, or the study of whist. I meant, how easy to some one else, — for I am too hopelessly devoted to old joys and favourite authors. I have not yet half exhausted the curious pleasures of listening to the old harmonies under the new skies. I read "Romeo and Juliet" with quite a fresh wonder beside a flowery creek where the kingbirds fluttered. I read Burns's greatest Elegy by the late light of a winter afternoon, while the snowflakes blew against the window-pane; and the verses seemed to glow, each a coal of fire from the poet's heart. The "Essays of Elia" were sent me last spring in two dainty green volumes by the kind editor who prepared them for issue among the "Temple Classics." I would have him to know that never did the tenderhearted fun, the gleaming, exquisite irony of Elia so play and lighten in my dull wits before. I am sure the long, idle evenings by the lamp, and the indoor atmosphere, helped in the happy effect. Charles Lamb should never be read save by lamplight and in winter. We have so many summer authors. When the weather was very hot last August, and the haymakers hard at work, I used to find great refreshment in the shady side of a big haystack, and Bacon's "History of the Reign of Henry VII." That cold-hearted, able monarch and his wiles, as described in easy, modulated English by the cold-hearted, able historian, had an agreeably frigid effect that would have been simply wasted in winter. Nicolo Machiavelli describes, something in the same cool way, the riots of his hot and foolish Florentines, in words that hit their mark like pebbles delicately aimed. He too is a summer author. But I may not transgress into the mazy paths of literature. I only mean to say this much, that for reading of books and pleasures of the mind in general, a ranche is the choicest place imaginable.

Still, to every woman there is something more attractive than the gratifying of her special tastes, sporting, literary, or domestic. Every woman seeks her vocation, and, consciously or not, desires a sphere in which to reign and serve, a place that no one else could fill, her own niche among "the polished corners of the Temple." Now the greatest attraction of the West is that it offers such scope to the woman who really knows her *métier de femme.*

It is hard to say how far social and physical conditions can extend their sway against claims of instinct; but we all know that the present state of things in England is somewhat out of joint. Socially speaking, women are a drug on the market, simply from their exceeding numbers. They feel it too, and try by all kinds of curious means to create to themselves new standards of value, of importance. All this is unnatural and unpleasant, and it makes the change to a country where a woman is, socially speaking, a thing of value simply as a woman, a very welcome change indeed. Of course it may be slightly demoralising too, if the woman's vanity should mislead her into setting down all the warmth of her welcome and the interest she arouses to the credit of her own charms, instead of to the scarcity of her species. But I think the most tough-skinned vanity would not secure her long from feeling the prick of an all-surrounding criticism which addresses itself to take note of her work and ways from very unexpected quarters and from unfamiliar points of view, but with a keenness of interest really less indulgent than the passing comment of indifference which is all we have to expect at home.

I sometimes amuse myself by imagining certain women I have known set down for a time to live and learn in the North-West. Especially I should like to transplant her one of those firm believers in the natural depravity of man and the born superiority of woman. She would arrive — the woman I mean — with a high purpose, and very, very kind intentions towards her countrymen exiled in these wilds. She would be all for touching and softening and civilising them, poor fellows! hardened and roughened as they must be by years of hard work among wild horny cattle and bucking horses. Well, that woman would have a good deal to learn; and the first of her lessons would be, respect for the primitive virtues. She has probably held them very light or taken them almost for granted hitherto; courage, honesty, and sobriety she has supposed to belong to every man of her own class by nature, or at least to cost him nothing in their exercise. Give her the object-lesson of young men in this country with all the desires and tastes of youth, and with recent memories of a life of ease, working with a daily self-denial, working hard and living hard, cheerfully, patiently, and courageously, yet without the least notion that they are in any way admirable beings, and possibly it may occur to that superior woman to ask herself if her own life can show anything as worthy of honour as this daily courage, industry, and self-denial? — if it might not actually profit by the example of the poor creature man? How delightful it would be to see that woman in the end touched and softened herself, and with a dawning colour of modesty about her moral pretensions! In time she might even come to revise some pretty theories about the nature and habits of men which she has taken on trust from Mrs. Sarah Grand and her like, to compare them with living examples, and let experience teach her more wholesome views. That were "a consummation devoutly to be wished."

Elizabeth Lewthwaite

Women's Work in Western Canada

It has always seemed to me such a misdirected stream of philanthropy, which carries out of the Old Country a class of women for whom the demand at home so infinitely exceeds the supply (I need hardly say I allude to domestic servants) and leaves to drift as best they can, that vast army of gentlewomen, daughters of professional men, impoverished landed gentry and others, who by their birth, tradition, and upbringing are so ably qualified for Colonial life and surroundings. Few who have thought at all about the subject will deny that education and good breeding almost invariably mean increased power of endurance and of adaptability to altered conditions of life. I cannot do better than illustrate this by the experience of a friend of mine, a delicately nurtured woman, who, on marrying a rancher in Western Canada, took out with her the maid she had had for some years at home. After trying the life for barely six weeks the latter told her mistress she was going home, as she could stand the life no longer; and go she did, leaving her mistress, for whom she had professed much devotion, absolutely bereft of womanly help in a far-off land. On the other hand in the several cases which have come under my own observation, where the companion was of gentle birth, the tale has been a very different one, generally only terminating on the happy marriage of the employee; and yet in both cases the life and work were practically the same. You engage a servant very often at great personal inconvenience, for more often than not the accommodation of your house is so limited that you have to spend half your time in her company, when suddenly — perhaps because you have wanted your own horse and "rig," unknowing that she had intended going out that afternoon; or she has heard that Mrs. So-and-so offers, in addition to the wage you give, "the privileges of the family" — whatever that may mean — off she goes at a moment's notice, neither knowing nor caring what becomes of you. There is no doubt you would much rather be without her, but still the work is too heavy for you alone. Whom then can you have? This is where Mr. Brice's argument supplies an answer.[1] Have a woman of your own class of life, one who would be a friend, take an interest in your affairs as you would in hers, and be a congenial companion in a land where distances are great and women few. It is a crying need in the Colonies to-day, and is bound to become ever greater in the days that are to be.

As much misconception seems to exist with regard to the surroundings, the duties and the social conditions, which a gentlewoman might expect to find in Colonial life, I will try to give as briefly as possible my own experience.

Having five brothers settled in Western Canada, three on a wheat farm in Assiniboia, two in business in Vancouver City, B.C., I decided four years since to go out and see them, with no very definite idea of ever making my home with them; for, like many others, I thought the life would be quite impossible for one who had never been over strong and had no special aptitude for domestic life. So it was arranged that I should go out to Vancouver for the summer, calling at the farm near Indian Head *en route*, whither I should return for the harvest in August and September.

The novelty of the journey made it a delight, as travelling in the Western Hemisphere is made wonderfully comfortable considering the immense distances that have to be traversed; and after the first night I slept splendidly, being almost sorry when the fourth morning at 5 A.M. I found myself at my destination. But here, misery of miseries, was a crushing disappointment, there being no one to meet me. Here had I come thousands of miles by sea and land, and yet because a stupid alarm clock had forgotten to "go off," I nearly turned tail and came straight back again. However two of my fellow passengers with more sense than I had at my command, suggested my accompanying them to the hotel and waiting till people began to wake when I might go to the Rectory, where I was sure of a welcome. No such desperate measure proved necessary, for hardly had we left the station when two men appeared, racing down the long straggling unkept looking street, who proved to be my belongings, and all was forgiven at the sight of a familiar face.

We went up to the Rectory, and imagine my amazement to find myself in a charming little drawing-room, which might have been transplanted from any spot at home. Pretty hangings, numbers of pictures, books galore, lovely plants, and a piano. Could I really be in that Godforsaken land, which one's English friends persist in terming the Backwoods? It seemed incredible. The same surprise awaited me at breakfast, where everything was equally reminiscent of the home I had just left. Pretty flowers, nice silver, and identically the same food. So much for Revelation number one. But Revelation number two, speedily to follow, readjusted my ideas, and revived once more the adventurer's spirit. When I saw the carriage (or "Rig" as it is called) which was to take me to my brother's house, I could have verily believed it had come out of the Ark. How it ever held together was a mystery; yet it lasted for twelve months after that, and even then was sold in part payment for a pony to an Indian, who considered he got far the best of the bargain. This relic of the past was drawn by two large farm horses whose harness left much to be desired. The jolting — for it was just at the thaw — was positively awful, almost worse than being at sea, but we got over the ground in an unconscionably short time, arriving at the Shanty without any mishap.

Here, indeed, my expectations were more than fulfilled. Lowly though my ideal had been, it was a world too high. The rubbish that was round about was amazing (and this is a characteristic of most bachelor's establishments, all that is not wanted being simply pitched outside), empty cans, socks, and other specimens of the masculine wardrobe, odds and ends of machinery, a pan or two, empty boxes, hens and cats, pigs and dogs, till I hardly knew where to step. And then — when I got inside — even now I can hardly look back without a feeling of horror. I saw at once I must accept their arrangement and stay at a neighbour's house for the few days I meant to stop on the prairie, where it was plain to see the difference a woman's presence made. Here I used to spend the night, going to my brothers' each morning to spend the day, cooking, cleaning, mending. Since then I have been told this anecdote: Anxious to know what I was like, a neighbour sent over her husband to "prospect"; on his return, "Tom," she said, "what is she like"? "Oh, she's right enough I reckon." "Does she seem stuckup"? "Nay," was his reply, "I know nowt about that, when I got there she wor carting t'dirt out o't shanty by t' barrerful." And that's just about what I was doing. But the air was so brilliant, the experience was so novel, and we were so thoroughly happy that the toil, incredible though it may seem, was a real pleasure.

After ten days of this, I went on to Vancouver for the summer. Of my stay there, delightful though it was, I need not speak, for it was too much like life in any town at home, Vancouver being an up-to-date go-ahead city, with all the necessaries and most of the luxuries of civilisation. One instance of woman's successful work there may be given.

A lady, formerly in very comfortable circumstances at home, a pupil of Madame Sainton-Dolby, owing to serious financial difficulties determined, in a new country, to make the most of her training; so, giving up her home in London, and armed with only one letter of introduction, she arrived at Vancouver in May, 1897. After trying to get singing pupils, with very little success, she was glad to accept a post as nursery governess in one of the best known families there. Here she became acquainted with many people, and, on the promise of a certain number of pupils for music and other subjects, she resigned her engagement, bought a little house for which she has now fully paid, and is at the present moment making more than a livelihood, an example of courage and energy worthy of emulation. With barely four years' work she is able to save, and is possessed of a nice little property steadily rising in value. This, however, is perhaps an exceptional case; but nurses both for children and the sick are much in demand, and lady helps could no doubt readily obtain berths if the salaries they asked were not so exorbitant. It must be remembered that in a new country where every one has to make his own way, it is often impossible to give the £50 or even £60 which is demanded as wage; whereas if £25 or £30 were asked, this sum would be gladly given in addition to a most comfortable home, for work which, in the towns at any rate, is by no means onerous.

In September I returned to the Prairie, where a new era had already dawned. A small building, about twelve feet square, used previously as a granary, had now been done up, and made a charming little room. A trestle bed, a wash-stand, two tables, and a chair or two constituted the furniture, together with what was intended to be a looking-glass, suitable, no doubt, for a mere man, but certainly not calculated to increase a woman's vanity. Some curtains, a few photographs I had with me, and a book or two, soon gave the little spot an air of Home. The bed covered with a rug made a capital sofa by day, when friends came to afternoon tea in truly English fashion. This time the visit was prolonged for two months, extremely busy and happy ones, all through the harvest, when my brothers often worked for fourteen hours a day. Was it not something to be able to have nice hot meals ready for them when they came in absolutely tired out, instead of their having to get what came first to hand in miserable comfortless fashion? Towards the middle of November I left for Vancouver with the understanding that when I returned in the spring I should find a nice little home waiting, which I did, and the old order was entirely changed, though we leave the old Shack still standing as a contrast to what the present has brought forth.

Since then the conditions of life have tremendously improved. The country is becoming much better settled, farmers are better off, and with increased demand and competition, prices have come down; an infinitely greater variety of commodities is obtainable in the shops, and the social side of life is brighter and gayer.

Our household consisted of three brothers, two hired men, who lived with us the seven busy working months of the year, and myself. I at once saw I could not manage alone, so persuaded another sister to come out in June, 1898, and together we went into our newly-finished house, which consists of two sitting-rooms, the larger being divided by curtains into dining-room and smoke-room — the smaller being my own special sanctum where the men are only admitted when their work is done, and a certain level of cleanliness has been attained. Upstairs are three good bedrooms, my old room at the Shanty being used as an extra one. At the back of the house is a large lean-to kitchen containing a small room in which the men wash when they come in from work. Last, but not least, is an excellent cellar where, even in the hottest summer, everything is fresh and cool. This delectable region is reached through a trap-door, where once I nearly killed myself by stepping on a sheep's head (inadvertently left there by the butcher of the family) and rolling in a horrible fright to the bottom of the steps.

As economy of labour is the aim of a woman's life out there, the next question was how to furnish the house on this basis, so we decided to have all the floors covered with linoleum or Japanese matting, so clean-looking and so easily washed. The majority have their floors painted, but as this entails their being redone each year, we felt that our plan would be more satisfactory in the long run. Furniture suitable for its environment is easily obtainable and very cheap. Besides which, the men themselves are often good carpenters and make many simple things. Our smoke-room couches and tables are all home-made and do extremely well. We did not do everything at once: the first year the absolute necessaries only were procured, other things coming in due order, until now we have attained to carpets in three rooms and the indispensable piano — such a comfort in the long winter evenings.

Now for the work which seems so appalling to those at home. They cannot or will not understand the multitude of appliances for the simplification of labour, reducing it to a minimum. Instead of having half-a-dozen fires there is one stove in the basement which warms the whole house; in the winter it is kept in night and day, so there are no fireplaces to be cleaned each morning. A little mop is used to wash up with, so that you need never put your hands in water. And even for washing floors, there is a mechanical arrangement which obviates the necessity of going on your knees: and so on in every direction.

We rose about 6 A.M., and when we got down found a good fire, lighted by one of the men, and the kettle boiling. As we had laid the breakfast-table the night before, we merely had to fry the bacon, etc., and make tea for the 6.30 or 7 o'clock breakfast. After the men had departed we cleared away and washed up: then the cook-sister would sweep the dining-room and prepare the dinner, look after the poultry and do the thousand and one little things which always seem to crop up: churning, perhaps, or bread-baking, or it might be merely giving an extra tidying-up of cupboards; the other sister, in the meantime, doing the beds, dusting our sitting-room, and so on, similarly to a housemaid at home. By 10.30 we were generally on the verandah sewing or reading, with an occasional visit to the kitchen to see that dinner was going on right. This meal, at 12.30, usually consisted of meat with one or two vegetables, milk pudding, and fruit tart; soup occasionally, and game frequently in the season, relieved our meals of the dull monotony which might otherwise have characterised them. After dinner we immediately cleared away and washed-up. By 2.30 our work was done, and after a short rest we would get our ponies and go off for the afternoon to see our friends, having prepared everything for supper in case we did not return. If we felt lazy we merely scrambled into our hammocks on the verandah, and waited for our friends to come and see us. A cup of tea at 4.0 enabled us to wait till supper at 6.30, after which once more wash-up and lay the table for the morrow: and then the cosy chat in the cool of the evening, or a drive to a neighbour's and bed at 9.30 or 10.0. Frequently we would go off to a neighbouring settlement for a picnic, a gymkhana, or a polo match, with a dance to follow. And now and again, that first summer, half-a-dozen friends would ride over, stay the night (sleeping on the sofas and even on the floor), to start at 5.0 the next morning for a wolf-hunt. This, however, was burning the candle too much at both ends and hunting now takes place at more reasonable hours. Ponies are ridiculously cheap; my three did not cost £20 all told, and the last is a little beauty who can do everything but speak.

There was one difficulty that confronted us when we started housekeeping, and that was: "Could we have our meals with the hired men, neither of whom at that time could lay claim to the title of gentleman?" We decided in the affirmative, for the idea of two distinct meals was appalling. We never regretted our decision; and our whole experience has proved that a lady receives from men of this class the courtesy and respect accorded her by those of her own rank of life. Never once had I cause to complain, and as each year brought us fresh men, not to speak of the multitude who came to see my brothers on business or pleasure, this in itself speaks volumes for their innate chivalry, as owing to the necessary intimacy of our lives it might be thought that the position would be awkward, if not intolerable.

At the end of twelve months our *ménage* had to undergo reconstruction, as my sister had to return to England, partly on private matters, but partly, truth compels me to admit, because the life did not suit her. The atmosphere so bracing to me, and, indeed, to the majority who go there, had an entirely reverse effect upon her; so from June, 1899, I had to face life alone, which enables me to speak most sympathetically of the truth of Mr. Brice's article. I would have given simply anything for some one to take my sister's place. It was not the amount of work that distressed me, but the lack of feminine companionship. I used sometimes to long for the sight of a woman's face.

Perhaps if I had tried very hard I might have obtained a maid-servant who would have condescended to work for me if she had no more pressing engagement; or I might more readily have obtained the services of a Doukobor woman. As she, however, knew no English, and I was equally ignorant of Russian, the experiment seemed too rash, though it has been tried with fairly satisfactory results by ladies who were in direr straits than I. I did, in a weak moment, take in a wayfaring lad, who, after trying to instil into my heart the virtue of long-suffering, decamped as silently as he came, taking with him nothing more serious than half-a-dozen boxes of sardines. After this it seemed better to wait till I could come home and persuade some girl friend to join me.

Mine is no exceptional case. On the contrary, it is the rule, even for the married, for little children, with all their winsome ways, need a lot of looking after, and leave very little time for the poor tired mother to have much rest. To such the assistance of a gentlewoman who would relieve her of some of her responsibility, and give her the chance of getting a day's absolute rest now and then, would be incalculable.

It may be said, "But how about the girl who comes out: is she to have all work and no play?" On the contrary, in many cases where the experiment has been tried, the remark has often been made by outsiders that the employee seemed to have a much better time than her employer. This, of course, ought not to be; but it is easy to see how the mistake arises. The lady is so thankful to have a nice helpful girl of her own class with her, that she wants her to have the most favourable impression of her new home and so sacrifices herself for the sake of the new arrival, letting her go to this picnic and that dance, in the hope that it will make things pleasanter for her.

What, then, does a girl lose by going out there, so far as externals are concerned? Is she musical? there is the piano, or, at any rate, the universal parlour organ. And it is wonderful what a lot of harmony you can extract from one of these unpromising instruments. I have known of most enjoyable dances with this as the sole music. Can she sketch? There are scenes even on the dull monotonous prairie of radiant beauty. Or, perhaps, she is a great reader. Here she gains decidedly, for nearly every book published at 6s. in England may be got for half price there, and every house gladly constitutes itself a lending library. And for friends — what may be lacking in quantity (to put it baldly) is more than made up in quality, for more absolute and disinterested friendship could nowhere be surpassed, and I, for one, can never be sufficiently grateful for the kindness I have received.

The great drawback, of course, is that where distances are so tremendous, your life is bounded by your immediate neighbourhood. When one only earns two or three pounds a month, one does not care to spend it all on a long railway journey, even though it be to hear Albani or Gadski, or perchance Ysaye. This is what one misses, music, pictures, plays, so near to us all in England. To some, the absence of this side of life amounts to positive pain. Yet, after all, is this so terrible a drawback? Think of what is offered instead. A home where she is treated exactly as a sister might be; when her share of the work is accomplished she can, if she so wish, go her own way, see her own friends, and, in fact, do as she likes. As to salary, in the part that I know best £25 to £35 a year is more the rule than the £50 Mr. Brice names, though this is obtained further west, but prices being proportionately higher, little is gained. Out of this she need spend very little on her dress, and incidental expenses are few. Does not this seem a more inviting prospect than wearing out one's life as a typist or nursery-governess, or that nondescript being, companion or lady help, which is often all a girl with no specialised training is competent for in the Motherland?

The very variety of the work destroys its difficulty, for I take it that it is monotony we dislike rather than work itself; and of monotony there is very little, where such a multitude of interests occupy our minds.

Mr. Brice urges that if a sister join her brother she should go out the year after he does. Might it not be well however, if she go out at all during the early years of her brother's settlement, that she go at the same time he does, finding a home (on mutual terms may be) in the same locality if not in the same household. Then when he takes up land the following year, she would have the necessary experience to begin housekeeping at once with him, knowing all the little "tricks of the trade," which economise labour so marvellously. By so doing she would prevent his ever having to "batch" and drifting into those habits of carelessness, —

if not worse — that take such ages to eradicate. And I dare wager that she will save enough in their first year's housekeeping to pay for the building of the extra room which she perforce will need.

Few but those who have actually lived out there, can realise the miserable conditions under which so many of our brothers live. I have not spoken of their work, it has been described far more ably than I could attempt in many books treating of Colonial life. When I think of how grateful they are for all one does, I wonder a sister is not in every bachelor's house, until it is a bachelor's house no longer. And this brings me to another point on which I hope I may be allowed to touch.

Hundreds of young Englishmen go out to seek their fortunes year by year: where are the women who ought to be their helpmeets? Not in the lands to which they go most certainly. So the young man, tired of "batching," either comes home for a wife who too often does not understand the life to which she is going, and the tragic tale of *Hilda Strafford,* that vivid story of broken hopes and unsuitable environment is told once more; or he marries the girl on the spot — too often alas, an ignorant, uncultivated girl, whom he is ashamed to bring home to his people, who even if she make his home comfortable (which by no means is invariably the case), can never be in touch with the finer side of her husband's nature. It may be thought that a man who lives as most ranchers and struggling farmers do, far from the centres of intellectual life and thought, would speedily lose all refinement and graces of civilisation. On the contrary, though externally this may seem to be the fact, a "bachelor's shack" being often synonymous with disorder if not dirt, yet morally and intellectually he is generally on a level with, if not superior to, his brother at home, provided this was the case when he arrived in the Colony. It is too often forgotten that the Colonies are the "dumping-ground" for the ne'er-do-wells of the Motherland; so, naturally, cut off from the only rock which might steady them, they too frequently merely go from bad to worse in the land to which they have been sent.

To sum up then: whom do we want? Not, most decidedly, the woman who looks forward to nothing but a "good time" as she would express it, and talks of work as menial. As if any work is menial where everybody takes their part. But we do want those who will be kind and helpful, willing to take the rough with the smooth and not always expecting all the plums of life. Robust health in England is not a necessary qualification, though of course desirable, for the prairie atmosphere is so pure and invigorating that many delicate folk on their arrival become new creatures; and I have often been amazed at what fragile, delicate-looking women are able to accomplish. I should not advise girls under twenty-one to go out, nor over twenty-eight; and if they have a small income so much the better, for private means grease the wheels of life out of all proportion to their amount. Fifty pounds sounds so much more as two hundred and fifty dollars, and has a correspondingly elevating influence on your spirits. The knowledge, too, that if anything went very badly wrong you have the wherewithal to return to England, acts as a very useful tonic, and generally prevents the occurrence of any such event.

I do not hold that previous training of any kind is absolutely indispensable, though of obvious value; for if a girl be willing to learn, she can learn out there just as well as at home; and, as it is more often companionship that is desired than even assistance in the work, one understanding the kind of life and willing to undertake its responsibilities need not be debarred because of her ignorance of detail. A cheerful, happy temperament will be worth all the technical knowledge in the world. But if training can be obtained in the Motherland so much the better; and I should specially recommend —

(a) A practical course of plain cooking, including bread making.

(b) Laundry work, especially the getting up of starched things, though as far as I am concerned I have never done this, for we get our things well and most reasonably done. The wives of many of the poorer emigrants are often only too thankful to do your washing, or will come to your house at a charge of fivepence an hour. Besides which, in most of the towns along the great railway line the ubiquitous Chinaman has established his little laundry and does starched things most beautifully though his prices are frequently high.

(c) The elements of dressmaking, such as blouses and plain skirts. Materials are reasonable; but though ready made (especially men's) working clothes are particularly cheap, better things are very dear.

(d) Butter-making: though I do not follow Mr. Brice in recommending her to learn to milk. She will find she has quite enough to do without this, if she attend properly to the house, poultry and probably the garden. This little bit of advice was volunteered me by an old pioneer when first I went out, and I am sure he was right. If she once learns she will always have to do it, and as the generality of English women in the Colonies almost invariably overtax their powers, it is well to preach moderation where it can be effectually put into practice.

In this connection I should like to mention the Leaton Colonial Training Home, near Wellington, Shropshire, where girls are most efficiently trained for the duties of Colonial life at the very low fee of 10s. or 15s. a week for a three or six months course. Anyone who underwent a course in this excellent institution could be quite certain of finding very readily a welcome in any colony, and would know exactly what would be expected of her. I can only hope that it is my ignorance which prevents my alluding to other institutions of a similarly practical kind.

I have entered into such trifling details, for I find how extraordinarily ignorant people are of our surroundings. Since my return a lady of good social standing, who has a son out there, confided to me how delighted she had been to find, when he came back, that he had not lost all his manners. She had evidently quite expected he would use his knife as a salt-spoon, and come into the drawing room in his shirt sleeves. Another, on hearing we had iron and brass bedsteads throughout our house (with spring mattresses) was incredulous. "But my dear, I always pictured you as sleeping on the floor with a bundle of hay, or the feathers from the birds you killed, as a bed." And there was quite a plaintive air of disappointment that it wasn't true. So first of all we must enlist the sympathy of the Press. Through its good offices more could be done in a week than individuals could do in a year. When once the ignorance is dispelled, I do not think we shall have to wait long for the realisation of our hopes, and the supply of gentlewomen such as I have faintly described may approximate more nearly to the great demand there is for their services. The sympathy, too, of active ladies in the Motherland would speedily find a response in those of the daughter countries. Personally, I can speak of at least one (living in Toronto) who had made this subject her own, and who would most cordially co-operate in any effort originating in this country, and who has already done much to make the needs known in Eastern Canada.

One of the chief drawbacks, no doubt, to any wide scheme of emigration for gentlewomen is the very obvious difficulty of bringing both employer and employee into direct communication. In the Report for 1900 of The United British Women's Emigration Association, practically the only Society which makes this its object, it is stated that during the preceding twelve months this Association and the societies working in connection with it, sent out 345 single women, of whom the largest proportion (109) went to Canada, but of these a large percentage were domestic servants: a mere drop in the ocean of our needs, thankful though we must be for the work the Society is doing. If only all Agencies for the employment of women could make known the wide opening there is in the Colonies, and the protection afforded by the above Association to girls and women going to distant lands, a far greater number would surely offer their services, and find a fuller, freer life than could ever be their lot in the over-crowded Motherland. But the Colonies themselves must take the initiative and make far more widely known the organisations which already exist, and in every chief town of every Colony let there be well known Central Agencies, with their Correspondents in every quarter of the kingdom, to whom both employers and employed may apply. These, if kept in constant communication with the many Agencies for the employment of Gentlewomen in the Motherland, would act as channels of supply for the ever-increasing demand in the daughter countries, and at no very distant date there will be a very different tale to tell. At present, unfortunately, so few persons (comparatively) know of these organisations that, unless the Press makes known their existence, few will be able to avail themselves of the means already at hand.

1. Arthur Montefiore Brice, "Emmigration for Gentlewomen," *The Nineteenth Century* (April 1901).

PART THREE

The Wheat-Boom Years: 1905-1914

From *A Woman in Canada*
Commentary

The traditional roles of women — "mother, sister, daughter, sweetheart, wife," in Mrs. Saxby's survey of the possibilities as she saw them — set the boundaries for the early phases of the debate over opportunities in Canada for Britain's redundant women. Early in the new century, however, several converging forces brought a notable change in emphasis and tone in books and articles devoted to this issue.

Simply to identify these developments hardly does justice to their individual complexity, or to the nuances of their interrelations. One of the most important, obviously, was the dramatic rise in the numbers of British emigrants to Canada in the decade prior to World War I. "Declared settlers" from the United Kingdom as shown in annual dominion immigration returns hovered around the 10,000 mark for most of the 1890's, but in 1902 the figure jumped to over 17,000 and then to more than 50,000 in 1904. The year 1908 saw 120,182 declared British settlers enter the country, and this figure was matched or bettered in each of the four years (1911-14) before war brought emigration from Britain to a halt.[1]

Moreover, a significant proportion of these newcomers settled in the prairie West. The census returns for the three prairie provinces show that from 1906 to 1910 inclusive, 87,654 people of British origin arrived to swell the population, compared to 69,654 from the United States and 81,684 from continental Europe. The figures remained in the same proportions from 1911 to 1914, making Britons the single largest component in Western Canada's immigrant population from 1906 to 1914.[2]

A second factor of importance was the coincident expansion of the popular press on both sides of the Atlantic during the years of Western Canada's greatest inflow of settlement. The date 1896 is often cited as marking the onset of this expansionary phase in Canada's national development. This was also the year in which Alfred Northcliffe launched his halfpenny *London Daily Mail* and revolutionized the newspaper business, spawning in the process a wide range of imitators and competitors. The making of news rapidly became a full-scale industry, while the profession of journalism opened its ranks as never before to women of talent and ambition. And when news-hungry journalists in Britain looked overseas to North America where so many of their compatriots now lived, they found Clifford Sifton's well-oiled immigration machine more than ready to ingest them into its works. Parties of writers for all manner of daily, weekly, and monthly publications made regular tours of the prairie West at the invitation and expense of the dominion government. From this practice emerged a number of books on Canada compiled expressly for British consumption, such as James Lumsden's *Through Canada in Harvest Time* (1903) and J. F. Fraser's *Canada As It Is* (1905; reprinted five times and then issued in a revised, updated version in 1911).

Along much the same lines, although with a rather more specialized audience in view, was Marion Dudley Cran's *A Woman in Canada,* published in London and Toronto in 1910 to generally enthusiastic acclaim. Having already visited Canada once before as a private citizen, Mrs. Cran was asked by dominion government officials to undertake a longer tour, paying special heed to opportunities for women. The substance of her report to the Canadian authorities is contained in her book, but portions of it also appeared as articles for several English magazines and newspapers, while at least one of her "Prairie Studies" (not included for reprint here) was published in the *Regina Leader* (and provoked some outraged letters to the editor) while the author was still in Canada.

Marion Cran was born Marion Dudley in 1875 in South Africa, the daughter of an Anglican minister who soon returned with his family to England. Although she trained as a nurse, it was in journalism and later broadcasting that she made her name. Her list of publications is a long one; throughout the 1920's and 1930's she published a book almost every year, variations on the theme of gardens, on which she was an expert. In 1939 she was awarded a Civil List Pension by the British government for her services to literature. She died in September 1942.

A Woman in Canada has the faults of its virtues. Cran writes in an intimate, impressionistic style that will charm some readers and irritate others. Having served for a time as an art critic in Edwardian London, she occasionally slips into a rather blatantly arty manner. On the subject of proper care for childbearing women in Western Canada, however, she writes with force and directness, and both for her cogency of statement and for her disinterested personal efforts to improve maternity nursing in Canada she deserves respect. First in these selections from her book of 1910 come some general comments on the Prairies and two of her five "Prairie Studies." They are followed by her description of opportunities for women in poultry-farming and market-gardening. Finally, there is a chapter entitled "The Fly in the Ointment," in which she offers her personal solution to the mystery surrounding the apparent reluctance of educated British women to settle in the West.

One final note on *A Woman in Canada.* On page 213, Mrs. Cran alludes to a speech that she made to the Women's Press Club of Winnipeg in 1908. She chose the subject of women's suffrage "because I saw it was a topic that both interested and shocked." Interested, because the leading members of the Winnipeg Women's Press Club — Cora Hind, Marion and Lillian Beynon, Isobel Graham, Nellie McClung — were then weighing the merits of an open campaign on the suffrage issue; shocked, because of the violent turn The Cause had taken in Britain since 1905 under the leadership of the militant suffragettes. That she should have chosen the topic at all, however, indicates something of the distance the women's movement had travelled in the twenty years since Jessie Saxby's visit in 1888, a difference even more startlingly apparent in these sentences from Mrs. Cran's foreword (p. 22): "Canada wants women of breed and endurance, educated, middle-class gentlewomen, and these are not the women to come out on the off-chance of getting married. They may be induced to come to the country if they can farm or work in some way to secure their absolute independence. They want, every nice woman wants, to be free to undertake marriage as a matter of choice, not of necessity."

1. W. A. Carrothers, *Emigration from the British Isles* (London: King, 1929), p. 316.
2. *Census of the Prairie Provinces, Population and Agriculture* (Ottawa: King's Printer, 1918), p. 279.

Marion Cran

A Woman in Canada

We go into a homestead for tea. The farmer's wife is a busy, rather silent woman with four children; her face is nice to look at with its harsh mouth and gentle eyes. That mouth looks as though it had tasted trouble and found it bitter; her eyes, a little tired, but so kind, look as though she has much love in her life. "It's rather a busy time just at harvest," she says; "you must please excuse if you find things rough."

"I should think you are always busy," I reply.

"Yes," she says, "when it's not cooking it's washing; when washing's done there's ironing, and what with the housework and children and sewing and dairy and all, I have no time to spare."

"Do you do all that without help?" I ask, marvelling.

"Yes," she says, "there's no help to be got out West; I could keep a girl, too, if there was one to be had. She would soon pay for herself out of the extra butter I would be able to make. I have to keep the cows down small now, but I like a big herd. I had a girl once from the old country, but she married in a month. They always get married." She sighs, and I am silent. I know she has touched on one of the great problems of the West — the dearth of female labour.

Back to Mr. Larcombe's farm — across twenty-five miles of prairie, purple and gold, with the warm, wild wind on our faces and the wild hawk overhead. From there I wander over many hundreds of miles of prairie, by rail and rig, through many weeks, watching, noting, questioning the conditions of life which British women are so loath to accept, apparently, since they are so scarce. I sketch people and places as I find them, generally at the time and on the spot. Before I go on with the prairie studies I think I will quote an article, "to be continued," which appeared in a certain *T.P.'s Weekly,* by "A Transplanted Englishwoman." Here it is —

"Frances" spoke truly in a recent article when she said that no girl should go to the Colonies without having some idea of the conditions of life she will find there. I would, however, suggest that a cheaper and more practical method of gaining experience than by taking a course at Swanley College could be had by spending three months as a working member of the household of an English or Scotch agricultural labourer. Provided choice is made of a cottage many miles away from towns and villages, where the wife has to make her own bread and see to a few animals, I think most of the conditions of colonial life (I speak of Canada) can be experienced. These conditions can be roughly summed up as discomfort, inconvenience, and "doing without." Every labourer's wife is well inured to these conditions, and for this reason I would never have the slightest hesitation in advising a working-class woman to go to the Colonies, whereas I cannot think of one middle-class woman of my acquaintance at home whom I would care to bring out here — that is, to live as wife, sister, or daughter on a homestead.

People at home talk vaguely of "roughing it in Canada." That sounds somewhat romantic, and calls up visions of cowgirls flying across the prairie on horseback, picturesque in wide-brimmed hats and loosely-knotted neck-scarfs — red for choice. I will endeavour to put into cold, unromantic words what "roughing it" really means for the middle-class woman. Let us first take the house prepared for her by her male relative. It is of logs, and looks somewhat picturesque in a painting. As a matter of fact, dirt appears to her — especially if she arrives in spring — to be its most prominent feature. Mud is ankle deep, and the cow and chickens are wandering around the back door, adding to the filth there accumulated.

In time, of course, there will be added a fence, but at present the male relative has so many things to do. The spaces between the logs are chinked with moss, and then plastered with a clay-and-sand cement which at intervals cracks and drops off in bits, having to be done each autumn. Inside the bare logs have been covered with building-paper — the colour of a grocer's sugar-bag, yellowish-white — tacked on in somewhat unsightly fashion. Flies and spiders find a cosy home in the moss behind the paper, and frequently there are worse things. The roofing of the house is of boards and tar-paper, and by the second summer it begins to leak, so that whenever it rains it is necessary to put pots and pans under the drips. The most unpleasant places for these drips are the stove and the beds. On the prairie, where the houses are frequently roofed with sods, the drips consist of liquid mud. Of course, in the fulness of time the male relative will get the house shingled, but — he has so many things to do.

The floor, of course, is bare, the boards are unplaned and uneven, and there are large gaps between them in places. The native Canadian drudge laboriously scrubs her floor, but no sane woman who can scrape up a dollar wherewith to buy floor-paint need do this. A painted floor is easily cleaned with mop or wash-cloth. The house generally consists, for the first few years, of one large room, a part of it partitioned or curtained off for a bedroom. An Englishman will generally stand out for a board partition, for it is unpleasant to be having a bath or lying ill in bed with nothing but a curtain between one and the living-room, which is practically open to any passer-by who calls at the door. There is a door on each side of the living-room — no passage or porch between door and outside world — so that every one who goes in or out, when the temperature ranges from zero to forty-five below zero, gives those inside a taste of the fine bracing air out of doors. Those who suffer from cold feet, in spite of felt boots and three pairs of stockings, do well to comfort themselves with the thought that in six or seven months the warm weather will have come, and it will be pleasant to have open doors. At the approach of winter one cuts old coats and trousers into strips, and laboriously tacks them down the cracks in the boards of which the doors are composed, for, having been made in a hurry out of green wood, they have, of course, warped and begun to gape.

In many cases one of the worst discomforts on a new homestead is the incessant trouble about water. This is one of the numerous points we have in common with the old country agricultural labourer's wife. Time was when I thought — with my class — that "poor people" could at least keep themselves and their houses clean, for water was cheap. I know better now. In some parts of the West the water is so alkaline as to be unfit for either washing or drinking, and even the well-to-do farmers have to be dependent on rain-water in a cistern. In the bush, however, water is good and plentiful if means are taken to secure it, but the homesteader, as a rule, digs a shallow well at first, instead of going to the trouble and expense of boring. In a dry season it probably runs dry, and one goes to a neighbour's for drinking-water, and waits for rain to provide washing-water. This is in summer. From November to April one melts snow to provide all the water required for drinking, for washing, and for such animals as are kept. This is a tedious and messy process, for a pail of snow will only make half a pailful of water.

It will be understood that a bath under such conditions becomes a luxury, and one is never so wasteful as to throw away the water after one's weekly tub. It serves to mop or wash the floors on cleaning day, or to soak the dirtiest of the clothes on washing day. In time, of course, the male relative will provide an adequate water supply, but — he has so *many* things to do, and, besides, he hopes to build a proper house in a few years' time, and when he bores he will prefer to do it near the new house. Washing day in winter comes round all too quickly. It is prefaced by melting numerous pailfuls of snow, until one gets half a barrelful of water. There are, of course, no coppers in Canadian houses, either in the cities or in the new countries, and the water is heated in a tin boiler on the stove. If one is short of pails and tubs, one must just carry dirty water out in the midst of operations from a steamy atmosphere to the arctic temperature outside, and before the clothes can be shaken out to hang on the line they freeze stiff. One, of course, learns to manage things so as not to go outside until everything is finished, shaken out, and put in position to hang out as expeditiously as possible, and one puts on coat and warm gloves before starting the hanging-out performance.

Such discomforts as being many miles from a village and post office, of doing without various articles of food, such as fresh meat in summer, milk if one has no cow, and fresh vegetables for eight months in the year one soon gets accustomed to, just as one gets accustomed to eating in the same room as one cooks in, finding everything in the house frozen solid on January and February mornings, and keeping muslin and wire mosquito- and fly-screens over doors and windows in summer. It is, of course, quite unnecessary to lengthen out on the things which every woman *must* be able to do in rural Canada, and this applies to the civilized old settled districts as well as to the new places. She must cook, clean, wash, bake bread, make butter, milk, mend her menfolk's clothes and make her own, attend to a garden, and in summer go out every day and pick wild fruit — blueberries, strawberries and raspberries — to preserve for the winter. No tame fruit is to be had, and an average provision of preserved fruit for two people for nine months will be two hundred quarts. This is not jam, but stewed fruit put in jars which seal hermetically, and which are to be bought at every village shop in Canada.

[Mrs. Cran then comments:] I have many quarrels with that article. The writer advises any working-class woman to go to the Colonies — and not the middle-class women. I strongly oppose such advice. The working-class woman does not bring the intelligence to bear on domestic emergencies which a cultured woman can, out of her ignorance how can she reduce disorder to comeliness, and make the prairie home a beautiful thing? It can be done. I have seen it. Then the next generation deserves some attention. If ignorant women of our lower orders go out and marry — as they will — farmers, who are often men of decent breeding, their children will go down, not up, in the scale of progress; a woman of refinement and culture, of endurance, of healthy reasoning courage, is infinitely better equipped for the work of home-making and race-making than the ignorant, often lazy, often slovenly lower-class woman. I know; I've washed too many of them in hospital days.

Then the squalid picture of the hovel drawn by the transplanted English-woman galls my kibe. There *are* such shacks; no man ought to ask a woman to share one; no woman ought to be silly enough to do it, unless she chooses to deliberately, and then she ought not to grumble. There are plenty of comfortable farmhouses on the prairie where the farmer's wife will welcome her and pay well for help. Let the transplanted Englishwoman go to her. She will work less hard than in the piteous hovel described so graphically, and under infinitely more comfortable and healthy conditions. Let her earn good money and leave that "busy male relative" to miss her enough to build a decent house, and board his floors, and look after the well-boring and all the rest. Even if the male relative is her husband I'd say the same. In fact, I would say it more urgently — such a hovel is not fit for child-bearing, both mother and baby would suffer. Every woman who works, and domesticity *is* work, has a right to ask for decent working conditions, and if she cannot get them, to leave any man, husband or no, and work for herself until he can provide them. The labourer is worthy of her hire. I have no patience with the women who go to ill conditions and grumble about them instead of bettering them. There is no *need* to stop and be miserable. No one can compel you to.

I asked one woman on the prairie who slaved to keep her shack in nice living conditions, "Aren't you sorry you came?" She went to the door and looked across the sunny acres. "No!" she said. "this is all our own. England could never have given us this. We shall soon be more comfortable."

The "transplanted Englishwoman" talks of doing without fresh vegetables for eight months in the year. There is no need for it. I have something to say on market gardening later on — but what on earth is to prevent her growing her own vegetables? The relative afore-mentioned will spare her an acre or two near the shack where she can grow "roots," as they call them over there, and store them for winter use as her neighbours do, in a cellar or "root-house."

It is bitter to find individual incompetence described as general conditions. To do the lady justice she does say in her next and concluding article that there is hope for those who stick to their drudgery — the hope of ultimate betterment.

T. P.'s Weekly, however, does not publish only grumbles. Here is a letter from a worker of evidently cheery soul who makes comfort out of what may readily be turned to hideous discomfort. A very different story this man tells.

To the Editor of "T. P.'s Weekly"

Sir,

After living in Canada for six years, and having resided in the provinces of Ontario and Manitoba — I am now in Saskatchewan upon a farm of my own — I think I may claim to have a good knowledge of the country. Like "Successful Man," I emigrated to Canada independently, which seems to be the only way to avoid trouble. The Canadian Immigration Department specially advise against dealing with private agents and advertisements such as ended so disastrously for the "Three Who Failed."

Arriving at Winnipeg, I applied at the Government Bureau for a position, and was sent out to a country town in Manitoba with a letter of introduction to the postmaster, asking him to place me with some farmer needing help. Unfortunately, this old postmaster got in a temper, saying he had "no connection with the Immigration Department." However, he stated the case to some farmers that had just called for their mail. They told me of a man whom they thought needed help. As I had only thirty cents in my pocket and was practically stranded, and night drawing near, I of necessity paid the farmer a visit. His hospitality was all that could be desired, and, after keeping me overnight — I suppose to "size me up," for I was pale-faced and anything but sturdy-looking — told me he did not really need a man, but directed me to another farmer; and, after walking fifteen miles from place to place, I finally obtained a position at fifteen dollars per month.

I was not altogether "green" at farm work, but being new to the country was to my disadvantage, and Canadian farmers, like most employers, will not pay any more than they can help. After serving six months in my first berth I changed from place to place, always getting highest wages — fifteen dollars for winter and thirty dollars for summer. I always selected the larger farms, for on them they usually have some system and pay highest wages, and a man learns quicker. On the smaller farms, where there is only one man, he has everything to do; system is lacking, which often makes the working hours long. I have worked on large farms of 2,000 acres and upwards with as many as ten other men, each having four horses under his care and to work.

"Successful Man" said he "always avoided the bachelors" because of their "wretched establishments and the absence of female help." It is true some of them are negligent, but not all of them are as black as he has painted them. I myself am a bachelor, not through choice, but rather force of circumstances, and know the situation only too well. I am constrained to put aside my natural modesty to modify the statement that in "these establishments" there are "no properly-cooked meals, no regular hours, general disorder, dirt, etc." I have known many to be systematic, orderly, and excellent cooks; and some I have known to receive great praise at the hands of women for their household management. Recently I had a threshing machine with a crew of sixteen men (and this is the average number in the West) to do my threshing; and I had to do all the cooking alone for them for three meals. Through force of circumstances I have become fairly proficient in this art, though this is the first time I have been put to so severe a test.

As to the absence of women, which "Successful Man" mentions, it is not the fault of the bachelors. The bachelors are a great majority, and the women are not in the country. Any woman who ventures here will receive more than her share of attention, and, most likely, be promptly appropriated by some bachelor anxious for a happier state. The crying need of Western Canada is women; it is like that heathen cry which comes to the missionary — "Come over and help us." Though Canada is not altogether "heathen," it needs the missionary spirit of women to make it a crowning success, and no doubt many of the teeming multitude of British women would profit by this golden opportunity. The life, though strenuous, is not altogether mono- tonous, for one can have one's hours of leisure in which to cultivate the mind as well as the land, if the man so desires.

Yours faithfully,

J. G. S., Sask., Canada.

That man deserves a good wife! I have lingered to quote and comment because there is so much written one way and another on the prairie farm-life that English readers must often be rarely puzzled to know what to believe. Every one writes sincerely, I think, from the individual point of view. Every reader may be sure that in himself alone is the stuff to make this picture of Canada come true, or that.

The trail is what one might call hummocky, the heat is fierce, and I am getting my skirt covered with grease from a new kind of cartridge. My face and hands I gave over to perdition after the first ten minutes with them, but the extension of damage to my skirt is less easy to bear as I am "travelling light," and it will be ten days before I reach Calgary and my trunk!

The little smokeless bullets I used at first were hardly big enough to kill, and after I had suffered seeing half-a-dozen little furry gophers die slowly in great rebellion, I open a box of black-powder cartridges and become a pillar of grease! — and mercy. I am really driving out over this sun-smitten prairie to see an Englishwoman who has newly settled in Canada, and learn from her of the conditions, but the journey is considerably gilded by the loan of a 22 Winchester and the presence of a driver who connives at gopher-shooting. We dawdle along and shoot from the rig whenever the boy turns with a "Say! there's a dandy shot," and I see a pretty squirrelly person sitting by his hole staring defiance with his cheeks bulged with stolen wheat. I would recommend gophers to any one who prefers a rifle to a shot-gun — they give quite as good sport as rooks in May, and that is saying a good deal. We lose our way once and I am electrified to find a patch of prairie roses in bloom. They are the loveliest things of wonder, in that desert of scorched grass — from dead white to deep red they grow on low bushes a foot or so high and smell with a wild, warm sweetness impossible to describe; we find the trail again and see at last the place we are looking for. Out on the livid grass it stands, a mean black shack of wood and pulp-paper, a lowlier shelter than many a farmer's beast would have in England. My heart sinks with pity as we approach — how can anybody live in such a shell here in this arid, treeless desert? The rig draws up and a man comes out of the doorway, I get a glimpse into a stifling den of flies, and am reminded of the accommodation in a gipsy's caravan — this looks no bigger. There is a small tent in front of the shack — I suppose for sleeping in in dry weather. The man listens to my story and takes me round to see his wife; he is a nice man, deeply tanned, with humorous eyes and a strong chin. I like his face. His wife is sitting the other side of the shack in the shade, nursing a fat baby. As I sit beside her I am wholly prepared for an outburst of grumbling, and, indeed, I feel I have no right to expect anything else. But lo! like the roses in the gasping prairie there blooms nothing but courage and cheerfulness from her tale.

"Lonely! not a bit now I have my baby! But even without him there was plenty to do. A farmer's wife in Canada must expect work. In seeding-time she will be up at 4 A.M. to get the men their breakfast. Then she will have to milk, and separate the cream afterwards, if they have a separator. If there are several cows it is quite a back-aching task. Then there will be the house to clean, the breakfast things to wash up, the beds to make, and she must not waste time over that part of her day for there is dinner to cook for hungry men by 11:30. After washing up again the afternoon will mean bread-making, or clothes-washing and ironing, or jam-making, or butter-churning — one of the endless things like that anyway, and at 7:30 or 6:30 (according to the season of the year) she must have "tea" ready. Tea is nearly as big a meal as dinner and the last meal of the day. After that she must wash up, then milk two cows and separate her cream before she can think of going to bed. Probably there will be some darning or mending to do even then. That is a straightforward day, but it is greatly complicated when the children begin to come."

She has told me the tale of labour quite simply. Her eyes are happy, her face is beautiful with health and courage.

"We only came out a year ago," she continues; "in a week or two we will move into a good house — this is very uncomfortable — my husband has bought another farm and it has a house on it. Isn't my boy beautiful? but he was born before his time. You wouldn't think so, would you? I had to go so far to reach the hospital that the journey upset me, and I was very afraid for him, he was nearly a month too soon."

The baby is a magnificent chap, worthy of unstinted praise and gets it, though he dislikes my way of holding him and clamours to get back to the arms he is growing to know. "Do you think he will smile at me soon?" she says. "I am so glad to have him, but the women suffer much out here in these wilds for lack of proper nurses. They want qualified midwives who will turn to when their patients are settled, and do housework for them. It is a dreadful thing to know how many prairie women go through their confinements alone; I was very lucky, I was able to get to a hospital, but lots of them can't." I ask her if she is homesick for the old country, and she saddens for a second. "Will one ever lose that feeling, I wonder? It will come all right. We are getting on, we are not going to give in — we have never thought of doing that."

The man comes out of the shack with tea and bread and butter for me — he has prepared it all quietly while I was talking; as he returns to his work the young wife watches him very fondly. "Englishmen make better husbands than Canadians," she announces, and I observe that the latter would not like to hear her say so. We laugh and talk on about the life, the people, the country.

I discern in her a reserve of cheerfulness that promises success for both in the venture. Her laughter is not forced, it bubbles continually from some inner fount of joy. They came from the Midlands, and neither of them understood land culture, in general a foolhardy experiment. But these two young English people are on a fair way to success — I cannot exactly say why. They may be intelligent above the average, they may have brought considerable capital, they may, or he may, own to some streak of farmer blood which helps him to learn readily, it may be unusual industry (a quality which always brings success in Canada), or it may be — who knows? — that old-fashioned love has them in grip, and makes everything seem easy for each other and nothing too hard to win. I have pictured them exactly as I found them — I cannot hit on what made them so interesting and so nice in their squalid shack. I only know that their eyes were kind when they looked at each other, and they were very happy in surroundings which many would have bitterly resented. I realize one thing as I look at them and say "Good-bye" — the hardness of a settler's lot is infinitely lessened if he has a wife to smile with him. A grumbling woman could have made life hell for both on that blazing, shadeless plain.

If I were to come next year I should see them in a nice house, with granaries and cow-sheds; with more acres of prairie broken into grain, and a small fat person toddling round who has learned to smile at mother.

Going, I sniff industriously — it almost feels as if I can smell mignonette! I accuse them inwardly of having made me homesick with their peaceful English voices; but a few yards from the shack I see a plaintive tribute to our common nationality — a square yard, not more, of prairie land hedged round with pegs and string, where bloom gloriously mignonette and nasturtium.

My conscience stirs uneasily — in all my wanderings through this beautiful busy country I have not found an Englishwoman to tell me in close detail her experiences of Canadian domestic life as she found it on first landing, white-hot with eager industry — and ignorance. They would be useful reading, I know, to intending immigrants, and till I find them I feel I have hardly obeyed the official instructions to "describe Canada from a woman's point of view." A difficulty I have never foreseen confronts me, for the feckless settlers have nothing of value to tell, little but self-revealing grumbles to offer, and the workers have so much to do that they will hardly talk about it. It is quite near the end of my sojourn in the country before I find what I want: an English girl who came out two years ago to keep house for her brothers, and who tells her story vividly while she gets tea ready in the little wooden house out on the prairie. She is young and pretty, I watch her work with pleasure; she has curly red hair and a pleasant voice, her hands are red and rough, an honourable sign in this country. Far away on the horizon is a crimson ring of sunset, in the middle distance a straw-stack burns with a pale yellow flame.

"I'll tell you of my first day," she says. "I can never forget how odd it all was. I got to Regina at two in the morning, and whenever I think of the city I see it as I saw it then for the first time, silent and grey, with its unpretentious rows of wooden houses. My brothers had been 'batching' it, and welcomed me gladly; they are not farmers, they work in the city and had had many discomforts to put up with. I started right into work at once — I got up that same morning to make their breakfast; they were asleep still, and I wanted to please them from the first day they had me there. I went into the kitchen to make the fire, but could find no wood, no coal, no water; I looked about for the bundles of tidy sticks one always has in the old country, nothing to be seen. Then I remembered I must not expect comforts, and went outside to hunt. I found a shed with coal, but all the wood was big round pine logs, hopeless for kindlings. I hunted for a chopper. It cost me a long time and a cut finger to splinter enough for my purpose, and when I tried the stove — oh! I wish you'd seen how clumsy I was. I tried to light the fire from the front like we did at home, but I found it worked from the top, and after my eyes were smarting with smoke and my temper ruffled it began to draw. Then for the water: I looked everywhere, there was none to be found, no taps, no barrel, no anything! I took a pail and searched round about for a well, but at last had to call one of the boys and he took me down to the well that supplies several of us here — a good four hundred yards away.

"It was with real dismay that I realized how every drop of water I used must be drawn from the well and carried all that way. At last I got them some tea and bread and bacon, and sent them off to work with a list of wanted stores. We are too far from the shops to be really comfortable here. After they had gone I looked round. First to wash up the breakfast things. There was no sink, no sign of a sink; earnest search revealed a pail full of tea-leaves, potato-parings and refuse hidden behind a packing-case — evidently this must be my portable sink; but where to empty it? I went to the door and surveyed the blank prairie; at last I took a spade and dug a deep hole far from the shack, for the boys had evidently emptied the 'sink' out of the front or back door, or anywhere handy, during their reign, and the method did not commend itself to me. With a pail and tin basin I made shift to wash up; then made the beds, cleaned the dusty windows, scrubbed the kitchen floor, and then made for my great work. Early in the proceedings I had spied in one corner of a room up-stairs a heap of dirty clothes, socks full of holes, tailless shirts and other bachelor signs, which made my female heart to bleed. The tablecloths looked as if they had been used to clean boots with — at least two months' washing stared me in the face. Half-a-mile or more away I spied a neighbour's shack — there I went to borrow a wash-tub after a hopeless search for the thing at home, and I first drew four pails of water up from the well, putting three of the pails straight on the stove to heat. The neighbour, a slatternly Irish woman, with tousled hair hanging about her face, and gifted with a dingy, sore-eyed child, lent me her tub with all the good-will in the world. With indescribable back-ache I washed the pile of clothes and linen from pure black to pale grey, the best I could compass, and then was hard put to for a clothes line. At last I remembered a cord round a trunk up-stairs, and unknotted it with sodden fingers wondering where to fix it to — there was no pole, there are no trees here! Finally I strung it between the house and woodshed, and hung out the washing to dry. There was hardly any food in the place, I boiled some potatoes and made a 'hasty' pudding for my dinner. When the boys came in with the stores I prepared their supper and listened with seemly humility to their expressions of admiration and delight!"

Funny little woman with the red hair and red hands! What will the "boys" do when she marries? She has refused two offers already for their sakes, but she can hardly be expected to do that for ever. I look round me, and see how beautifully she keeps the house; outside she has rigged up a primitive boot-scraper to save her shining floors, a clothes-line stretches proudly between poles beyond the back door; endless homely contrivances bear witness to her ready wit and industry. The "boys" must marry too, in self-defence! But wives are scarce in Western Canada.

Although I am anxiously looking out for "bachelor" women on the prairies I do not seem to find any. I mean by this phrase women who are working the land "on their own," singly or in clusters. At last it is borne in upon me that there are no women on the prairies except the wives and daughters of farmers, and they are scarce enough; but travelling as I am doing at this stage of my visit, week in and week out, over soil so rich, I am constrained to wonder if there is any reason why women should not come out and work it as well as men. No one questions its fertility and abundant profits, nor the fact that hundreds of healthy English-women are encumbering the old country and leading profitless lives. The labour of "homesteading" would be very great for women, I can understand their shirking it; and the lure of 160 acres of free land is not so golden, when faced in detail, now that Canada is fast settling up, as it is impossible to homestead within easy reach of the railway, a most important matter where the question of carrying goods to market is concerned. The distance, too, doubles the expense of con-veying lumber for fuel and building purposes, furniture and implements and stock to the farm; it also makes the homesteader a very lonely person. To "make good" on a free farm a woman would need either much courage and capital, or considerable male labour, besides agricultural skill.

Land, however, can still be bought at any price from ten dollars (£2) an acre and upwards within a few miles of the railway, and only those who have been over here can appreciate the opportunities for money-making in Canada. Women in England have no conception of the openings there are for them in the great North-West. Given health and industry, there is a fortune waiting for them in that marvellous prairie loam, just as surely as for the men who go out to grow wheat and run stock-farms. Above all there is a splendid opening for our women gardeners. Plenty of women now-a-days train in agriculture and horticulture, but the demand for their services is at best small in Great Britain, while it is urgent round the rapidly growing prairie towns. These towns are utterly unlike anything English; built of wood, they spring up like mushrooms wherever some accident of rail or water in the locality makes them convenient centres of access to the outer world. Thither come the farmers and ranchers to sell and buy, to bring their sick, to fetch their mail, to hire the labour which is so dear and scarce in the North-West — and to "see life."

They are excellent centres, moreover, for the sale of market garden produce, which at present is, like labour, both dear and scarce. The Canadian housewives use tinned goods to a tremendous extent because their men prefer the big gamble of wheat-growing to the steady, if slower, road to fortune offered by vegetable, fruit and flower growing. Here, then, is the opportunity for Englishwomen. Let them come out in twos and threes, unless any single woman has herself sufficient capital, and (just as important) courage for a lonely life; let them settle within marketable driving distance of such cities as Saskatoon, Regina, Edmonton, Calgary, etc., and they will find awaiting them every facility for a life of independence and certain ultimate success in the grandest climate in the world. The brilliant bracing air, the bustle of industry and of hope which pervade the prairies are beyond my powers to describe. If they would prefer to try such a centre as Winnipeg they must be prepared to pay bigger prices for their land, or else to settle near the smaller towns, like Birtle, which is eight hours by rail from Winnipeg, where excellent land is to be bought for ten dollars (£2) an acre. Mr. Larcombe has 800 acres at Birtle, where he raises excellent wheat, yet he finds it pays him to devote more and more of his land every year to growing potatoes, beets, tomatoes, pumpkins, etc., for the Winnipeg market. He would be an invaluable and willing adviser to any one proposing to compete with him; it sounds altruistic, but the market is large and grows yearly larger; also he is an ardent Imperialist who keenly desires to see British settlers on Canadian soil. It is possible to settle within an hour, by electric car, from the city on the Assiniboine River, but land there fetches 250 dollars an acre. Winnipeg offers a greater market for fruit, flowers and vegetables than any city in Canada. It imports hundreds of car-loads yearly from the United States, all subject to 33 per cent. duty, not to mention the high freight rates. The soil is magnificent, a warm quick vegetable mould which has been known to produce 650 bushels of potatoes to the acre. Figuring that out at 50 cents a bushel shows a yield of 325 dollars an acre, and 50 cents is a low estimate. I met a man here in September who had just received 1.25 to 1.50 dollars per bushel for his last load! All vegetables sell readily. Some of the companies will do the first year's ploughing for buyers of market garden lots, and take payment by instalment as profits come along; personally I should always suggest the advisability of starting fair with sufficient capital to be unencumbered by any such debt, although many a wealthy Canadian of to-day began in that way.

Land round the other cities I mentioned can be purchased now for twenty-five dollars to thirty dollars an acre, generally speaking, and they offer a steadily growing market. Round Saskatoon land may be bought for anything from ten dollars to twenty-five dollars an acre, in accordance with its proximity to the city, a factor the value of which to a market gardener it is unnecessary to emphasize. The soil is of marvellous fertility — three to four feet of loam over clay — and one or two of the townspeople have begun to grow their own vegetables, in despair of getting them any other way. In Mrs. Hanson's garden at Saskatoon are cucumbers, carrots, tomatoes, marrows, asparagus, celery, onions, beets, radishes, turnips, potatoes, strawberries, raspberries, currants and gooseberries. The season is short, and housekeepers who can get fresh vegetables store them in "rootcellars" for the winter — they are also very clever at pickling them. As evidence of the rapid growth of these prairie cities I may mention that Saskatoon had 200 inhabitants six years ago, and has 10,000 to-day. The story of the transformation of Winnipeg I have already narrated. Edmonton is one of the most beautiful and prosperous of the prairie cities — and Calgary, "the capital of ranchland," is another wonderful place for such a venture as I am advocating. It stands at the feet of the Rocky Mountains, is warmed throughout the winter by Chinook winds, fed by a glacial river of indescribable beauty, and boasts, even in Canada, an atmosphere of exceptional brilliance and exhilaration.

For the benefit of such of its subjects as live by the soil, the Dominion Government, as I have already said, supports nine experimental farms, of which two are in Saskatchewan, two in Alberta, and one in Manitoba, so that the prairie provinces are well supplied. The importance of these farms to settlers is beyond count — there experiments are ceaselessly in progress for the identification and destruction of weeds and pests, for the breeding out of flowers, fruit, grain and vegetables which will stand the hard North-West winters, or ripen before the earliest frost, or in some way render the grower immune from climatic hazards in his ventures. The farms exist solely for the use of the people, and results of successful experiments are made public property at once; advice is given free, and the literature they publish is of extraordinary value to those interested in the land. I have spoken of these farms before, but the matter will bear repetition in connection with market gardening.

I am particularly struck with the possibilities for women market gardeners at the Manitoba Hall in Winnipeg, where I am in time to see the Horticultural Exhibition. There I find an old familiar friend, Beauty of Hebron, and Early Rose, and Early Jersey Wakefield, among other potato tribes. The latter were sown on June 17th, and win first prize on September 1st. Strange pear-shaped tomatoes, too, I see; Swiss Chard, an unfamiliar vegetable, with stalks like flat white rhubarb ending in a leaf similar to that of a cabbage with white veins; petunias, asters, carnations, zinnias, stocks, sweet peas, cacti and a few pathetic half-wild roses. Pumpkins and citrons are here, and home-made wines and jams in abundance — yellow misty dandelion wine that carries me back to thirsty childhood hours in the hay-fields, when sunburnt peasants drank dandelion "beer" out of big stone bottles, and we children clamoured vainly for that nectar instead of tepid milk. One never-to-be-forgotten day I persuaded an infant brother to accompany me to the stone jar, and we drank furtively, like the dwarfs in the old myth, of that Odhaerir, honey-sweet and just as fatal, for the Odin-eye of a parent discovered us later disgracefully fuddled under a briar hedge. I am straying from my subject, however, and will not pursue the story; it is hardly a creditable one, and nothing whatever to do with Canada; moreover, the rest of it is painful even in remembrance. To return to Manitoba Hall, I see parsnip wine, bronze like an Austrian copper briar rose with the sun on it; cherry wine, black and opaque; white currant, a warm orange; raspberry vinegar, homely pickles; and one exhibit round which I hover fascinated — the sweet herbs! Thyme, summer savory, sage, marjoram with flowers like "cherry pie" or heliotrope, and sweet basil, with its pale green spikes and small white flowers, indissolubly connected with memories of Keats and Isabella.

Herbs are always quaintly attractive with their beautiful names, their odd perfumes, their virtues and sobriety. English cooks ignore them in the most unintelligent fashion, few will use rosemary for veal stuffing, or put chervil, tarragon or dandelion into their lettuce salads, thereby missing countless subtleties dear to a discriminating palate. Mint and parsley they will admit in their dishes, but the difficulty of getting an English cook to put a chopped chive-spike with mashed potatoes is beyond belief — sometimes they will rise to borage for Cup, but chives for potatoes — never. As Schloesser has it, "once upon a time, when things went more slowly and life was easier, the culture and culling of the simples which went to make the olitory, or herb garden, was as much a part of female education as a nice deportment." It is with considerable admiration, therefore, that I linger by the herb stall in Manitoba Hall and see that Canadians are not above growing herbs. There is an immense market for market garden produce out West — flowers are dear and sell well; vegetables are greatly needed; it seems an infinite pity, therefore, that any one should think of inserting such an advertisement as appeared the other day in a Surrey paper. A trained woman gardener offered her services free in exchange for a house! It sounds incredible; but it is a fact. Nor is it unusual in England. Here is a woman, trained expensively, ready to haggle her skill for a home! Why does she not go out West, where many a farmer would gladly pay her well to "run" a few acres for flowers and vegetables, while he and his men attend to the wheat growing? She can save money and ultimately buy her own land; it is easy to save in these wild places of the world, where there are none of the lures to spend which make saving such a dire and difficult game in the old country; there are no after-season sales, no entertaining, no taxicabs, no theatres; it is hard to spend money indeed; and there is every inducement to make it. It is easy to acquire land in a slow, sane, industrious way, and work it profitably. Market gardening requires no such outlay as wheat farming; that is a venture which does not begin to pay till 160 acres are tilled, a feat which takes some doing in the bush-covered parts of the prairie with only a scrub-plough to help. The ploughing of a few acres, on the other hand, is not a very formidable undertaking, and returns in flowers and vegetables would be steady.

Before I left England a woman I know asked me to look out for an opening for her out West. Her comely face, drawn into puckers of anxiety, haunts me as I travel; I make inquiries on her behalf, and get five offers for her services on the prairie lands, one in Nova Scotia, none in British Columbia. Four out of the five would-be employers are anxious to engage her as domestic help, practically as servant, a post at which I beg no reader to sniff. Every woman is a servant where labour is so scarce, and the wives among them throw in their travail and child-rearing as well! The wages offered range from ten to twenty dollars a month. The fifth offer is to run a poultry department on a large farm of 800 acres near Winnipeg. The farmer wants to keep poultry, there is a good market for it in the city; his daughters are already fully occupied with the housework and dairy, and he would like an Englishwoman "for company" for them as well as to manage the poultry. He says he will "deed" her five acres to work on, make them wolf-proof, although he cannot promise they will be hawk-proof, and give her fifteen dollars a month, to become twenty if she likes the work and stays on, and as perquisite all the eggs to sell that are not wanted for the house or for sitting. I remember the worried face in the Devonshire rose-garden —

"Auntie is very kind, but what am I to do when she dies? I have no trade; I look after the fowls for her; she gives me five shillings a week for that, and I have to dress on it. I can't save. I am thirty. I shall never marry now. No one wants an old maid. . . ." I remember her, and tell the farmer I think I know an Englishwoman who will suit. I picture her round, rosy, good-tempered chubbiness in this land barren of women, and tell myself that some lonely farmer will learn one day how clever she is in all female arts, sewing, cooking and filling a house brimful of domestic comforts, and I write to her detailing all the offers, keeping the best till the last; but she does not come.

What is the fatal inertia which makes our women remain parasites on the community? Do they fear to travel? Why do they persist in staying in a country where they are not wanted, just because they were born in it?

I never learn why the Devonshire girl goes on living with an aunt who thinks herself a philanthropist for keeping her. The only reason ever offered is, "It seems such a dreadful long way away from every one."

Wondering I have passed from Province to Province. Wondering at the homes to be made, at the husbands to be found, and at the scarcity of women all over the West. That sounds bald, "husbands to be found," unattractively phrased. I will not retract it, nor re-phrase, nor modify. Whatever may be urged to the contrary by the enforced bachelor women of my own land, I know that in their secret hearts most of them think of marriage as the ultimate goal. An honourable wish, by no means to be hidden with shame. Every healthy normal woman has it. If we are in England, as I believe we are, evolving a race of practical neuters we are making for evil, not for good. They are the "oddities" of Kipling's "Mother-hive." Our little Island on the edge of Europe is overcrowded with people, chiefly women, and a vast Continent in North America is at its wits' ends for inhabitants, especially women. Now, why does not plus go over to minus and level things up a little, in order to make both countries more comfortable?

First one sees in England a surplus of women working hard, working savagely day by day for bread and bacon, working at a ridiculous wage with no hope of ultimate independence, no hope of marriage or motherhood, no hope of anything but the moment's pence for the moment's meal. One sees, too, the middle and upper class women suffering in the press of humans more acutely (because more intelligently) than these, their factory sisters.

Then over here we see a vast majestic country, rich in wine and oil, in bread and bacon, yielding abundantly under cultivation, giving to all who labour with a spendthrift hand. We see the thousands of acres of prairie lying desolate for want of people; the black loam, virgin to the plough, covered with lilies and roses and golden-rod instead of the fruits of the earth — for want of labour. We see the farm homesteads and farmers' wives suffering from lack of servants to cook and mind the house, the farmers themselves frequently leading wretched lives for lack of women to wed. It all sounds so simple of remedy. Wondering and watching I have passed through Canada, telling myself that Englishwomen have never realized the *room* in Canada. There is a wonderful lot of room — room to live in, to be lost in, to make money in; room to learn the wild ways of the world in, room to cast the fetters of civilization, and room to work — most splendid of all, room to work!

There is room for so many women in the West that the heart aches to see them cramped and struggling there in England; it is paralyzing to travel through both countries and note the crying need in one for the surplus of the other, one is impelled to ask if it is ignorance or cowardice that keeps them away.

And at last I found what I felt all along must exist; a hardship to be faced which makes women justly shrink from the country. First from one prairie wife, and then from another I heard a cry about the hardships of birth on the homesteads. Myself a trained maternity nurse as well as a mother, I know what lack of skilled attention must mean at the hour of travail. And wherever I went I asked how the outlying districts were supplied with midwives. I heard many stories of courage, stories of disaster. One I can never forget, the story of a woman whose first two years on a lonely farm were childless and whose reason began to totter under the stress of loneliness until she found she was to have a baby. The prospect of such an interest changed her life, she was engrossed with hope; it was not possible to obtain a nurse and difficult to get a doctor to the distant homestead, so she and her husband made arrangements for her to go to the nearest hospital forty miles away. She drove over the rough road, the baby was born prematurely and died. I picture her return, to loneliness. I talked with many doctors and nurses, one midwife told me of a case where the lonely young couple found themselves suddenly ushered into parenthood, the nearest doctor was twenty miles away, and they had not been able to get a nurse for love nor money. They were entirely ignorant of obstetric work — the baby was blue and they were frightened. Thereupon, with the placenta unborn, it was put in a hot bath; visions of inverted uterus rise, and appal the initiated. Countless unrecorded cases as terrible must occur. On Pender Island, British Columbia, there are eighty children of school age, so the population must be fairly large. The island has no nurse or doctor. The Jubilee Hospital in Victoria has no maternity wing; at Duncan, on Victoria [Vancouver] Island, a district of forty miles is fed by two doctors. The doctor at Davidson in Saskatchewan has a circuit of sixty miles; there are no nurses at Yellowgrass and Wood Mountain; the city hospital at Regina has only three private rooms for maternity cases, in the Catholic Hospital where the Reverend Sister Superior Mary Duffin and her devoted band of grey nuns work day and night, there are only four private rooms, and even they cannot be spared in the Fall when typhoid is about. These are a few facts and represent little of the case. Within driving distance of a city a woman near her confinement may consider herself more or less safe. Some one will be found to help. But the wives on ranches and farms at any distance, and there are hundreds of them, must spend hideous hours looking forward to the day of trial with every prospect of scrambling through alone, at the risk of the baby's life as well as their own, or else relying on the attentions of some half-breed whose knowledge of the elementary rules of cleanliness will be less than nothing. The percentage of lacerations is enormous — one would expect that under such conditions. Any obstetrician reading this will realize what I mean when I say that such neglect leads to the train of evils which necessitates the building of gynaecological wings on hospitals. I was filled with concern to learn of the hardships Canadian mothers are called upon to endure, I felt I could not ask too many questions to find out the reason. Doctors, of course, are necessary; wholeheartedly I repeat necessary at confinements, but every doctor and every mother knows that the nursing which follows after his duties are over have a tremendous part to play in recovery. A woman should not have to drag out a day or two's rest by herself after the doctor has left and then get up and begin her house duties, as many of them do, of those I mean who are lucky enough to get a doctor at all. The maternity nurses I found had in nearly every case gone through the full three or five years' training and were disposed to sniff at maternity work. I can thoroughly understand their point of view. Maternity work is unexciting and very laborious, it is day and night work and very exacting. Fully trained nurses prefer fever or accident work, and when they undertake maternity cases charge exorbitant fees. The general hospitals are in nearly every instance averse to maternity wards. They say, and quite justly, that maternity work should have a separate building and staff.

The prairies suffer greatly in this need of their mothers, but British Columbia even worse, as it is so isolated in settlement and so much more difficult of travel.

I found the nurses were not in every case certain of obtaining their fees, and there was again a difficulty I could understand in the way of meeting this pressing need of maternity assistance; under stress of fear and love any one can pardon a man for promising any fee to have his wife tended, and understand too that with fear allayed and a new expense safely launched on a slender purse, that however willing he might delay payment and perhaps need a nurse again before the first obligation was discharged. A common fee is twenty to twenty-five dollars a week, and forty or fifty dollars make a hole, for there are many expenses to think of besides; the doctor, laundry, travelling and all the rest. The nurse's point of view has my sympathy too. She does not want to work hard for a problematical forty dollars when there are plenty of certain ones to be had. With all these facts before me I realized one certain thing, that the need of efficient nurses cried aloud. That it spun from mouth to mouth never questioned, that no great band of facts was necessary to back up a plea for attention from the Government because all in authority know the need is there. It struck me that the only way to get at these lone farms was through some subsidized band of itinerant midwives, a sort of mobile corps unattached to any given town or building, but working coherently under the direction of the Government. Women who have thoroughly trained at Queen Charlotte's Hospital or the Rotunda of Dublin are capable of undertaking cases unattended by a doctor, *if need be;* they have not been through the devastating General Training which, in a very large percentage of cases in Great Britain, leaves a woman a gastric invalid with varicose veins, or if it leaves her healthy nearly always makes her too superior for maternity work. I hope that does not sound ill-natured. It is a fact. And one cannot in reason blame nurses for feeling so when they have given arduous years to a complete training, and have emerged fitted to deal with the intensely interesting inch-by-inch work of fevers and the exciting work of surgery. Here and there in unfortunate instances they may get a taste of everything in maternity work, but fortunately that is comparatively rare. Moreover, as I have already said, the fully trained nurse wants fully trained fees, and many of the settlers' wives could not possibly afford them if they could find an unengaged nurse who was willing to come. The fully trained nurse also has been through her purgatory of drudgery in the hospitals, she has washed and cooked and scrubbed and polished, and is now a nurse, not a superior ward-maid. Therefore she would be useless practically in the little prairie shacks where she would have to do all the domestic work as well as the nursing.

Looked at from every point of view it seemed to me that the women wanted out West were the qualified midwives trained by such reputable hospitals as I have named. They would accept a reasonable fee of ten dollars a week. At Edmonton I saw the Honourable Mr. Oliver, Minister of the Interior, and put my idea before him. He listened with perfect courtesy, and considered without haste what I said; he admitted the need of such a scheme, but declared finally that he thought it a Provincial rather than a Dominion matter. He said it was the business of the Dominion Government to bring settlers into the country, but the business of the Provincial Governments to look after them when they had once settled.

So I then went to see the Honourable Dr. Rutherford, Premier of Alberta. He also listened very patiently and asked me to put the scheme in writing so that he might submit it in session. He agreed with me that if one Province took up the idea the others would probably fall quickly into line. So I wrote a long letter asking if it would not be possible to establish a body of nurses under Government auspices at every small town or hamlet through the country, from whence they could radiate to the surrounding districts. Such nurses could be guaranteed a minimum fee for every case where the homesteader was unable to pay, and would take ordinary fees in the ordinary way where possible. The homesteader would be under obligation to repay to the Government as soon as possible, and the nurse would not be working for nothing. The nurses in return for such protection would be pledged to take each case in turn as it applied to the office without picking and choosing. The settlers' wives, then, would only need to write in to the nearest branch stating circumstances and asking for a trained midwife at such a date for such a period. I also suggested that no nurse should go to a case for less than twelve days, a useful safeguard for the health of many mothers. Further, I asked if it were not possible that such a body of maternity specialists be attached to the existing order of Victorian Nurses, acting as an endowed Government body, but incorporated with the present order.

I mentioned that in the old country many more women are trained for maternity work than there is work for; and that it should be possible to select from among them women who can bake bread, sew, cook and run a house, women who *knowing the conditions in the West* would be willing to come for the sake of guaranteed employment, and who after settling the patient would turn to and mind the house.

So having heard nothing from Alberta I approached the Premier of British Columbia, who put the matter in council at once, and at least did me the honour to reply. Here is the letter I received —

Provincial Secretary's Office,
Victoria,
15th October, 1908.

"MRS. GEORGE CRAN,
     "c/o Supt. of Immigration,
     "Department of the Interior, Ottawa.
"MADAM,
     "I beg leave to acknowledge the receipt of your communication of the 9th instant, in which you outline the suggestions offered in your conversation of recent date regarding the bringing of nurses to this Province for extra-hospital work. The matter was laid before the Executive Council at its last meeting, and I am instructed to say that after very careful consideration the Provincial Government feel that they are not in a position to accept suggestions. The matter was thoroughly discussed, and the consensus of opinion was that this being a matter of immigration is one which lies entirely within the province of the Dominion Government at Ottawa.
     "I have the honour to be, Madam,
          "Your obedient servant,
          "H. E. YOUNG

"(Provincial Secretary)."

This was a game of battledore and shuttlecock, the need of the women being the shuttlecock between the greater and lesser governments. I hoped that Saskatchewan might prove more kindly about things, but the Premier was away for the General Election when I reached Regina, and the public health official makes tuberculosis his hobby. He assured me in the airiest way that the women were amply provided for, yet he lives in the province where maternity nurses are scarcest and where one doctor, aforementioned, has a circuit of sixty miles whereon to lavish his attentions. At Winnipeg I was advised to get the municipalities to subsidize the nurses, but my experience of governing bodies inclined me to regard that project with prophetic disappointment, and I went on to Ottawa, where is the head-quarters of the Victorian Order of Nurses, determining to lay the matter before the committee and ask for consideration at its hands. The Victorian nurses visit the sick and work, therefore, on short circuits; they, as they exist at present, are in no way able to meet the need I poignantly felt to be an urgent one for the widely scattered mothers of Canada. I saw the committee and detailed my scheme once more, and knew directly I spoke to the matron that I had met prejudice. The pity of the whole position is this, that while the fully trained nurse is more than a trifle scornful of maternity work, she is violently antipathetic to the "half-baked" sister, the midwife who has taken only the short maternity training and is not qualified for all branches of nursing. I have noticed that prejudice over and over again, and always with resentment. They might scorn the maternity nurses to the crack of doom and welcome if they were willing to do the work themselves, but they are not. They oppose the idea of giving maternity nurses a definite status, and themselves leave the work undone, Meanwhile, the mothers suffer. Any scheme for alleviating the distress, which none denied, was unwelcome to the Victorian Order of Nurses. Their work is great, it is well done, their nurses have worked hard to get their diplomas and are worthy of honour. But they met the maternity problem with prejudice. If an argument is advanced that the accidents and sicknesses of adults are more important than bringing to birth of the next generation, I wholly disagree. It is the race that is involved in maternity work, not the individual. A pregnant woman is a national asset, a national glory, a national responsibility. It is the next generation to which we owe allegiance, should show mercy and consideration, to which we should bend our energies and skill.

Interfering people are intolerable. They seldom compass anything. They are always a nuisance. Frankly I believe I was an interfering person in the matter of the neglected Western wives. Canada is not my country, nor was it any of my business to right its wrongs. I met my deserts. Yet the blood chills to think of the lonely mother-women, of the effect on their babes of the unnecessary harshness of the birth hour and the nervous expenditure in the anticipation of it. As Mr. Woods of the *Calgary Herald* said in speaking of the subject, "It grips one beyond reason."

Her Excellency Lady Grey was good enough to interest herself in the idea I mooted before the Victorian Order of Nurses; she mentioned the Cottage Hospitals sparsely dotted about the prairies and British Columbia, but realized their inefficiency in this one particular when I told her how women will come in eighty and a hundred miles for attention to them and yet many hundreds go unattended. Women within possible reach of a doctor, nurse or hospital may be counted provided for, but the women I grieve about are those who can only be reached by such an itinerant body as I have sketched. There are many farmers' wives with children who cannot go to hospital for their confinements as their man is out at work all day and they are unable to leave the house and children. To such women a maternity nurse representing a fortnight's rest would be an inestimable boon.

I am telling English women straightforwardly what to expect at present if they go out and marry on a lonely farm in the North-West. Also I can tell them that every woman who goes out to stay makes it easier for her sisters, for the evil will remedy itself with population. To British women trained at Queen Charlotte's and the Rotunda I would say there is plenty of work to be had if they will take the good and the bad and set about things carefully. It would not be a bad plan to advertise in one or two prairie papers before going out so as to secure one or two cases to go on with and not trust everything to chance. Better still, to find the names of one or two doctors in outlying districts and write direct to them. I hope it has been perfectly clear through all this talk of midwives that I never suggest them as a substitute for doctors, only as allies, and in cases where a doctor is unprocurable by reason of the patient's poverty or distance I maintain that their trained services would be infinitely better for all concerned than those of some terrified ignorant neighbour or dirty half-breed. I beg no one to misapprehend me on this point.

If such British women are prepared to go out and put up with the inconveniences of primitive homesteads, to be housekeeper as well as nurse, and to accept moderate fees — say ten dollars a week — they will find work in plenty. I would recommend them to insist on payment before leaving, and if cash is scarce to take payment in kind — say wheat or live stock. It sounds harsh, but it is only fair to the nurse who may suffer if she has a kind heart and is not armed with stern advice. In the majority of cases her fee would be gladly and punctually paid. A lady whose advice on the subject would be of great value to any one who has courage to face life under such conditions is Miss Beynon of the *Winnipeg Free Press*. She appreciates to the full the dearth of women in the North-West and has many practical hints to offer. There is this to be said, that every maternity nurse who has practised in Canada and marries there will be fully aware of what she is undertaking, and will probably take good care to live within reach of assistance. My sympathies are very much with the English girls who have gone out, reared in that pernicious ignorance of physiological facts which is counted among the many over here for innocence, and has learnt at bitter cost of unnameable suffering the penalties Nature exacts for ignorance — the unforgiveable sin of ignorance.

The care of the lonely mothers, then, as far as I can see, devolves on the individual courage and skill of their British sisters. Had my suggestion found favour with any governing body it would have been a comparatively easy matter to select the suitable women to go out. Any one who knew the North-West could have obtained permission to lecture at the best Maternity Hospitals over here on conditions for nurses out there, and having told in sober truth the whole story the volunteers alone would have been considered, thus eliminating all but those with the desire for pioneer work. From those again the matron would have been asked to remove the names of those below a desired standard in health or efficiency. They would need to be strong, reliable, clever nurses, but if there were a guarantee of steady employment it would be a small matter to get all the picked women needed — steady work is a great attraction to an English nurse.

I do not think government aid would be necessary indefinitely. After a while some of the nurses would make money and start maternity homes here and there; which in their turn would make good training centres for the next generation of nurses, and so the situation would gradually work out of itself. So it will still. Things always do, but meanwhile the women suffer and the children suffer, two sorts of suffering that are exceeding bad for a young race. Canada, so fatherly in its government, so sane and sensible, so wise and patient in most of its measures, is here in this particular extraordinarily callous and short-sighted. All over the country one finds schools, well built, well managed, the scholastic system in Canada is really a remarkable one. Yet it neglects its children at the fountain head of being and hopes for a contented healthy people. I would reverse the system, I would look after them physically first in every possible way, and then set to afterwards with schools and book-learning.

Here I am, then, at the end of all, seeming to say to women, "Don't go! there are flies in the ointment." But I do not say anything of the sort. To the right women there is only one word, "Go."

But the women Canada wants are rare in English communities. There is the real trouble.

The English woman is used to large crowds, to a busy communal life. In Canada she would have to bring courage for loneliness, she would needs find companionship in her husband and children, in her cattle, in the housework, in the very beauty of the wild itself. The English women are used to specialized labour; they are artists, or stenographers, book-keepers, nurses, journalists, dairy-women, doctors or what not. The Canadian woman will drive a team of horses when her man is too busy to work the hayrake or binder, she will be baker, house-maid, cook, mother, seamstress, nurse to her neighbour five miles off when she is ill, she will run the dairy, sell the butter and eggs, and keep the farm accounts all in her own person. The English woman rises at 7:30 to 9 A.M.; the Canadian woman in the West at 5 A.M., sometimes earlier, rarely later.

The woman who makes good in Canada is energetic and brave.

The average English woman is lazy, fond of ease, and she lacks courage to face new conditions. Now how to do any good with such a need and such a supply?

In all these large questions one has to speak in masses. The *mass* of English bachelor women is, I am persuaded, unfitted by our complete civilization to face the toils of settlement in a new country. But the exception, the fearless, enthusiastic, clean-bred exception, must exist in her thousands. And to her a direct statement of fact is the strongest appeal. The woman who has faced an unvarnished history of conditions in the country and is still anxious to emigrate is the woman Canada wants.

Let no woman come from England to the Canadian cities; they are over-full already, there is no work for them there, and at best Canadian city life is but a parody of English city life. At the risk of offending I will tell the truth. But if any woman cares for work let her come to the prairies or British Columbia and labour with her hands like the rest. It is a great call for women. There must be some who have the courage and the health to leave the ready-made comforts of the old country, and come into this wild beautiful West, giving their best of mind and body for the race and for the Empire.

Here is the end of the book. The *au revoir* end, because in bones and blood and longing heart I know that somehow, somewhere, I shall again tread and write of that lovely land. What do I remember of Canada now that Quebec has faded away — Quebec with her ramparts and plains, her history, her mighty river — I remember the foaming rapids of Lachine; the enamels; the rolling wheat of the prairies; the fruit orchards of British Columbia and Niagara; the mines of silver, lead, copper, gold; the thrill of the whirling spoon in salmon waters; the cry of a stricken quarry in the bush; the scarlet bunch-berries on the mountains; the snow and the sun and the dominant brilliant sky. I remember these and so much more of loveliness . . . I remember, too, a people given over to work and hope, a people kind and prejudiced and courageous, a great Government which gives its children schools, experimental farms, free homesteads, a Government which subsidizes the hospitals so that charity in sickness does not exist, and the best medical attention may be had of all, a Government which works sanely on commercial lines for the good of the greatest number, and for all its sense neglects its women and babes at the hour of birth, leaving them untended on the outlying home-steads, a Government which makes at the same time a great hue and cry about race suicide. I remember these things.

Every August as harvest comes I must suffer the restless desire to stand on the prairie and hear again the rustle of miles of wheat — I shall long to board a train and lean from the end car to smell the pine and cedar, to see the silver rails slip from our wheels, the wooden houses, the great barns, to feel the space, to lave in silence.

If any woman, reading this, wants to go to a beautiful country and carve out her own fortune from its deep loam, I shall be happy to tell all I can that may help her to Canada, and if that is little I can at least put her in the way of getting information from the best sources.

There is money to be made there, at farming and horticulture; at domestic service which entails in Canada no loss of caste; at maternity nursing; and there are happy homes ahead for many, especially for women who do not settle too far from civilization for safety and comfort.

If I had to earn my living I would go to Canada.

In the summer of 1905 Georgina Binnie-Clark and her sister Ethel came to Lipton, Saskatchewan, to visit their homesteading brother. Like Elizabeth Lewthwaite ten years earlier, the two women found their planned summer sojourn turning into long-time residence. Georgina Binnie-Clark lived in Saskatchewan from 1905 to 1914 and again from 1921 to just before the outbreak of World War II. She died in England in April 1947 at the age of seventy-five. Ethel Clark spent upwards of forty years in Canada before her death in 1955. The two sisters owned and operated a wheat farm just outside Fort Qu'Appelle, and the story of their coming to Canada and entry into prairie agriculture is told in two books from before World War I, both written by Georgina.

The second of these two books, *Wheat and Woman*, has recently been reprinted.[1] It deals directly and at length with opportunities for educated middle-class gentlewomen in Canadian wheat-farming, opportunities circumscribed only, as Georgina Binnie-Clark saw it, by the failure of the Canadian government to permit single women to apply for homestead land. A single woman herself by choice, she was in many respects typical of the class she wrote for. She was born in 1871 to Arthur Walter Binnie Clark, a Dorset inkeeper-turned-landed-gentle-man, and his wife, Maria Clark. Binnie-Clark was educated at home by gover-nesses, but she may also have attended one of the colleges for women that sprang up in considerable numbers during the 1880's and 1890's in England. For at least a year, perhaps longer, she pursued musical studies in Germany and France.

Sometime around the turn of the century Binnie-Clark began publishing short stories and articles in English magazines, and by 1905, when she set sail for the New World, she apparently considered herself a professional writer. So much, at least, one gathers from the opening chapters of *A Summer on the Canadian Prairie,* published in London and Toronto in 1910, and certainly this book is not the work of a novice. In many respects it falls readily into the travel-and-social-commentary genre that was so popular at the time. Where it stands apart is in Binnie-Clark's evident literary sophistication and her sensitivity to the subtler aspects of social relationships among Saskatchewan's farming population during the early years of settlement. The chapter from *A Summer on the Canadian Prairie* given here concerns the experiences of Georgina herself, and of her sister Ethel (re-named Hilaria for the purposes of this semi-fictionalized and comic narrative), as they take stock of their position and their prospects in the West. (Lal is the name given here to Georgina's brother Lou; the "British Workman" is Lal's remittance-man partner Hicks. Neither is treated with marked respect by the narrator.)

Following this brief excerpt from her first-published book, which was written primarily as an entertainment for British readers, are three more samples of Binnie-Clark's writing on the subject of emigrant British women, all rather more earnest in tone. The first comes from the *Imperial Colonist,* whose files list several articles by Georgina Binnie-Clark between 1907 and 1912.[2] Among them are "Horticulture as a Career for Women" (February 1908), "Women's Chances in the West" (March 1909), and a three-part piece, reprinted here, entitled "Are Educated Women Wanted in Canada." (February-April 1910). In addition to this latter article, two other papers delivered as speeches are also included. "Conditions of Life for Women in Canada" dates from October 1909 and was delivered to the annual meeting of the National Union of Women Workers at Portsmouth, England; "Land and the Woman in Canada" was given before the members of the Royal Colonial Institute in London on 8 April 1913.

1. *Wheat and Woman* was reprinted in 1979 by the University of Toronto Press in its Social History of Canada series, with full historical and biographical introduction by Susan Jackel.
2. Several of these articles are cited by A. James Hammerton, *Emigrant Gentlewomen,* chapter 6, "Emigration Propaganda and the Distressed Gentlewoman, 1880-1914," pp. 148-86. I am grateful to Dr. Hammerton for providing these citations and so enabling me to locate these articles.

Georgina Binnie-Clark

Hilaria's Adventures — A Night Out

"Why, I believe you have the blues at last! What's Hilaria got to say?" asked Lal.

"Aren't you going to read your own letters?" I said. "No, I haven't the blues, but I'm afraid I shall have to make the trail again to-morrow."

"You — why? I don't think the horses are south."

"I want to wire some money to Hilaria."

"She said in her last letter that she was going on to the Graylings'. Why does she want money? Wired, too! Surely they would let her have some, if it was anything desperate. New clothes, I expect — Hilaria's disgustingly vain."

"All women worthy of the name care how they look," I said. "It appears that she didn't go on to St. Paul. She did her best to get nursing-work in Winnipeg — only there was none to be had there. She writes that if there had been, she hardly thinks she would have got a post worth having without a certificate. In a colony, too! One would have thought they would have been only too thankful to find any one who had put in nine months' training at the 'London.' "

"Well, what did she do, then? Is she stayin' at Mariaggi's?"

"Certainly not! She went off into the country as a farm help. She couldn't possibly do the work expected of her. Besides —"

"What?"

"There were creatures in her bedroom."

"Oh! Bugs, I suppose?"

"Hush!"

"Well, of course there were bugs — they are everywhere in this country."

"Lal!"

"'Pon my soul, it's true. I was eaten alive in my first billet. But you get used to them in time. There are worse things at sea than bugs. Hicks had to sleep seven in a bed in his first show, and he said he took *darned* good care to get in the middle! Good old Hicks! I wouldn't have endured the prairie a week without him. What's Hilaria gettin'?"

"Twenty dollars a month, but she is to have twenty-five through harvest and threshing."

"That's very good pay. They'll be awfully sick if she clears out before harvest."

"She has already decided to leave. She says the farmer's wife was kindness itself, and did all the cooking, but left her the house-work and the laundry. The second day she was there she had to wash seven blankets! And then not being able to sleep at night! She is awfully keen to get back. At present she is staying at the Women's Home of Welcome. Most clean and comfortable, with baths and things; but Winnipeg is hot and dusty. She says that the shack and the prairie will be *heavenly* after her adventures."

"Now don't pile it on!"

"You can read it for yourself, if you don't believe me."

" 'How often I think of the prairie and the dear old shack! Does the 'British Workman' still meditate like Hamlet beside the stove? I hope he appreciates your cooking.' By Jove! she has soon changed her note. If I had turned tail at the first bug, where should I have been to-day?"

"Where indeed?"

He went off chuckling.

"You will be starting early, won't you? I'll take the buggy down to the slough, and see if I can get off some of the dirt."

I was truly anxious about Hilaria. She was evidently unhappy, and I had always considered that she wasn't one to turn back unless she found herself in a *cul-de-sac*. Also I felt that she might be in difficulties about money. I had given her an emergency cheque for thirty dollars, but it was quite possible that in the far neighbourhood of some out-of-the-way wheat-town she would have considerable difficulty in cashing it. And the thought of Hilaria looking for rescue from toilsome days and sleepless, feverish nights was not to be endured.

At Fort Qu'Appelle I wired sufficient money to allow for sundry expenses and the journey home. I also paid the reply that she might let me know that it was safely received.

"I don't think that we can expect to get back the answer to-night," said the operator, "but no doubt it will be in to-morrow morning."

But the morning brought no acknowledgment, and by the mail came a letter telling me that she was leaving Winnipeg that night, so I concluded that my wire had failed to find her. I paid the hotel bill, and cashed my last available dollar to send a message to Winnipeg post office, where I felt sure she would call to give instructions about her mail, asking her to send me word to Lipton that all was well. Then, with fifty cents to my name, I set out on my thirty-five-mile journey home.

At Lipton there was no wire. I showed the outside edge of my anxiety to the depot-master.

"I guess she's all right! My, that's a terrible fire they had there last night —

makes any one anxious — sure thing! You haven't seen the account? Maybe you would care to read it? . . . Why, certainly."

Had I known more of Winnipeg I should have known that the fire was in the heart of the city, and the last neighbourhood in which Hilaria would be likely to find herself; but I had reached the spot where one's nerves lie at the mercy of the imagination. All the horrible deaths from fire I had ever heard or dreamed of blazed in my memory. I waited in hope until four o'clock, and then drove back to the Fort in despair, hoping to find reassurance in the telegraphed acknowledgment of the money.

In my ignorance of many customs of the country, which are not easily learned in the isolated life we had been living in a new settlement on the prairie, I had not grown used to the fact that in Canada you seek your letters and telegrams: they do not come out to look for you, as in England. I naturally expected that had mine arrived it would have been sent to the hotel.

The last glimmer of the setting sun was tinting the Lake as I crossed the bridge. All the inhabitants of Fort Qu'Appelle seemed to be sitting on the sidewalk in front of the hotel. I inquired if a telegram had been delivered for me, which simple question seemed to have the effect of provoking considerable mirth.

"Well, I guess it would hardly be sent to the hotel," said one.

"Where then?" I inquired.

"Well, the operating office; but that's closed, I guess."

"And the bank is also closed, I suppose?"

"This three hours."

I was evidently exciting a good deal of curiosity, and felt as though St. Peter had refused to unlock the gate at my bidding in full face of my friends. Before I realised quite what I was doing, I had run away, or rather turned my back and crawled over the bridge, at the most defiantly sulky pace of Charles Edward. If the English are difficult to understand, the Canadians are easily misunderstood. In a like difficulty to-day I should not hesitate to go to a local banker, hotel proprietor, or magistrate, and claim their assistance. Canadians are always kind and it is absolutely against the Canadian spirit to refuse hospitality at any time, especially in time of need; but I think it is in the English spirit to find it most difficult to ask for anything which may not be claimed as a right; and the more urgent the need the harder we find it to ask the favour. Of all those people sitting on the sidewalk I doubt if there was one who would not have instantly offered me generous hospitality had they known of my predicament, and liked the English all the better for the fact of one of us being so very much off the pedestal on which we are supposed to pose; but the fact remains that the channel of mutual understanding was closed, and Charles Edward and I went back over the bridge hungry, weary, and with a very swollen sense of wrong, leaving the little group doubtless discussing the question whether I was eccentric in the average degree of my nation, or "real downright silly."

I have no respect for a last coin, and as we climbed the hill I pacified my hunger with the assurance that I would breakfast at the Lipton hotel in the morning. True, the charge was thirty-five cents, whilst at the Fort it was only twenty-five; but time was an hour in front at Lipton, which is also a less respectable, and consequently less curious, town than Fort Qu'Appelle. Many strange birds from many countries roost there from time to time. None would take the trouble to put two and two together, and arrive at the fact that I must have spent the night under the stars; and if they did, the hum of affairs would silence the small and unimportant voice of my business. Fort Qu'Appelle and Lipton mark just the difference that lies between a wheat-town and a settlement minus a railway.

We turned off the trail about half-way. It was impossible to get into the close shelter of the bluff because of the mosquitoes. I took Charles Edward out of the traces and tied him to the back wheel, where he fed with joy, first munching his oats and then the grass at his feet. "The days are hot, the nights are cold." How often had I heard my brother and the "British Workman" quote the stock phrase of the stock delegate with a gibe. The moon and I shared the joke, as she rose in fullest glory to keep watch over us; and the moon in Canada never plays the part of the sleeping disciples as she does in England, but watches without the flicker of an eyelid until the day-break, and the glorious sun banishes its lovely satellite.

Luckily I had already learned to drive in a sun-coat, our first experience of the power of the sun having blistered itself through the average thickness of white silk shirts, which we wore in preference to those of any other fabric, finding it more easily washable. I wore the shortest of tweed skirts, and for my sins shoes instead of boots; so that there was only one place for the very light carriage rug, — the vulnerable precincts of my ankles. Judging from my earlier night-drive across the prairie, one might have dreamed that a night spent in the open under the Canadian stars could be nothing less than a poem — but the mosquito is stronger than death, since it can rob one of all joy in conscious beauty. I have no remembrance of that night but the fierce and unending battle with those myriads of piercing demons. It must have been between the hours of one and two that for the space of a few moments I was tempted to draw up the rug over my shoulders, and in the added comfort of its warmth was lured into a doze, from which I was roused by a concentrated fierceness of attack upon the exposed section of my lower limbs. Gloves of sound English reindeer protected my hands from their merciless assault; which was fortunate, since suicide, murder, blasphemy, anything but treachery to a friend, may be excused of a person with mosquito-bitten fingers. The shadows of dawn brought hint of the coming on of day. From here and there came the far-off crow of cockerels. Not a wolf had bayed through the night, which was a mercy, as I had not then learned that the prairie-wolf does not attack human beings; and even now the baying of a pack strikes weirdly through one to hit the note of melancholy. Sleep was out of the question in the coming of day, although the mosquitoes could hardly do more mischief — there could have been no blank space for a solitary bite. I got out and fastened Charles Edward once more between the shafts, and we drove slowly up and down the trail until the sun came up to right all wrongs, and coax one back to the effort of the new day.

In my own physical woes I had forgotten the anxiety for Hilaria. Hilaria's fate was in the lap of the gods: mine was in my weary, mosquito-bitten body, which yearned for sleep, or failing sleep, soap and water, and a cup of tea. Common sense reasserted itself with breakfast. I remembered that my father had been in direct communication with the Massey-Harris agent over the oxen deal. My bank draft had been cashed without a question, and in all probability there would be no difficulty in obtaining an overdraft. I crossed over to the station to see if by any chance a wire had arrived.

"You had an early drive from the Fort this morning," observed the depot-master.

"Very!" I answered. "No message for me? Then I shall make one more journey back to the Fort, and if I don't get news of my sister I shall go home, and wait until it comes."

"I guess you're right. It never pays to expect anything or any one on time in the North-West. Best to wait quiet, and take what turns up. Care to look at the paper?"

I scanned the list of the names of the injured in the fire, but found no hint of our own. As I handed it back, a woman with an air of trouble, which seemed foreign to her jolly, good-tempered-looking face, came quickly towards the depot-master.

"What! Ain't your friends come along yet?" he inquired.

"No. I guess I shall have to stay on at the hotel another night. Since they wasn't expecting me yesterday, they'll not be looking out for me till to-morrow, I guess. Wal, Lipton's a nice promising city, anyhow!" She turned towards me with a smile, which invited another, and a confirmation of her eulogy; but my mendacity was not equal to the last demand.

"I'm here on a visit to my sister," she said. "She's settled ten miles west with her husband and children — nice children, seven of 'em. It's a lovely country: they make good money. Guess they're right out of their reckoning of my day of arrival. I come up from Dakota. Guess I'll have to stop round Lipton an extra day. I observed you at breakfast this morning — I could tell you were from the old country, so I didn't make any advances. Though I guess the English is more affable when you know them. Been out long? You seem a bit lonesome like — guess you're waitin' for your husband?"

For the first time in my life I felt that he ought to be there. It was probably but the deviation of a strong current of opinion at that moment passing over the mind of my new friend from Dakota. I laid bare my state of single blessedness with profound humility.

Plate 19. This tableau, representing Great Britain and her colonies presented in Dawson in 1900 at a concert in aid of the widows and orphans of the Boer War, is characteristic of the ways emigrant gentlewomen supported the ideals of Empire in the West.

Plate 20. Hospital fund-raising: the Prairie Circle, a Cereal, Alberta, group, at their fair booth, c. 1912. These women raised funds to start the first hospital in Cereal.

Plate 21. Like her pioneer counterparts, Nurse Ruth Elliott was still carrying water for the hospital at Rockyford, Alberta, in 1921.

Plate 22. Market-gardening, poultry-raising, and other household chores may have been the more usual tasks recommended for women, but they were not their only occupations: here, a group is operating graders during the construction of the Grand Trunk Pacific near Viking, Alberta, c. 1907.

Plate 23. This lady, holding her spaniel and posing with a plow and team on the J.T. Dale Farm, south of Glenboro, Manitoba, c. 1904, appears somewhat overdressed for the occasion.

Plate 24. The horseless carriage: two unidentified ladies driving a McLaughlin automobile, 1915.

Plate 25. Marion Cran's *A Woman in Canada* was published in 1910, following a tour taken at the
request of the Dominion Government.

Plate 26. Elizabeth Mitchell's *In Western Canada before
the War* was based on a year's sojourn in the
West.

Plate 27. Triennial Convention of the Canadian Women's Press Club, held in Calgary in 1913. The numbers are surprising.

"Ah! Guess the farmers round can afford to pay pretty good for female help in these parts?"

Feeling a further exposure of ignorance to be ill-fitting, I rose to the true Canadian spirit for the occasion.

"I believe the highest degree of wages in the Dominion is the rule in this district," I said solemnly.

"For goodness' sake! Wal, thar! And homestead lands for the most part. Now what might you be getting?"

I confessed that at that moment I was earning nothing.

"Sakes alive! A likely-looking body, too. Not sufficiently domesticated, I guess. I've heard tell the English come out to get a livin' in the West, and all they can mostly do is dab the organ and speak foreign tongues — which don't set bread for themselves nor their employers. But you ain't one of that sort, I guess," she added consolingly. "Drove up from the valley before six o'clock this morning, they was saying at breakfast. Say now! I've got three nephews down Dakota — all batchin'! My, the lovely farm! and no female."

"How distressing!"

" 'Boys,' I tell 'em, 'there's no economy in sparing money over female help.' 'Say, aunt,' sez they, 'bring us along a likely woman, and she can do what she likes, and we'll pay her good money.' And that they will. And treat you like a queen. You bet they will. They're real nice fellows."

There was no mistaking the accent on the "you" for general: it was special and mine. I thanked her, saying that the prospect was as pleasing as her kind intention, but unfortunately out of the question.

"You would learn in no time. I guess you can bake?"

I wasn't going into details about my accomplishments, negative or affirmative.

"It isn't exactly that," I answered.

"Guess I understand. It's the fare. My dear, they'll send you that, if I give the word."

"I fear they would have to look hard for its value," I replied. "I could hardly expect them to advance me my fare back."

"Don't you worry yourself about that: it would never be needed! I can't say which of them it would be, but I guess you would get the pick. And they're real nice fellows, every one of them."

"I really can't desert my present post," I explained. "You see, I am looking after my brother and his friend."

"So that's it, is it! And what may your brother's friend be making?"

A picture of the "British Workman" in blue overalls, sitting on a portmanteau in the middle of the prairie with the eternal cigarette between his lips, and his hands in his pockets, gravely considering how he could raise a further fifty pounds from the respectable British guardian who lived in solemn British chambers in the neighbourhood of Lincoln's Inn, flashed to my brain.

"In my absence a good deal of work, I shouldn't wonder," I answered. "Men are so untidy, aren't they?"

"Ah, women's a lot to put up with, but we couldn't do without 'em on a farm."

"Couldn't we!" I said. "But I must be getting along, or the sun will be miles ahead of me."

"Well, good-day to you, and I'm downright pleased to have made your acquaintance. I've always said that I didn't see why the English should be more disagreeable than other folk. And they ain't!"

I chuckled over my compliments many times as Charles Edward and I made our way once more over the lonesome but beautiful prairie which stretches between Lipton and Fort Qu'Appelle. In the dust of circumstance, and the absence of that wire, my anxiety for Hilaria had crystallised to a less tender sentiment. Charles Edward made his way down the hill with great deliberation. Just as we were rounding the first corner there came the cheerful pipe of laughter. In a buggy perched between two Canadian youths, with discretion in her attitude, and the intention to get every scrap of amusement out of that or any other situation in her eyes, was Hilaria.

"You!" she cried. "Thanks be. I thought I might have to walk home from Lipton, and you know how I hate the thought of wolves." She explained me to her two companions, who made no effort to conceal their disappointment in being deprived of their guest. "I am so grateful to you both for offering me the lift, and I do hope you weren't too uncomfortable!" It is never what Hilaria says, but always how she says it. I have yet to meet the masculine entity for whom she cannot affect a tender interest.

"We are both most grateful," I struck in, in my most matter-of-fact tone. "Only, if I am to catch the mail, Hilaria, we must hurry."

"Oh, but I'm thankful you have turned up," she said. "I haven't a cent left, and had only just enough to get through with. You never know anything about a country until you haven't any money."

"I wired you money to that outlandish place the moment I received your letter," I said, not without resentment.

"Yes, but I left the very day I wrote to you. I didn't see being devoured alive by bugs."

"They are the bottom," I agreed, remembering a morning when I had watched the sunrise from the gardens of the Luxembourg after a night of horror. "Were they very awful?"

"Oh, I didn't get as far as that. The girl I was expected to share a room with said she had never seen anything of the kind, but another girl who stayed there the year before had told her she had suspicions. However, suspicions are quite enough to keep off sleep, and I wasn't taking any chances. And the work — endless! I scrubbed and washed up, and made the beds, dusted the rooms, and set the table. But when it came to washing blankets — blankets in July! — I made up my mind. When she had finished counting eight, I said I felt ill, and went upstairs to pack my things. I had only just money enough to get through with, and left my luncheon bill unpaid at the hotel. But they were quite nice about it. Of course I said we would send it along."

"We have to get it first," I reminded her. "But I expect we can at any rate reclaim the sum I wired you."

The local banker, who is quoted in Wall Street, and lives the simple life at the foot of the hills at Fort Qu'Appelle, smiled behind the curtain of his eyelids.

"So she got back?" he remarked.

All went well. We walked off with the necessary funds, and the promise of more if it was required. I didn't dream of asking the current rate of interest — just then it chanced to be ten per cent.

I was too late for the midday-meal, but bought crackers and oranges at the Hudson Bay Store, whilst Hilaria bragged of the menu which she had discussed just before we met.

"Quite such a nice salad I have never eaten," she said tenderly, "and the table-maid told me it was cabbage. It must have been a very special kind of cabbage, don't you think? But I was sold in my choice of a sweet. *'Cream of tapioca'* sounds most alluring, doesn't it? And it was nothing but a plain tapicoa pudding. Still, in spite of a high-falutin' name here and there, one can always get a good meal in Canada for a shilling. In Winnipeg meals are ever so cheap, but everything else is distressingly dear."

We wandered up the road that leads to the Springbrook trail. Hilaria's gossip over people and places and ways and means was most refreshing. In Winnipeg she had stayed at the Women's Home of Welcome. "Two such nice Englishwomen shared the bedroom with me," she said. "They were going on to Vancouver. One travels so cheaply in these days. Sixty pounds, I think they said, was the cost of their return tickets. Of course that didn't include sleepers or Pullman. They stay at the Y.W.C.A. and those kind of places, which are most clean and comfortable, and cost half nothing. I wish I had taken a return ticket. I shall never earn one in Canada. Make one's fortune indeed! I could make a living far more easily in England. It isn't that Canadians require you to do so much, although they are by no means moderate in their idea of value for money, but they seem to think it such an ordinary occurrence that everything should be extraordinarily well done."

"Wouldn't they have given you any sort of a salary at the Hospital, and allowed you to complete your training? You know even your friend the Matron allowed you were a fine nurse."

"But not on paper! It is your certificates and diplomas from morning until night in Winnipeg, if one has the ill-luck to be a woman; although men pull through on nothing at all. Canadians go to the States to train, because very few of them can afford to go to England, I suppose, since the Matron begged me to go back and finish my training at the 'London,' which she enthused about a good deal. She said if I came back with a 'London' certificate, age wouldn't keep me out of the highest position. Efficiency was everything. And they really are efficient over here. You should see the Canadian women in their white gowns — every bit as well turned out as the French contingent in the Bois. And they wash and starch and iron them themselves! I saw them. Every woman seems to wear white — babies, girls, women and grandmothers — and I didn't see a solitary turn-out that was not absolutely fresh and dainty."

"Then that accounts for their having so little imagination," I said, "because if they really do it all themselves, they can't have time for anything else."

"Well, they are wonders," said Hilaria with a sigh. "But believe me, Canada is neither my El Dorado nor yours. There is only one road that is really open — domestic service. Judging from my own experience, I should say that there the battle was to the strong. But they are kindness itself, and one shares all that comes along in the way of diversion. Oh, I forgot! One woman offered me thirty dollars a month to go as lady-nurse to her small girl and boy. She said she liked my *accent*! Did you ever hear of such impertinence? They were wealthy people — positively kept two women helps and a gardener-groom. But I was too tired for any fresh adventures when the offer came along."

"I can understand any one not being able to get anything to do, but I can't understand your failing in anything you arrived at. I should have thought your cooking alone would have dragged you through," I said.

"You see, the menu isn't confined to ducks, apricot dumplings, and rock cakes, even on a Canadian farm. Besides, I wasn't allowed to touch the cooking. Not that I wished it! It chanced that while I was there they gave what they call a box-social. Every one arrives with a present in a box. All the presents are of an average value. Then they draw. Oh, they think it is wild excitement! When the great event of the distribution of gifts had been got over, they gazed at my frock, and I gazed at their food. They all brought cakes — and such cakes! Not one of them but might have hailed from Buszard as far as appearances goes, and they tasted infinitely better than any cakes I have eaten from anywhere — the variety, the lightness, the flavour, and the icing — exquisitely done, *and* delicious!"

"Did they keep it up long?" I inquired.

"My dear, half of them remained to breakfast! You see, we danced. All the hired men in the neighbourhood came — of course there aren't any others, but there were many Englishmen — gentlemen — among them. These, I need hardly tell you, didn't dance. But the Canadians made up for it — how those men danced! Canadian men dance even better than Canadian women cook and do laundry-work. And I must say I liked them. Women are 'best goods' to them, you know — they value them, and well they may! Not that I would marry a Canadian for anything you could mention. In the nature of things they would expect too much."

"But, Hilaria," I protested, "surely we come in somewhere. I am quite sure that both you and your frock were much nicer than anything else at the box-social."

"We did very well," she admitted. "None of them were guys, but a Paris frock holds its own the world over. Still, the Canadian woman has annexed the cut that we all acknowledged to be such a fine point with the Americans; and from morning till night, in spite of the endlessness of the daily round, they contrive to be dainty. And after all, that is everything! I think we score over them in conversation, and probably as sportswomen. I doubt if they could come near us there — I am sure they wouldn't want to. . . . Can they hold their own with men? Oh, but that is such a very individual question. Men are so easily led by anybody the world over! Still, the American contingent hold on to their own, and continue to annex a number of ours, don't they?"

We turned in at sundown — both of us deadly tired.

"What a boon is bed!" I exclaimed from my heart.

"Oh, I had quite forgotten," replied Hilaria. "It will be those tiresome stretchers again to-morrow."

"For *one* of us. Just after you left the 'British Workman' and Lal sat on the weakling, and it snapped in the middle."

"I shan't dream of coming back to rob you of it. I shall sleep on the floor," she said heroically.

"Better draw lots," I suggested. "It is always more satisfactory. Oh, Hilaria, surely they are not going to have that miserable concert, knowing how frightfully tired we must be."

"You may be quite sure that will not be allowed to make any difference, and I really don't see any special reason why it should. I suppose it is a pleasure to them all, and we only come along now and again. That's the barber singing now — I really don't mind the music, if only they would spare their energy over the applause. Hush! that's the pretty girl with the green eyes and golden hair in a bun. 'The beautiful land of Nod.' I mean to be asleep before the end." And she was.

Georgina Binnie-Clark

Are Educated Women Wanted in Canada

To this question just now being constantly put to men and women who have personal experience of Canada, I will quote you the answer of a Canadian woman journalist, Agnes Laut, who says, "The need for domestic help is chronic and continuous. If all the domestics of the United Kingdom who are out of work passed into Canada for the next hundred years they would not suffice to supply the help that is needed at wages from £2 a month for common help to £6 and £8 and £10 for specialists. The question may be asked how is this possible in a country with a population under ten millions, but the statement is no exaggeration, and for this reason no domestic who is any good remains a domestic in the Colonies. They prosper, rise in life, set up establishments of their own and require domestic help for themselves." Another journalist wrote, "no greater mistake exists than that of imagining that, where women are concerned, the only use to which Canada can put home brains and home energies is in the field of domestic work. Many women who have wisely caught opportunity and started thankfully as home helps have drifted into other professions. Either the trade they have learnt at home is put to account, or, by taking advantage of the many excellent training institutions in their adopted country, they qualify themselves for a profession when they have ascertained when and in what manner are the best opening to be obtained."

May McLeod Moore writes. "Year by year the Canadian girl advances a little further into the labour arena. She is earning her living as a nurse, a newspaper woman — women have represented their papers in the Dominion House of Commons — as a teacher, as a doctor, as a barrister, as a farmer, as a clerk, as a stenographer and typist, as an insurance agent, as an artist, as a chemist, as a music teacher with the most modern methods, and in one Province the architect is a young woman. It would be difficult to say into what business or profession the Canadian girl has not found her way and stayed."

"But let us remember," says Agnes Laut — the Canadian woman who knows the conditions of Canada — "that only in domestic work is the newcomer certain of finding instant employment on landing. In office work, shop employment, teaching, farming — time should be taken to look about, to sift and weigh and examine and reject and choose from the hundred and one propositions that offer to the new arrival. Go slow in the beginning, to avoid regret afterwards; and in the words of the old prophet 'winnow not with every wind.' "

I have quoted from these several articles the opinions of Canadian women that you may know that my own opinion in the matter of Canadian openings for English women workers is not unsupported by Canadian women of trained thought and practical knowledge of the energy and effort required to make a living in these somewhat strenuous days. I entirely agree with Miss Agnes Laut in her broad invitation and in her deep strong word of caution, and personally, whilst conceding Canada to be the Mecca of that ever-increasing section of our population who on this side of the Atlantic come under the category of working gentlewomen, I would advise no woman to embark to Canada unless she is prepared to take up general or domestic service until an opportunity of special service presents itself.

No woman of refinement need hesitate to take up domestic service in Canada because of its circumstance, since there class distinctions are not, and rich and poor, gentle and simple, Canadian or immigrant, we are all of us working women, but one does need to consider domestic service most conscientiously from the point of their own efficiency, since the Canadian woman's definition of a good housewife or home-help is that she must know the way of every detail of the daily round. Housework, laundry work, cooking, baking; all these important duties present themselves in addition to the meaner tasks, and it is to be remembered that the Canadian housewife, although no mocker of the mistakes of English women, can be merciless to the slightest symptom of martyrdom — she expects the duties of the daily round and common task to be performed willingly, cheerfully and thoroughly. The first winter I was in Canada I stayed for three months with an Englishman and his Canadian wife in their charming home in the maple-groved shore of the western lake of Fort Qu'Appelle. The house contained three reception rooms in addition to its hospitable hall, four bedrooms, and two others built over the kitchen and scullery. The lady-help was an English girl, and I never dreamed that an English girl from any class could get through all sorts and conditions of household work as she did; but further acquaintance revealed to me that Canadian girls and women did their work quite as well, and put it out of sight more quickly. The English girl and I used to agree together that she was not quite up to Canadian standard, in spite of the fact that she rose in winter at 6:30, often in summer at sunrise; she baked the bread, did the general cooking, the laundry of the entire household, the greater part of the housework — we each attended to our own rooms barring an occasional scrub and polish — and she always contrived to appear at table as neatly and becomingly attired as a woman of leisure. She was always included in any invitations that came to my host and hostess, and was a very welcome guest among the neighbours. She took part in all the amusements and recreations that came to cheer one on one's way, and she also enjoyed the privilege of keeping her own pony, and rode whenever a successful navigation through the duties of the daily round permitted.

In process of time she left, and was succeeded by an Englishwoman of exactly the opposite type. This lady absolutely collapsed on hearing what was expected of her in the shape of daily toil, took the suggestion of the wash-tub and ironing-board as a personal affront, and in this way made herself exceedingly miserable. My hostess, I think, exhibited about as much patience as could be expected of a particularly well-trained and efficient Canadian woman; the lady was dispatched to the care of the Vicar's wife and the congenial occupation of looking after the Vicar's small boys, until the arrangements for her return to England were completed.

I am frequently asked do I think it just to expect such complete service from one person. I think it just in a Canadian woman, because I have visited many Canadian houses where the appointments, however simple, are perfect, the cooking excellent, the air of leisure restful, the conversation inspiring, whilst the white-linen frock of my hostess or her daughter might have been cut in Sackville Street and laundered by a "blanchisseuse de Paris." And behind it all lurked no expensive establishment of serving-people, but merely method, order and the habit of waiting on oneself.

Among the opportunities and special openings awaiting the Englishwoman immigrant in Canada I prefer to quote the information of others who have made the different professions a matter of special examination. Beginning with the prospect of Stenographers, we will go to that of Nurses, Women Gardeners, Shop-workers, Dressmakers and Milliners, School Teachers, Needlewomen, and I shall only give my opinion in the place where my experience warrants a statement.

STENOGRAPHERS

Agnes Laut writes: "It may be asked why I have not mentioned office women, when expert women book-keepers in Canada obtain from £2 to £5 a week and typewriters the same salary. I answer — because I do not approve of merely office positions for women, who wish to become permanently independent through their own efforts; and for these reasons: It is foolish for a woman who is bent on earning a competency to take up as her life work any kind of labour in which her usefulness is in inverse ratio to her experience; and that is the case with type-writing. The older a woman grows and the greater her experience, the less value she will become to her employer. If a woman can use typewriting as a step in the ladder, good and well; but for a life support it is to the wage-earning woman a broken reed."

Georgina Binnie-Clark writes: "Stenography does not offer a fair field to the English immigrant, as the Canadian girl has dropped straight down on it as an agreeable as well as a sufficiently remunerative occupation, and I think the cry of the shorthand writer is a fair cry of 'Canada for the Canadians.' She is required to be thoroughly efficient both in shorthand and typewriting, and the course of training at the various business colleges is thorough from start to finish.

So far, however, Canadians do not seem to have realized the force of the foreign tongue; doubtless as Canada's trade with the wide world increases, a knowledge of the French and Spanish languages is certain to be highly esteemed by the Canadian merchant; then the Englishwoman stenographer, equipped with one or more foreign languages, may find an opening and be able to leave a gateway. I noticed that even at the local stores of the railway towns there was usually at least one clerk with a fluent knowledge of German. The salary of the shorthand writer starts at about forty dollars a month, but, as I have remarked, the training is thorough, and an applicant who is not thoroughly efficient both in shorthand and typewriting would have no chance of obtaining a desirable post."

NURSING

A contributor to the *St. James's Gazette* in a special nursing article writes:—
"Nursing absorbs a good many emigrants of the better class. Although vacancies in the staffs of the various hospitals in the large towns are generally filled by local-trained nurses, there is a fair amount of work to be had by private nursing. The certificates of home-trained nurses are accepted by the Colonial medical authorities, although these have to be endorsed and a local licence procured before a woman can legally practise and is considered qualified to be placed on the register of the particular State in which she may wish to work. As regards salary, in one of the Provinces in which a mutual association for trained nurses has been established the pay varies from eighteen dollars a week for a non-infectious case to twenty-one dollars for nursing a contagious complaint, the cost of her personal laundry, however, being met by the nurse both when she is 'out' and when she is waiting for an engagement.

In the case of a prospective nurse settler, the prospect of being able to work up a good connection is a *sine qua non*.

A nurse's qualifications must in any case be thorough, and in addition to her three years' course of training, excellent personal health, untiring energy, and a determination to forget the traditions of her profession as it is often understood at home are necessary if any success is to be made of Colonial work. As a matter of fact, it is by her power to adapt herself to new conditions that the English nurse, transplanted into Colonial soil, makes or mars her career. There are, of course, wealthy families whom she may attend, and in whose houses she will receive as much personal waiting upon and consideration as is meted out to a private nurse in England; but there is no doubt about the fact that the majority of cases she will be called out to nurse are those where the expense of her board and fee stretches the family purse to the utmost, and luxuries will be few; also it is to be remembered that with the illness of the mother of a family matters are more than ordinarily disorganized; in such a case, the nurse has to rise to the occasion, and, besides looking after the invalid, may be obliged to undertake the ménage, and to the best of her ability tide over the time until the invalid is sufficiently recovered."

THE SHOP-WORKER

Agnes Laut writes: "Though the English shop-worker does not receive one-half, one-third, in cases one-tenth the salary paid in America, she is not worked to death by high pressure as she is in America, where a woman's nerve-energy finds it hard to stand the strain of pace. In Canada the pace is not so swift as in America by a length, nor the cost of living so high, although living expenses are going up faster than wages; and I recall the case of a clergyman's daughter who in ten years rose from an apprentice's salary of £1 a week to a salary of £300 a year, with two trips to Europe a year and all expenses paid. Among the shop workers, I do not think it possible for a conscientious woman in good health *not to rise* to a competency in ten years. By 'competency' I mean a salary that will enable her to live well, with trips during her holidays, and to save enough to be able to retire by the time she is fifty. The average salary for an experienced and competent shop-worker would probably run from £6 a month to £12 a month in Eastern Canada, and from £8 a month to £20 a month in Western Canada, having begun as apprentices at £4 a month."

DRESSMAKING AND MILLINERY

The same writer continues: "The competent dressmaker or competent milliner is ranked as an expert and a God-send in Canada. She can command her terms in the city, for the simple reason that if her employer refuses to pay her she can open an establishment for herself."

A contributor to the *St. James's Gazette* writes: "In dressmaking a private connection is essential. Starting a large establishment in an important town, where there are sufficient well-to-do people to pay very high prices is a venture which requires too much capital for the average emigrant, but the profession of visiting dressmaker is not to be despised; in some parts of Canada a moderate income can be gained by going out by the day, the remuneration is about 6/3, the work fairly constant and a clever needlewoman, with a genius for adapting remodelling, is practically sure in time of establishing a good *clientèle*."

The Bishop of London says: "From one town in Ontario came a pressing demand for respectable needlewomen who could earn from twenty-six to thirty shillings a week, board and lodging being thirteen to fourteen shillings."

SCHOOL TEACHING

Georgina Binnie-Clark writes: "In Canada school teaching is an adequately remunerative occupation for men and women. In cities the salary is usually higher than in the country districts, but here again conditions are compensating even in newly-settled parts of the country. It is always the *privilege* of one or another of the leading women of the district to board the school teachers at a charge of from three to four dollars a week, and the school teachers may rely on finding a hearty welcome in the most desirable home that the district can offer. Salaries are on an upward scale from thirty-five dollars, and many Canadian men and women now in high professional or official positions have earned the fees of their calling by a period of school teaching.

If a teacher is aiming at work in private and preparatory schools, her English degree or diploma will probably be accepted; but if at work in the public schools she must spend six months taking a special normal course in the methods of Canadian schools. This will use up a considerable amount of capital, and a further margin of time should be allowed to look round for the best place, but once ready to start she finds the minimum salary of her profession to be £6 a month. In a year, if she is any good, she will be earning £100 per annum. If she has average ability she can work up to £200 a year. It should always be remembered that Canada has a horror of the useless gentlewoman. Let me give one case. A few years ago in Winnipeg, a highly-cultured English family living on the outskirts of the city were found starving, with a violin of almost priceless value in their possession. They were accomplished musicians, but would not take other employment until they had had time to make their accomplishments known. What became of them I do not know; for with false pride they ordered the ladies of a Church Society, who had brought them food, from the house. I can imagine what kind of a story that family would carry back to England about opportunities in Canada."

OUTDOOR OCCUPATIONS

Agnes Laut says: "There is a still larger class of occupations open to women in Canada — to take up fruit farming, chicken farming, ranching, even wheat growing. The number of women who have done this successfully is legion. I recall a girl who went to the Territories to teach painting. Now the West is not old enough for art. The paints were laid aside, and as the head of her family of brothers and sisters she bought land near Regina. On that land the banks advanced money for building and implements. To-day the girl drives her own span, and is educating the other members of her family — which she could never have accomplished from art."

Mrs. George Cran writes: "Particularly is there an opening for our women gardeners. Plenty of women now-a-days train in agriculture and horticulture, but the demand for their services is small at the best in Great Britain, while it is urgent round the rapidly-growing prairie towns. No one who has not been over there can appreciate the opportunities for money making in Canada. And least of all do the women in England realize the openings there are for them in the great North-West. Given health and industry there is fortune waiting for them in that marvellous prairie loam just as surely as it waits upon the men who go out to grow wheat and run stock farms."

Georgina Binnie-Clark writes: "Personally I know that so far work on the land in Canada has not presented itself as an open field for female labour, but in many ways land work is far easier than housework, certainly more interesting, and there is no reason at all why women should not adopt it as a healthy, practicable and highly remunerative occupation. I worked on the land in my emergency; had I drilled myself into a state of efficiency during my first season in Canada, I should have been my own insurance against emergency, and my farm, my purse and myself would have been the better for it to-day. The work in the case of nearly every implement is perfectly straight forward and practicable; the only exception I make is the breaking plough; the manipulation of which calls for physical force, especially in breaking up stony land; but a day on the disc or the mower and rake should be quite a holiday for the average Canadian housewife. Sulky ploughing calls for a little more exercise of the intelligence, which makes it the more interesting. Walking behind the harrows is excellent exercise for either sex, but I should prefer to trust a woman to drop all rubbish on the skirt of the field and set fire to it. When the pickling and cleaning of seed is entirely given over to women, wheat will be gradually relieved of the parasite smut, which costs the farmer and the Dominion of Canada at present many thousands of dollars a year.

Men at work on the land earn anything from twenty-five to forty-five dollars a month, with board and lodging. It is true that they are expected to put in ten hours a day field work, besides tending their team of four horses, but out of work hours they are at leisure; their meals are prepared and served to them; they get a mid-day break, and can have eight or nine hours sleep if they choose; whilst Sunday is in deed, as well as in word, their day of rest. Should I be offered the post of general help on a Canadian farm at a salary of twenty-five dollars a month, or land work at twenty dollars, I should not hesitate to decide on the outdoor occupation, in spite of the lesser remuneration."

In another paper, urging the wisdom of the extension of the free land grant, now confined to men only, she writes: "Woman so far in Canada has had no opportunity to establish her relation to the land — to demonstrate her power as a worker on the land. In urgency and emergency, but beyond either in the daily need for care, order, and patient cheerful industry which crops, stock and implements demand, I have from the point of view of an employer, yearned for the Advent of the Hired Woman on the Land."

In closing my paper I feel that I cannot impress upon you too strongly the healthfulness and hopefulness of the conditions of Canada which await any project formed to help the educated women of Britain to the opportunities of the Land of Promise. Neither can I sufficiently congratulate you on what you have already accomplished. You have established a system by which work and the comforts of a home await our emigrants on landing in Canada, and the work of the British Women's Emigration Association in our great Colony is already considered to be "above suspicion," which is a far higher degree of commendation than a gathering of English people can quite understand. The reason is that, in the organization of the emigration of the women of Britain you have not only paved the way for her to pass over, with generosity and kindness, but you have fenced it inch by inch with thought, and the wisdom of justice towards the country which is in deed and in truth a land of promise to our working classes, gentle and simple. Emigration is without doubt the soundest and the happiest solution of our ever-deepening problem of unemployment. The question of the wisdom of State-aided emigration is altogether too complex to warrant the expression of my opinion here, but there is no man or woman who, of their better fortune, has helped a single member of our unfortunate or unemployed classes to Canada, but has served Humanity.

Georgina Binnie-Clark

Conditions of Life for Women in Canada

In the present phase of the development of Canada, the immigration of English women is a matter of vital importance to the Canadian race, and bound to affect Canada in her future career among nations.

To-day the great need of the North-West is the need of the service and the influence of woman. Nevertheless, hitherto in its programme of invitation to the English emigrant, the Canadian department of immigration has offered very little inducement to Englishwomen to emigrate to Canada.

It gives a definite promise of adequately remunerative occupation to those women who are prepared to accept such work as in England we are accustomed to associate with the duties and the position of the domestic servant; further than this it seems afraid to commit itself. The direct consequence is that in the main, the number of English women who emigrate annually to Canada are drawn from the ranks of women employed over here in domestic service, or from those women of the cultured classes who have no choice left, and who accept the alternative of "domestic service" with the grain of bitterness in the heart which does not contribute towards the wisdom of success.

The Canadian department of Immigration has much to learn of the capabilities of the cultured women of Britain; the working gentlewomen of this land have much to learn of the all-round meaning of the term "domestic service" in its relation to Canadian conditions.

It has to be borne in mind that in Canada there are no women of leisure, and that social classification is barred as being baneful to the development, and naturally distasteful to the free and independent spirit of the country. The individual is judged on personal merit as it appears in the light of Canadian opinion; and Canadian opinion so far neither aims to reach lofty height, nor profound depth; its key-note is progress running on the lines of common sense; it has a strong bias towards the liberty of the individual in its intention; in its nature and influence it is wholesome. It is a healthy, strongwilled child of keen intelligence with its eyes fixed, not on the stars, but on the place where the footsteps of To-morrow can catch up with the desire of To-day. Neither fame, name, nor colossal fortune will exempt the individual from this examination under the X-rays of Canadian opinion, nor can the individual be pressed by the accident of circumstance below the just reach of personal force and service.

In forming this paper I have divided my subject into three sections:—

Conditions of women who serve for hire.

Conditions for married women on the prairie.

Opportunities for women on the prairie.

No woman should dream of emigrating to Canada unless fortified with the courage of hard work. From their childhood Canadian women are trained to the household work of their own homes, in fact they are born into the enclosure of the beatitude of those who have learned to do things for themselves. A leader of Canadian society would, generally speaking, be highly recommendable as a competent housemaid, a well-trained parlour-maid, and excellent cook, an efficient laundress, and possibly a clever dressmaker, in any household of any country; in the housewife's battle of the daily round and common task, the palm of victory seems to me to be indisputably in the hands of the Canadian woman; yet she is never the bond-slave of her domestic concern, but contrives to combine the roles of Martha and Mary with ease as well as generosity.

What then will be the natural attitude of the Canadian employer towards an English working woman, gentle or simple, accepting a post in her household with the responsibility of domestic service? Firstly and always, she will be unfeignedly glad to see her. Canadian women seldom love their tasks so well that they do not prefer to share them with another; besides, they are naturally sociable and kind-hearted. Secondly, she will be her critic from every point of the daily round — nothing will escape her observation or her intuition in domestic detail. She is generous in her admiration of the intellectual gifts and graces, and has a fine appreciation of the advantages and acquirements of women brought up in an European environment; but she also has scorn for the frequent helplessness of the cultured woman in the duties of the daily round. She will be no mocker of the mistakes of her imported help; on the contrary, she is always rather pleased to teach and to help; but she is by nature entirely frank, and can be merciless to the slightest symptom of martyrdom.

Apart from the obligation of her service, the domestic help will, generally speaking, take her place as a member of the family, in the city or on the farm. From the social point of view the English are looked upon as an acquisition in Canada; the "help" will always take part in such public amusements as occur in the district of her employers, and will usually be included in any invitations which fall to their lot. I spent my first winter in the home of an Englishman who had married a Canadian woman; occasionally she launched out into the — in Canada — rare form of entertainment — a dinner party. Everything was prepared as far as possible beforehand, but in a meal of several courses some small culinary attention is always required before each. The English help was present in her evening gown, and changed the meats and the plates without a tinge of self-consciousness, assisted by the English youth, also in orthodox evening dress, who at the time was earning his winter's keep in exchange for such duties as wood-chopping, stable-work, water-hauling, stove attendance, and occasional aid at the washing machine. He, by the way, was the son of an English clergyman, and his brothers were officers in the British army and navy.

What I would endeavour to make quite clear is that the ultimatum of "domestic service" need prevent no woman of refinement from emigrating to Canada. On the contrary, it is an excellent position from which to feel the pulse of the new country, whilst watching for opportunity. The English gentlewoman need never fear to accept service in a Canadian household because of its circumstances; but she does need to consider it most carefully and conscientiously, from the point of her own efficiency to fulfill the tasks of the daily round. These duties are reduced in Canada through the simple manner of living, and also by those many ingenious devices curtailing and facilitating human labour, which naturally occur to the mind of man and woman in a country where human labour is the most expensive item in the market; but, as an English girl, who had turned her back on blanket-washing once remarked to me, "It is not that they expect an extraordinary amount of work of you, but they expect the most ordinary thing to be so extraordinarily well done."

I have dwelt on domestic service as it is the one calling which directly or indirectly concerns all immigrants; but there are openings for all sorts and conditions of women workers in Canada, if only they will resign themselves to accept domestic service until their vision is accustomed to the new environment where opportunity lurks on every side. There is room for school-teachers, stenographers, landscape-gardeners, vegetable and fruit gardeners, trained nurses, dressmakers, milliners, shop assistants, buyers, but efficiency is the watchword in the female labour market of Canada, and they love it stamped with the hall-mark of a certificate. A Canadian journalist was talking over some Englishwomen to me, who as Canadian immigrants had proved failures. She mentioned among others a girl to whom she, with others, had shown help and kindness. She said the girl had come over with the idea to teach dancing and drill. "Where is your diploma?" demanded my friend. "And would you believe it," she added, "that girl expected to come out here and induce Canadians to pay her to teach their children to dance without a diploma!"

I find among Englishwomen, whose experience of the conditions and nature of women should give weight to their judgment, a strong tendency to sympathise with the complaint of the married woman on the prairie. It seems to centre in the lack of congenial society, aggravated by the incessant toil attached to unfamiliar household duties, and the general superstition that comfort and refinement are impossible within severe climatic conditions. Those household duties are difficult, and the bitter side of them seems to be in the fact that the Canadian woman of refinement will get through them so easily and beautifully, that she doesn't appear to work at all; but the woman of average intelligence and resource need not be uncomfortable in Canada. Comfort is a positive instinct with Canadians, but to be comfortable in a country of severe climatic conditions one must get on to that country's lines of comfort. For instance, an open British grate with a scarlet fire from British coal warms the heart; a few home-cut logs in the cheapest of Canadian stoves will warm one's back, even though there be an inch of ice on the window-pane, which for some reason or another the English settler may have omitted to protect with storm-windows. It is the custom to furnish modern and orthodox Canadian houses with a furnace, and, by means of pipe and register, its heat is evenly diffused throughout the building; but in the drawing rooms of the English and of many Canadians there is also an open grate with the heart-warming fire on the hearth "for remembrance."

One view of the complaint I cannot share is that the condition of isolation, now less generally attached to prairie life, owing to the rapid development of the railways, should be so much harder for the woman of refined and cultured tastes and accomplishments, than for her fellow-countrywoman, who has been brought up to all sorts and conditions of domestic work. It is our good fortune to have been born in the era of the intellectual emancipation of woman. Within certain conditions of wealth and early training, every opportunity is now offered to woman for her advance in knowledge and in taste. Are we to possess the royal advantage of life as a weapon, or merely as a defence against the intrusion of the undesired? Is advance in knowledge and taste to mean the fence of exclusion, or the gateway of expansion — hindrance or help? I think if one has really found the courage of life in the wisdom of knowledge and treasures of taste, in which it is our special privilege to be environed in Europe, it will not desert us on the prairie which some have named the wilderness. On the contrary, whether it be in the preparation of those three commonplace meals for hungry toilers, or the Monday morning warfare of the washing machine, the wrestle with the understanding of the nature of a plough in the turning of furrows; whether it be gathering the standing grain into the sheaf with the binder-reaper, or the harder work of gathering the sheaves into stook; if one has truly lived by the inspiration of the ideal in Europe, it stands by with the strength or sweetness of the moment, to overcome the difficulties of the daily round in Canada, in the home or on the land. In the nature of humankind mind is the propeller; the woman of trained hands may know better what to do, but the woman of trained mental power ought to know better how to do without.

During the working months the wife of a Canadian farmer should have breakfast served at six o'clock, five is the better hour, because it will allow for a long rest for man and beast during the mid-day heat. The men are supposed to be on the land for five hours, and to return to the house for a twelve o'clock meal of meat and vegetables, with pie or pudding. The greater part of the household duties can be accomplished in the morning, so that between the mid-day meal and six o'clock supper, which usually consists of cold meat and potatoes, with cakes and preserves, or stewed fruit, there is ample time for rest and recreation. After the evening meal the milk must be set, and the wants of the stock supplied, but by eight o'clock one's time should be one's own again. There will be extra men during the harvest, but as a rule they bring their own rugs and blankets and sleep in a granary, so it is merely a matter of extra cooking. During the thrashing-season there is usually a party of from eighteen to twenty men, and if weather is bad and operations cease, they may be one's guests for several days. They justly expect to be well fed, not only with plenty of beef, but Canadian women have spoilt them with a wide choice of the excellent confectionery for which they are famed. I saw that they had the best of meat and as much as they cared for, with a plentiful supply of stewed fruit, scones, potatoes and bread and butter, but my finest tribute has never scored a higher point than excellent intentions. In winter, work on the land ceases with "freeze-up"; the farmer has little to do beyond cleaning the stable, feeding stock, and hauling his grain to the nearest wheat-market. The small farmer seldom keeps hired men round during the winter, so that his wife will probably be left alone during wheat-hauling days. This fact has to be faced. I have known women who cannot face it.

The true sportswoman will neither be dull nor bored on the prairie; riding, driving, shooting, wolf-hunting, skating, snow-shoeing are within the reach of all. The woman with a business instinct has a fine point of vantage on her husband's farm, because grain is all over the place, and eggs and poultry command a ready sale and good prices in the railway towns; and even in new settlements there are always many bachelors, thankful for the chance of purchasing bread, butter, eggs and household commodities of all kinds. Hog-raising and bacon-curing are also fine sources of wealth on a Canadian farm. Many women have paved the way of husbands through the dark wilderness of bad wheat seasons with contributions from such profitable, although frequently neglected, sources of wealth.

I think none has ever heard of the complaint of a child on the Canadian prairie; it is the happiest nursery in the world. All young things, babies, beasts, birds and buds seem to adore life and each other; and if when school-time comes, mothers are inclined to think wistfully of the attractive training ground of our English public schools — the wheat of the wilderness, the oats and the barley, the pigs and the poultry will also contribute to the realisation of that desire of the heart, if they are given a real chance. In any case the education provided for every child within the Dominion by the Government is sound and thorough, sufficient to insure the state against that bitter reproach of its child prophesied by Emerson in his claim for the national right to mental training; "This which I might do is made hopeless through my want of weapons."

To the sincerely exclusive, and I think everyone has sympathy with sincerity in any form, the entertainment of gossip is seldom available in Canadian farm life, nor can one for obvious reasons find solace in the attraction of charming frocks and luxurious surroundings which avail in Europe. Good gossip, charming frocks, and delightful surroundings *are* among the joys, and within the inspiration of life; but if one feels that they are indispensable to content, that the new life cannot offer sufficient compensation for the surrendered delights of the old, it is not wise to decide that one's years of youth and vigour shall be spent on a Canadian farm. None can tell how immeasurably a woman's help and influence can contribute to a man's welfare amid the stress of his early wrestle with new conditions, but it seems to me that the spirit of true comradeship is an essential condition to the happiness of married people, in the more or less isolated and always active life on the prairie. By a comrade, I mean the one who, visible or invisible, is always at the other end of the load. We are not all endowed with this fine quality of enduring sympathy, and it is still within the wisdom of love to refuse to become a married woman on the prairie.

I have said that the scale of remuneration for human labour in Canada is adequate; I mean that it allows for one's physical well-being in the present, and leaves a fair margin for saving towards the provision of the independent future, which should be recognised as the righteous claim of every honest human labourer. Canada offers especially fine opportunities for the investment of savings, in the fact that she is still glad to part with her most valuable securities on the easiest terms of payment. My attention was attracted to this condition in the fact of a young girl having purchased a plot of land in the city of Winnipeg. She had borrowed her fare to go to Canada, and within a week had found a situation as table-maid at one of the smaller hotels; she received a salary of five pounds a month with board and lodging. She paid twenty dollars (£4 4s.) down for her plot of land, and completed her payment at the rate of ten dollars a month. In her fourth year she contemplated building, but came home for a holiday instead; the last news I heard of her investment was that building operations were in the immediate prospect.

But the finest investment in Canada is my own battleground, the land. I spent a summer in a homestead settlement, and saw that wealth did really wait on human effort on the Canadian prairie, and saw, too, how sadly new settlement conditions lagged for the need of the disinterested women of enthusiasm. And whatever we English people lack, we are charged with the vital spark of enthusiasm. It is true we have a tendency to seek a sphere for our gift in the fuel of other countries, but what would be the warmth-giving value of a world-wide quarry of coal, but for the vital spark to set it alight?

I bought an improved farm of three hundred and thirty acres, worked it for three years through good seasons and bad. During this time I contributed to various periodicals on the subject of Canadian farming as a profitable and practicable profession for Englishwomen; and much correspondence came to me from all sorts and conditions of women eager for the chance of a fresh fair start.

At the end of my fourth season I was able to state that I had made a cent per cent profit on the year's working, and I wrote to ask the Minister of the Interior, the Hon. Frank Oliver, to extend the land grant of 160 acres to those of my country-women whom the officials of the Canadian Government should pronounce to be sufficiently capable, and to be possessed of, or entrusted with use of sufficient capital to work the land.

I gave him a sketch of my own up and down career and added,

> Woman has not yet had an opportunity in her relation to the land to demonstrate and establish her power as a worker on the land. In urgency and emergency, but beyond either, in the daily need for care, order and patient cheerful industry which crops, stock, and implements demand, I have from the point of view of an employer just yearned for the advent of the hired woman on the land.

> From the point of view of a woman who has worked every implement, ploughed the land with interest and enjoyment, tended fourteen head of horses and cattle and a number of pigs without help through the long and trying winter of 1906-7, I write, after another season's experience of the frequently combined duties of housewife and husbandman, as I wrote in the article of an English magazine two years ago: "Should I be offered the post of general help on a Canadian farm at a salary of twenty-five dollars a month, or land work at twenty dollars, I should not hesitate to decide on the outdoor occupation, in spite of the lesser remuneration."

> The extension of the free land grant to women should have the same effect on a new settlement that deep-ploughing has on the prosperity of the grain-grower: it should work towards Unity, the first condition of prosperity and content. Untrammelled by the special care of husband and children, the woman settler would find leisure to think and work for the general welfare of her settlement. Frequently the coming of the church, school, or any institution, thought into substance for the good of a community, is discussed in a new settlement from the personal point of view of every family man or woman who finds time to discuss such matters at all: the bachelors preserve an air of detached superiority until there is a murmur of the school tax coming their way; then one hears little else but the absolute unfairness of bachelors having to pay it.

> Miss Agnes Laut, in addressing the Women's Canadian Club at Winnipeg on the Canadianizing of foreigners, held that every hamlet and village should have its women's club. Every new settlement should especially have its club, and it could be easily arranged so as to offer facilities for the discussion of matters of special interest to either sex. The coming of the woman-settler would mean the coming of the Club; Church and School will hurry along the footprints of her trail, certain of her aid and sympathy in spite of tithe or tax; certain also of her unbiassed judgment in matters relating to the general

welfare. Stock-raising and dairy work will begin with her beginning; from the outset various threads of life will knit the homesteader to the homestead, and both to the settlement. From settlements where the government rules to plant women-farmers, or women-farmers plant themselves, it is safe to predict a flourishing and effective future: it means the dawning of the hope of the long-deferred advent of the spirit of Content in newly-settled districts of the prairie.

English women may not have so direct a claim on Canadian land as the women of Canada, but any country would be the richer for the coming of such Englishwomen as would be prompt to avail themselves of an offer of free land in Canada. Women of trained intelligence, nerve, energy, patience, good-will, foresight, perseverance, courage, power of endurance — limited capital — good comrades, not easily driven back from their purpose — Englishwomen, not drawn from any particular class but forming a class of themselves summoned together from all classes by the bugle call of the decree, or desire, to labour for a living — or for life.

I received the answer that, unfortunately, "Homesteads for women" other than widows and the heads of families was against the law of Canada.

I approached the law-giver — unfortunately we approached Ottawa on the same day; he, after a lengthened visit to the West, I on my hurried way to England. An interview was only to be had by waiting, and a grave personal anxiety did not permit of my waiting. I had almost given the matter up as hopeless, when a few weeks ago, I received a note from the Minister to tell me that he would be glad to see me when I was passing through Ottawa, that he might go lengthily and thoroughly into the matter. I can only say that from all one hears, the cause cannot await the judgment of a clearer or more disinterested intelligence. Some prophesy that the eventual issue will rest with the fact whether women *really* want this free land grant.

Judging from the personal communications I have received on the matter, many are eager for it. For the rest, I only know that it is in the nature of Englishwomen to love outdoor pursuits. I feel that there is a grave and ever increasing necessity for Englishwomen to support themselves in youth, and to make provision for old age. In the wisdom of friendship and the power of wealth, schools of land culture and industrial farm training have been established by women for women in our land. I am told that marked success has crowned the goodwill in the experiment.

In Canada there is land waiting for the labourer, and in the Colonies a combination of capital and labour is a wealth-compelling force. The influence of woman since the earliest phase of her emancipation has tended towards the cleansing of the Augean stable. Nowhere is this cleansing influence more vitally needed than in the chamber of finance — the anteroom to the hall of wealth — the place of Power.

Georgina Binnie-Clark

Land and the Woman in Canada

In the present profoundly interesting phase of the history of the British Empire the cities of Canada are being built up. Canada has arrived at the prominent phase of her development: the period of the digging of foundations is of the past. Any of us who may have shared even in the final stage of this last and most fascinating phase of development — the pioneer or sporting period wherein one is accountable to none for the manner of accomplishment, and to oneself only for the sum — must recognise that it is at an end. The bricks-and-mortar phase of the development of Canada has already risen to such prominence as creates standard, invites competition, and attracts the attention of the world; and as each digger of the foundations scans the animated surface of the once silent plains of the Prairie Provinces it seems clear that it is time to fall into the order which governs form, or to shoulder one's spade and get off into the unknown country where a further stretch of the Empire is calling for the pioneer.

Nowhere is this change more searching than in the way of the field. Just a hundred years ago the colonists of the brave and gallant pioneer John Douglas, Earl of Selkirk, reached the banks of the Red River in the near neighbourhood of the locality from which now rises the city of Winnipeg. The chief stone in the foundation of Winnipeg, the central producing force of that vast and wealthy territory of the British Empire known as Western Canada, is the kind and chivalrous thought of a Scottish landowner who had sufficient imagination to place himself in the miserable circumstance of his very poor and long-suffering land-working neighbours, and the sympathy and thought to find for them a way out of it. Without labour and population the value of natural resources cannot be proved. The Selkirk colonists formed the nucleus of the population of Winnipeg, which in 1911 was returned at 200,000. The labour of the Selkirk colonists (crowned by the very few bushels of wheat from "that precious and promising crop," the record of whose preservation in that year of suffering, toil and strife (1812) marks one of the most interesting, pathetic and significant crises in the history of the British Empire) marked the first phase of development in Western Canada. "Do not forget them!" said His Royal Highness the Governor-General in addressing the people of the West on Selkirk Day, just after he had performed the ceremony of the stone-laying of the Selkirk Memorial. "Do not forget them. But give a thought from time to time to those courageous men and women who first showed the world what lay beyond the Great Lakes."

From the harvest of "that precious and promising crop" of the Selkirk colonist to the harvest of 1910, wheat held complete sway over the agricultural lands of Western Canada, but there have been very few women-farmers in the wheat-mining phase of the development of Canada.

I have watched many women work their way through every sort of agricultural labour in connection with grain-raising, and firmly believe that a large percentage of women are, with very little training, perfectly able to seed, and harrow, harvest and market the crop, and to plough and cultivate the land. But every woman who wants a 160-acre field in Canada — no matter how competent she may be to work it — must buy it at the current price per acre, which is no longer inconsiderable; but every man who wants a 160-acre field in Canada — no matter how incompetent he may be to work it — can have it for the asking. So that if frost or other disaster prevents the harvest of the man's first crop he can just walk on to the well-paid job which is always waiting for him; but the woman, even though she may be able to carry forward her land payment for the year, must meet the interest of six or seven per cent due on the full sum of deferred payment; and although she also would have no difficulty in obtaining work, it would be domestic work at from twenty to forty dollars a month according to her ability; whilst last year anything in the form of a man who could take the smallest part in the harvest, threshing, or building industries, was earning from two-fifty to three dollars a day.

Canadian women have taken up this matter of the land grant with a deep sense of the injustice of a law which, whilst seeking to secure the prosperity of the country in enriching the stranger, ignores the claim of the sex which bore the brunt of the battle in those early and difficult days when our great wheat-garden of the North-West was won with courage and held with endurance. No pen can depict the fine part that woman played in the spade-work of British expansion in this, the supreme place of prosperity among British lands; but history occasionally throws over the past a search-light which discovers the claim of the woman to her share in the land which, over a hundred and thirty years ago, woman helped to win by spirit and to hold by toil.

In grain-raising and horse-raising over a big acreage it is necessary for a woman to have a true vocation for farming, because the ruling factor of farming under these conditions is "something to sell once a year." Frequent disappointment would mean failure to the farmer merely in search of a livelihood, although not to the farmer living and seeing life. But farming in Canada is particularly in the process of change. The pioneer phase of the development of a country is the time in which one learns by doing and lives by doing without; but demand creates supply. Even in the heart of winter on the prairies it is possible to do without everything but shelter, fuel, flour, water, and clothing; and when it is remembered that the population of the Prairie Provinces is chiefly made up from the labouring classes of the British Isles, the countries of Northern Europe, and the United States of America — people who went out with little or nothing in the way of capital — it is not astonishing that, until the phase of development (marked by the building of the cities of Canada) which is caused by the centralisation of population in obedience to the claim of industrial forces it was difficult to sell for money anything that could possibly be dispensed with. Wheat hitherto has been almost exclusively grown by the pioneer farmer, because it was the only product that could be relied on to find a market for ready money. The Duke of Marlborough, in his recent letters on "The Land Question," seems inclined to invite confidence for wheat-raising in Britain, on the strength and continuing strength of price. One of the conditions he borrows from the future to support his argument is that as we Canadian farmers bring under cultivation the unturned acres of the further North, climatic conditions will operate against cheap prices; but if by adverse conditions the sword of early frost is intended, that is the condition under which we have contributed to the world's granary our splendid share of the finest wheat in the world, whose hard quality we owe to extreme heat and to extreme cold. Emerson says "the way to conquer the foreign artizan is not to kill him but to beat his work." We do not bank on price but grade in Canada. Price cannot command grade, but No. 1 Northern can always afford to wait for the market. If soundly granaried it will even improve in grade, although it may slightly shrink in weight. In the future it is reasonable to anticipate that the United States must look to Canada for bread; but before Canada contributes to the bread of a kindred or neighbouring nation she has to take up the work of supplying the present demand of her industrial population, not merely with bread, but with a choice of meats, poultry, milk, eggs, bacon, butter, cheese, potatoes, vegetables, and fruit.

Agriculture, though usually the first born, is but the twin industry of manufacture. Each in its own degree is the channel and test of commerce, the chief corner-stone of industrial value; but the supreme test of each and all in a country of great natural resources is population.

In 1901 the population of	Winnipeg was	42,340	.. In 1912,	200,000
" " "	Regina "	2,645	.. " "	30,210
" " "	Edmonton "	2,652	.. " "	53,383
" " "	Calgary "	4,907	.. " "	74,000
" " "	Saskatoon "	113	.. " "	27,527
" " "	Prince Albert "	2,275	.. " "	12,280
" " "	Moose Jaw "	2,152	.. " "	25,000
" " "	Medicine Hat "	1,975	.. " "	5,579
" " "	Vancouver "	26,133	.. " "	185,600

To go outside the Prairie Provinces: Victoria, 20,816 in 1901 and 65,000 in 1912; and to go east: Fort William, 3,997, in 1901 and 25,000 in 1912, and Port Arthur, 3,285 in 1901 and 15,654 in 1912.

Wheat always has been, and I think always will be, the centre of interest in farming in Canada. In such splendid measure did the soil of the Prairie Provinces yield its raw product that it is doubtful if wheat would not have remained the sole marketable product of the Prairie Provinces but for the side issues it created as an article of commerce, the industrial forces it set into circulation to centralise population and to demand the building of the cities of Canada. For example at Fort William, the city at the head of the Great Lakes, 5,500 men, with a pay-roll of over three million dollars, are required to handle the work of grain transportation from the railroad to the waterway. Those men represent just one section of labour and of population — but a very definite and important section of the population of the twin cities of Fort Willam and Port Arthur. They have to be fed; they earn excellent wages, frequently within a year or so of their arrival in Canada they are in a position to buy a site and build their home. They are not mere diggers of foundations, but workers on the surface, and they demand the best of food, of education, and of social conditions. They say to the farmer, "If you will produce these our daily requirements we will pay you in money, not once a year, but once a week," and the call is the same from every city in the North-West — the call of the industrial population of the bricks-and-mortar phase of development in Canada for the commercial farmer.

Never has there been a better opening for the woman-farmer of commercial instinct than there is in Canada to-day. Industrial development has selected the great cities of the North-West. A great population is gathering in those centres, and the land and the farmer must make ready to supply their great demand for food.

The first consideration of the woman-farmer contemplating this business of farming should be the relation of her plan of produce to her market. She should study the map and digest statistics, especially as to population, and, above all, she should grasp the facts and the promise of industrial development.

The commercial farmer is not to farm for mere livelihood, she is to farm for independence. The lowest sum that a woman should take as the symbol of independence should be £5,000. She should take as her maximum of time twenty years, and she should select the years from twenty-five to forty-five; that is, she has to start on five, fifty, or a hundred acres of land on a capital of one hundred, five hundred, or a thousand pounds. Every year that woman is to earn her living, her clothing, her holiday for twenty years, and at the end she is to be in possession of £5,000 and live where and how she will.

Firstly, I will be the woman of a hundred guineas capital, bound for a five-acre plot in Western Canada. I must beware of the place to which I wish to go, and also of the place where I am wanted to go; I must go where I am wanted because I have to make my living and £5,000 out of the food of the industrial population. I am told that I shall find the winter absolutely unbearable in the Prairie Provinces, the people more useful than delightful, and the conditions altogether unattractive for an unattached woman. I remember that the Archbishop of Rupertsland said that, in the hard times of the Selkirk colonists, the women were "the best men of the lot," that nothing ought to be unendurable, that delightful society always accommodates itself to a corner of one's baggage, that the term "useful" is a recommendation in itself. I weigh the verified inducement to the twin cities very carefully, but pass on through the cities of the Prairie Provinces, not because I am afraid of the winter, but because I have only a hundred guineas to work on, and I know that in Vancouver Island I can still select my five acres in the neighbour-hood of the industrial population, or even within feeding distance of the beautiful city of Victoria, and there I can work on my land, not for seven or, at most, eight months out of twelve, but all the year round and in the most exquisite environment, under the most perfect conditions for my business that the heart of woman can desire. I can grow bulbs by the seashore, fruit of varied and perfect kind, vegetables for which there is always demand, and with just a little thought for form — to which colour will always lend itself on Vancouver Island — I can conceal the lumber and slender dimensions of my shack with one of the loveliest bits of garden in the world.

I have an introduction to a real-estate man who has grown up with Victoria and knows the island from end to end. I tell him that I can pay a hundred dollars down on my land and no more, and that my business is to supply the demand for food supply in the most promising locality in the island. Two acres of my five I reserve for my shack and its concealing garden, my poultry- and pig-houses and cow-shed and runs. The remaining three acres I hire a man and team to break and put in shape for crops at five dollars an acre. In two and a half acres I sow barley, because it will mature in less time than any other grain, and should yield me at least a hundred bushels of pig feed, and there is no finer feed for pigs than chopped barley. I am sufficiently a gardener to know that potatoes, although they will grow fairly well in newly-ploughed land, should only be expected to contribute a marketable crop when they have considerable depth of soil in which to root. In the remaining half-acre of my prepared territory I put in potatoes, sow rhubarb, lettuce, cabbage, carrots, onions, parsley, &c.

With 125 dollars I shall buy a cow, and, if possible, a mother sow with eight small pigs, and with the remaining dollars purchase hens. I shall have to feed the cow and the pigs and chickens, but for my milk, without any labour but milking and a little stable cleaning, I shall get ten cents a quart, and with my experience of milch cows on the prairies she will yield me at least twelve quarts a day: that will mean a revenue of at least seven dollars a week, leaving me sufficient milk for my own use and my butter and milk food, so that if I put aside twenty-five dollars from my capital for feed, the gap that may probably occur between that and my barley chop must be filled from revenue.

I have 235 dollars left for my buildings, plant, and bank. My shack is to cost a hundred dollars only, lumber and labour; to my buildings, plant, seed, and tools, I allot the other hundred, learning to work by doing, and to live by doing without. I supply myself with a bag of flour and tea and sugar, and for the rest I look to eggs and milk and their fair exchange. In the autumn I shall kill six pigs, reserving two for spring produce. If I have the luck that befell Miss Jack May and her partner in the first year of their experiment on their ready-made farm, my sow will have produced another family, but my 100 bushels of barley chop will provide sufficient keep to ensure the steady physical progress of the pigs from day to day without interruption. If I sell my six pigs to the butcher I shall expect to get eight or nine dollars a hundred dead weight, and I expect my pigs in November to weigh 150 lb., and I shall draw in from seventy to eighty dollars cash, but if I pay the local butcher a dollar a pig for killing and cutting up, and sell meat fresh or pickled I shall make at least double the sum minus the butcher's fee of six dollars. But in any case I shall arrive at the opening of my second year fully prepared to demonstrate my belief in pigs and potatoes, and out of the food for the miners or lumber-men or even the population of Victoria I shall expect to make at least a thousand dollars profit in my second year; and in my second year I shall learn to select the produce that yields me the highest margin of net profit; and from the compass of commercial instinct I shall build up my £5,000 in twenty years.

I should like to take my 500 guineas to the neighbourhood of Edmonton, because it is the most interesting and beautiful capital of the fertile province of Alberta, or to the neighbourhood of Calgary, because, within forty miles, at Strathmore, I can see at the C.P.R. Demonstration Farm what land and labour will yield as commercial produce in just a year or so. I can see fruit gathers on a strawberry-bed, where in 1910 we only dreamed that strawberries would grow. I can walk through glass-houses counting many hundreds of cucumbers, tomatoes, and carnations, on the place where in 1909 we wondered if the glass-proposition could possibly be worked to pay. I want to settle near Medicine Hat when I face the fact and read the figures of what the Rosary Nursery Garden has achieved with five acres of land and a number of feet of glass in less than four years; but I abide by my determination to be governed by my judgment of industrial conditions, and I take my 500 guineas to Lethbridge in Southern Alberta. In the year 1910 the coal mines in the vicinity of Lethbridge, and up the Crow's Nest Pass line tributary to Lethbridge, yielded over six million tons of coal. The pay roll of the men connected with the mining and shipping of the industry averages 750,000 dollars. Seven thousand miners and their families are already here.

I am warned that Lethbridge is within the dry-belt; I observe that it is the centre of the dry-farming movement in Western Canada. This movement marks the splendid effort of man to reclaim all that is scientifically reclaimable of the desert or insufficiently watered land of the world. The leading factors of the dry-farming process are conservation and selection. Persistent and patient must be the experiment to prove the best method to conserve the natural rainfall and enrich the soil, and more persistent and more patient the experiment to select and to develop drought-resistent plants, with the object of conserving moisture at both ends of the proposition, so that agricultural result may be insured against drought, and the arid or semi-arid district, which frequently owes its superlatively fertile soils and incomparable climate to a low rainfall, may be induced, through these careful methods of culture, to yield the harvest worthy of early and superlative promise. I hear in Britain that this theory of reclamation is beautiful, almost ideal — but will the end be worthy of the labour? I read that at the International Dry-Farming Congress and Exposition, held in 1912, the 2500-dollar prize for the world's best bushel of hard winter wheat was won by Henry Holmes, a farmer living seventeen miles from Lethbridge and the first prize in every hard wheat class was captured by a farmer living in Lethbridge's tributary territory.

Precisely as in Vancouver Island I am prepared to pay one-fifth of my capital as my first land payment, but I shall hope to get my fifty acres very near to the city. I buy three milch cows because I was talking with one of the best commercial women farmers (and her husband) in the Canadian Pacific ready-made farms, four weeks after their wheat-crop had been badly hailed in the Crossfield Colony. They had been out six months and they had proved their household expenditure to be covered by the dairy produce of three milch-cows, and had at once bought six more. They were then making sixty pounds of butter a week; out of this produce they had bought sixty hens and were prepared to buy winter feed for their thirteen pigs, two of which were expected to farrow within the month. I buy six sheep because I see a farmer at Lethbridge who, having his crop hailed out but insured, went at once to Montana with the insurance money, spent it on ewes, put them to winter in the hailed grain, sold the spring lambs at a great profit for food, and still had his flock of ewes to the good. I put 250 dollars aside for land-cultivation because I mean to grow oats for a brood-mare and oat-sheaves for my cattle, barley for my pigs, and a little wheat for my hens, and to carry out my pigs and potatoes foundation on a larger scale. But I shall have my land-culture, my seeding, my harvest, and my threshing done in that first year. I do not want the expense or the trouble of hired service, and in any case I prefer to spend the winter alone or with another outdoor woman interested in the same sort of work. I put 750 dollars aside for buildings, as I want my cow-stalls, piggeries, and hen-houses to be comfortable, but my shack is to be as simple as at Vancouver Island, although built with sufficient substance and care to resist the cold. One hundred guineas for my land, one hundred and fifty for my buildings and plant, seventy-five for the breeding and seeding and harvesting and threshing of thirty of my acres. One hundred guineas for milch-cows, pigs and hens, leaves me £75 for feed and bank, and unless I see a very great bargain I shall postpone the pleasure of my brood-mare until the spring, when I shall need horse labour on my potato patch of at least five acres, and also a conveyance to carry my produce to market; but all this in my first year I can do without. I sell no grain; my fifty-acre proposition for my £5,000 intention can spare no profit to the middleman.

To the neighbourhood of Regina I take my thousand guineas; for I hope to select my hundred acres in the Qu'Appelle Valley.

Through Fort Qu'Appelle runs the Grand Trunk Pacific line from Winnipeg to Regina. I can ship my food supply daily from Fort Qu'Appelle station. I know that, within the limit of my own sojourn in those parts, the population of Regina has grown from 5,000 to 40,000: that it has become the centre of the largest distribution of farm implements in the world. It is the political and ecclesiastical capital of Saskatchewan and bids fair to become one of the first educational centres of Canada. All that I can produce on my hundred acres I can certainly sell to Regina and in seven years I have learned by experience all that I should *not* do in farming in the Qu'Appelle valley. Even if I only come in at the finish, I belong to the pioneer contingent of farmers in Canada; and although I consider that wheat-raising should be left to farmers of large capital and men nursed by the Canadian Government with 160 acres of free land, I shall set aside just ten acres of my hundred for wheat; and I shall keep that ten acres clean as a garden and use the harvest for seed for which there is always a good sale in the valley. Twenty acres I shall break for oats, which will yield me oats and oatsheaves for my horses and sheaves for my cattle, and in twenty acres I shall sow barley for my pigs. Thirty acres I shall fence off for pasture, ten for potatoes, and the remaining ten acres I shall keep for my shack and vegetable gardens, horse and cattle stable, pigs and poultry houses and runs. One-fifth of my capital I pay down for land, one-fifth for horses, and they will be all mares even though they are charged with a further payment. You cannot raise horses without land and capital, because you cannot expect your revenue to begin for at least four years, but it is the most delightful and remunerative line in Canadian farming, entailing very little labour on the farmer. I shall start on my hundred acres with four brood-mares, six milch cows, ten sows, a hundred hens, twenty turkeys, which I calculate, with my first land payment, will take up half my capital. Five hundred dollars I spend on my shack, which is to be a two-roomed bungalow with a lean-to kitchen; a thousand dollars on my farm buildings, granary, fencing, and plant. I shall buy a disc, harrows, and wagon; but for my ploughing and harvesting I shall hire horses, implements, and labour; and for my bank (for such hired service, feed, and food, for the first six months) I shall set aside the remaining fifth of my capital.

I have not referred to the steady and substantial rise in land values in Canada, because no commercial proposition should contain the element of chance. The land and the population are there waiting to be fed; the commercial farmer is needed; but it is the duty of those who advise the British woman to seek independence in Canada to do everything in their power to secure definite results to the undertaking which is urged as worth her while.

Life on the land in Canada is not easy, but it is worth while. Patience, endurance, and energy it requires of everyone every hour of the day; but it is set in the atmosphere of Lucas Malet's wind of promise — "that strong, clean, untamed wind, a wind as it seemed of promise still reached out of the uttermost north, bringing good tidings, bidding fear and distrust to cease, calling aloud that the world comes round to those who can dare even more surely than to those who can wait."

From *A Home-Help in Canada*
Commentary

In 1911 the Colonial Intelligence League for Educated Women was added to the
ranks of voluntary associations devoted to assisting women to emigrate to the
colonies. This association found its clients among the rapidly rising number of
women graduates of Britain's colleges and professional schools, for many of
whom there were no positions available at home. One of the League's first
projects was to sponsor an enquiry into a certain widely advertised occupation
for middle-class women in Canada, the home-help. Reports had filtered back by
disgruntled British emigrants that home-help meant nothing more nor less than
general servant in the majority of Canadian homes; the phrase was merely a
euphemism designed to placate middle-class British women, whose lingering
allegiance to genteel traditions prevented their openly hiring out as servants. To
find out the truth of the situation, the Colonial Intelligence League enlisted the
services of Ella Sykes as an investigative reporter. Her plan was to go to Canada
and pretend that she was an impoverished gentlewoman in search of work. In this
way she would find out at first hand what being a home-help involved.

Ella Constance Sykes is somewhat less than representative of the majority of
the writers whose work is reprinted here, for she belonged by birth to the English
upper class. Her birth date is not available, but it was probably between 1870 and
1875. In 1894 she accompanied her brother, Sir Percy Sykes, on travels through
Persia, and she achieved some notoriety as the first woman to ride overland from
the Caspian Sea to India. From these experiences came two travel books,
Through Persia on a Side-Saddle and *Persia and Its People*. In 1915 she made
further travels to the East, and between 1920 and 1926 she served as the Secretary
of the Royal Asiatic Society and lectured to various geographical and other
societies. She died in March 1939.

The result of Sykes's six months in Canada in 1911 was a book published in
London the next year entitled *A Home-Help in Canada*. In her preface, Sykes
outlined the circumstances behind her novel adventure:

I was greatly impressed by a letter in *The Times*, that put in forcible words the
hard lot of many of the million surplus women in the United Kingdom. It
showed how the labour of educated women was too often a drug in the
market, and how difficult — nay, often impossible — it was for a girl to earn
enough to support herself comfortably and lay by for old age, and as a
remedy for this state of things it mentioned the openings in the Overseas
Dominions.

As the ideas in the letter appealed strongly to me, I resolved to go out to Canada in order to investigate what openings there might be in the Dominion for educated women. Shortly before I started, it was pointed out to me by a candid onlooker that I should gain far more information if I would go as a home-help for part of my tour, thus getting practical insight into the conditions of life.

I confess that the idea was distasteful to me, for I had had little experience in the domestic arts, though I had undergone some "roughing" when travelling in Persia, and had always been strong. But, as the answer to my objections was that "evidently I wished merely to dip my fingers into the water, and shirked taking a plunge that might be of real use to the women I wanted to assist," I decided to go, and am now deeply grateful for the somewhat unpalatable advice, as I have learned so much from having followed it.

This book is the plain, unvarnished record of what I saw during a six months' tour in 1911. Practically all my remarks apply to Western Canada, as my experiences were mostly limited to that part of the Dominion and must not be regarded as typical of the Eastern provinces.

Sykes's record of her five incognito engagements in Western Canadian homes as a temporary domestic worker is indeed plain and unvarnished; it is also intelligent and even-handed in its assessments of the drawbacks and opportunities she encountered. Sykes warned her countrywomen in unequivocal terms that "Canadians are, as a rule, remarkably capable, and have 'no use' for the incompetent, who will find the Dominion a hard country, with few to care whether they sink or swim" (xi). Her detailed descriptions of her duties and privileges as a home-help both in the countryside and in towns provide excellent documentation of her general conclusions on the subject, summarized in the section "Openings in Canada for Educated Women."

We begin with an excerpt describing Sykes's experiences and feelings as she waits in Winnipeg for answers to her newspaper ad, "Educated Englishwoman, inexperienced, wishes to assist mistress of farm in housework."

Ella Sykes

A Home-Help in Canada

The Post Office was always thronged with people waiting for their letters, standing opposite pigeon-holes marked A-E, and so on, or opening little private boxes and taking out their correspondence. One day, as I stood in the long *queue,* a pleasant-faced old gentleman bowed to me to take his place. I demurred with a smile, but he insisted, with the words, "I come from a country where the ladies go first; in Canada they go last!" To the latter part of this remark I must take exception, for I was never made to go "last" from the Atlantic to the Pacific and back, and not once did I have to hoist my belongings in or out of any railway car, meeting with the utmost kindness again and again.

He went on to inquire what I was doing in Winnipeg, and was quite distressed to hear that I was looking for a situation as home-help, but said that he could perhaps assist me by giving me an introduction to some clergyman, a friend of his. I did not feel inclined to respond to this offer, and thought that the incident was closed; but a few days later I came across the Englishman again, who put me to the blush by urging me to write to him for help were I hard up at any time — in fact, I had considerable difficulty in impressing upon him the fact that I was by no means penniless.

"I know an educated woman when I see one," he said, "and I feel that you are throwing yourself away as a home-help."

I longed to tell my good-hearted acquaintance that I was under no compulsion to earn my livelihood, but I feared to trust my secret to anyone, and, holding out my hand in farewell, I assured him that I was all right. "Do you think you will come through?" and there was real concern in his voice. "I am perfectly sure that I shall," was my answer, and I went my way considerably cheered by one of the most genuine bits of kindness that I have ever encountered.

It was curious how completely I had now merged myself into my part. It was no longer acting. I knew the despairing feeling of hunting for work and finding none, and I had a pang of disappointment as girl after girl went off to her post, and I, the incompetent, was left behind without one. I filled up time with washing my clothes, thus learning the use of a wringer and a washing-board, and the right way to hang the garments on the line, and was humiliated to find that I did everything in the wrong way if I followed the light vouchsafed to me by Nature; and I also helped to clear the table after meals and assist with the drying of the many cups and plates.

Part of my long delay in getting work was owing to the fact that the newspaper had twice omitted to put my "ad." into its columns, through some negligence, and thus I was twice thrown back, as it were. I was urged to take a post as telephone girl, where a salary is paid and teaching given at the same time, and also would I not be a waitress? In each case, even if I had not determined to go on the prairie, the stuffy, overheated atmosphere of the offices and hotels would have strongly repelled me; and in all probability I should have been "fired" the next day, as I heard again and again that English waitresses are looked upon as too slow, and are speedily hustled out of their posts by the alert Canadians, who seem to do their work with lightning speed.

One day I found a letter in my "ad." box to the effect that if I would call at such or such an office I should hear of a "position" (they never speak of situation) to suit me. Accordingly I went, and was interviewed by a burly Canadian, who did not trouble to rise from his seat or remove his hat as I entered. "Mother is old and past her work," he began, "and she wants a strong girl to take over things. My father has a whole section, and there would be him and my brother and the two hired men to 'do' for, and you would have to milk three cows and make butter." "As well as do all the cooking, bread-making, and washing?" I inquired. "Yep, it's a good bit of work," was the answer, and I declined the post with thanks.

[Finally, after two weeks of unemployment, Sykes's ad was answered by "a widow on a prairie farm, who did her own work and needed a companion":]

It was a lovely evening as my taciturn young driver and I started off to my future home. The prairie was undulating, with bluffs covered with poplar and wild cherry, and here and there reedy "sloughs," as they call them, alive with wild-duck. I had a sense of adventure as mile after mile separated me farther and farther from the railway, yet there was always an uneasy feeling that perhaps I might not please my new employer, and very probably would not be considered worth even the small salary of £2 a month. The silent yokel who drove me had been three years in Canada, but my questions as to how the Dominion compared with his old home in the North of England elicited the shortest and most reluctant of replies.

At last we reached a nice-looking wooden house, surrounded by a little garden, and a pleasant-faced lady came out, warmly welcomed and embraced me, and then led me into a spotlessly clean and well-appointed abode. I felt that I was indeed fortunate in my first venture, and enjoyed supper, which was graced by my driver and his brother in their shirt-sleeves. Mrs. Robinson then helped me to wash up the supper things, showed me to a prettily furnished bedroom opposite to her own, and promised to call me about six o'clock on the morrow. I had given her a reference, kindly furnished by the Honorary Secretary of the British Women's Emigration Society, but she declined to read it, saying that "one look at my face" was quite sufficient for her, so I felt that my new life had begun under flattering auspices.

Next day it was a curious experience to dress hastily and descend to the kitchen to help my mistress with the preparation of porridge and fried bacon for breakfast, and at half-past six the two youths appeared with pails of new milk, and tidied themselves for the meal. In the wooden lean-to, answering to the scullery, was a basin of water, and into this they plunged their heads and hands, and came dripping into the kitchen to dry themselves with the roller-towel hung on the door. They then combed their hair with the aid of a small mirror on the wall, and sat down, waiting for me to serve them with porridge out of the saucepan — excellent fare when accompanied by milk fresh from the cow. They never thought of lending a hand as I passed them the jug, cut the bread, changed their plates, placed the dish of bacon on the table, and handed them the tea poured out by my employer, eating my own meal in the pauses of waiting. I confess that it went somewhat against the grain to wait on them in this manner, and I had to remember that they had been up early milking and feeding the animals, and therefore deserved a good meal. As soon as they had finished, they swung out of the kitchen and off to their work of "seeding," while I rolled up the sleeves of my apron and donned a pair of indiarubber gloves for the wash-up.

Even this apparently simple operation has a right and a wrong way of tackling it, and of course I took the wrong way by putting a mixed assortment of crockery and silver into the pan. My mistress now showed me how to wash the cups and saucers first, then the silver, then the greasy plates, the knives receiving attention last of all, everything being piled on a tray to drain, and scalded with boiling water from the kettle in order to facilitate the drying operations, plate-racks being unknown on the prairie. After this the washing-cloth must be rinsed out (in many places a little mop is used), and I was implored never to use the dish-cloths for opening the oven door or for handling pots and pans. This was a lesson hard of learning, as they hung invitingly from the line, and the legitimate rag was never to be found when wanted, while I soon learnt from painful experience that every part of the stove was capable of inflicting a burn upon bare hands.

The washing over I went upstairs to do the rooms, but the way in which I made my own bed met with disapproval. The usual English manner of arranging the pillows was stigmatised as "most untidy," and I was shown how to place them in an upright position, Canadian fashion, and lean against them an elaborate pillow-sham, with the words "good-morning" and "good-night" embroidered on opposite sides of it.

We then descended to the "shed," as Mrs. Robinson called the scullery, and my employer churned a mass of cream, but would not permit me to assist her, as she was sure that I should "make myself in a terrible mess" if I did so — probably quite true, but humiliating. I was set to peel potatoes, to prepare rhubarb for pies, and to draw water from the well just outside the back door. To do this last job I had to let down a large milking-pail by means of a strap, and had hauled up two or three bucketsful when a catastrophe occurred. Presumably I had not fastened the strap properly, but anyhow the pail vanished down the well, disappearing with a resounding splash as it reached the water! I uttered a cry of despair that brought Mrs. Robinson out in a trice, and though she must have felt much vexed, yet she behaved nobly, and said that Jack and Harry had already lost two buckets in this way, and mine made the third; but she would persuade them to descend with a ladder and retrieve the whole lot, and meanwhile we must do the best we could with a very inferior pail. I felt most grateful to her for her forbearance, and later on, when the midday meal was ready, we strolled to the barn and found two fascinating colts eagerly awaiting their mothers, that were at work; and I cannot describe the neighing and whinnying that took place when the two teams at last came in (in Canada a pair of horses is always called a team), the mares wild with impatience to get to their little ones.

Dinner consisted of fried bacon, for the second time that day — it is the staple food on most farms — and we had a milk-pudding for "dessert," as Canadians call the second course. Tea, as is the custom throughout the Dominion, was served at every meal, and at first I got very tired of it, and used to supply myself with hot water from the stove close at hand, to the surprise of the others.

"Have you got 'nerves' that you won't take tea?" Mrs. Robinson inquired, with a scarcely veiled contempt.

"No, not yet," was my answer, "but I don't want to have them."

Later on I took tea like everyone else, and got accustomed to it, though I always reverted to cold water whenever I could be sure that it was safe to drink it. At one farm, when I asked whether the water was good, I was not particularly reassured by the answer, "Well, I can't quite say, but I have never heard of anyone getting typhoid from it."

Mrs. Robinson, not content with tea three times a day, partook of it during the morning, and again at four o'clock, and I told her frankly that this indulgence partly accounted for the frequent attacks of "nerves" to which she was subject.

I still remember how tired I felt that first day, and how glad I was when my mistress said that I could do what I liked till four o'clock, as she herself always took "forty winks" during the afternoon. I lay down for half an hour, and then intended to go for a walk, but hardly had my head touched the pillow when I was sound asleep, and never awoke until I was roused by Mrs. Robinson at half-past four. She was kindness itself, and had lit the stove and made her afternoon tea, making me feel ashamed at having performed my duties so badly, and firmly resolved to do better in the future. In England I was usually looked upon as capable, but here at every moment it was borne in upon me that I was very much the reverse, and this gave me a humiliating feeling of being out of my element.

[Miss Sykes stayed with Mrs. Robinson only ten days, there having been a "coolness" between them over a trivial matter. However:]

As the time for me to leave drew nearer, my employer liked me better and better, and said that she would miss my "bright face dreadfully," and now and again she dropped me a word of praise on the performance of the household "chores." One day, as I was scrubbing the back staircase, she exclaimed, "What a terrible come-down your mother would think it could she see you now!"

"I consider it a great come-up," I retorted with a laugh, and felt quite proud when she said later on that the stairs had seldom looked whiter.

We had always cakes or scones for tea, and I learnt here the excellent and speedy Canadian method of measuring flour, sugar, butter &c. by the cup, and small quantities by the table-and tea-spoon: I never saw weighing-scales throughout my tour, but at first found it difficult to translate the pounds and ounces of my English recipes into "cups" and spoonsful.

On Saturday we had a general clean-up. I washed with soap and water the shabby linoleum that covered the kitchen floor, and the smart dining-room linoleum was cleansed with skim milk, that gave it a wonderful polish; the drawing-room, a repository of countless knick-knacks, had to be dusted, and the carpet-cleaner diligently used here and in the bedrooms. The work tired me hardly at all when I got into it, and my chief concern was the fear that my hands would become permanently blackened from the cleaning of dirty saucepans, while the many washing operations made my nails terribly brittle.

The kitchen floor was partly covered with loose pieces of carpet that I was for ever displacing at first, arousing my employer's ire and caustic remarks about my "shuffling tread." One length went from the "shed" to the kitchen table, and there was a piece laid down for the feet of each youth, an attention that they much disliked; but I suppose it was easier to shake the mud off bits of carpet than to remove it from the linoleum. The pots and pans were kept in the "shed," and here it was that I scraped out the porridge saucepan every morning, a tiresome task anyhow; and as it had two holes that were stopped up with scraps of calico, it behoved me to be careful not to pull these out during my cleansing operations.

The kitchen table was covered with white oilcloth, and on it Mrs. Robinson mixed her dough for bread and pastry, without the aid of a board; but for meals we had a tablecloth, that the boys speedily soiled, owing to the uncivilised way in which they ate their food, and I should have infinitely preferred the oilcloth unadorned.

I had a hot position with my back to the stove, in which there was one large oven in the middle, and on the right a boiler that it was my task to keep filled from the rain-water tank at the back-door. Above the stove was a receptacle in which plates and dishes could be kept hot, and on either side hung a collection of pots and pans. The big block-tin kettle was king of the kitchen, and it behoved me to be careful of it, as when on the boil the steam from its spout was capable of inflicting a bad burn, as I discovered to my cost.

During the days of rain it was most difficult to keep the fire alight with the damp wood, and we had recourse to drying the logs in the oven; and when the weather suddenly got hot, the kitchen was a veritable Black Hole of Calcutta, and the hateful house-fly and mosquito began to annoy.

Sometimes I used to wonder whether it were indeed I who was cleaning out rooms on my hands and knees, or rubbing clothes on the washing-board, or ironing, or replenishing that voracious stove with pieces of wood. I must confess that though I gave my whole mind to my work, yet I found the life very monotonous, and it was hard at first to be ordered about, and not to be mistress of my own time. Mrs. Robinson and I had a curious kind of friendship. She liked me personally, invited me cordially to visit her later on, confided in me, and begged me to correspond with her, and yet she not unnaturally hated the amateur way in which I set about my work, and made me feel that I did nothing right and was thoroughly incapable.

But my depression vanished when I awoke up one morning to feel a warm wind blowing and to see the snow melting fast. The birds were all singing, and a wren was actually building its nest in the pocket of an old coat of Jack's that he had left hanging outside. The trail had been so bad on account of the snow that perforce I had stayed two or three days longer than my week, and now that the roads were drying I made a personal appeal to Jack to drive me to the station the next day, for I knew that he and Harry would miss me, and I had a lurking fear that he might tell Mrs. Robinson that it was impossible for me to leave for the present, in order to prolong my stay.

We had quite an excitement on my last evening, as I persuaded one of the boys to go down the well and make an effort to retrieve the three lost buckets. This he accomplished finally with the aid of a rake, tied on to a long clothes-prop, and I alternately watched his efforts, which seemed to be attended with considerable risk, and gazed at the young moon and stars in a wonderful sunset sky, and at the long line of prairie, purple as the sea where it lay on the horizon.

And now the time for my departure had arrived. Mrs. Robinson had a meeting of the "Women's Auxiliary," a charitable society, at her house that afternoon, and came up three times to my room as I was finishing my packing, to urge me to come down, as "the ladies all want to see you." When she paid me my wages she gave me a little homily on the subject of untidiness in my work, saying that she was speaking for my good, and that I must improve if I intended to be a success in my next situation; but she tempered her severity with a word of commendation of my willingness, and said that I had learnt a good deal while with her. I listened in a humble silence, and did not "answer back," though I wished that she could have understood with what an immense effort I had earned the money that she handed to me!

At last the buckboard made its appearance. I bade farewell to sunny-faced Harry, who said, "Let us hear how you get on," as he wrung my hand; and Mrs. Robinson embraced me, gave me a little souvenir, and was genuinely sorry to say good-bye to me. The colts insisted on accompanying their mothers, and impeded our progress a good deal, one of them soon beginning to lag behind; but Jack had no pity for it, and rather cruelly remarked, "It would come though it wasn't wanted, and so it must just take the consequences."

I was delighted to be off after ten days of indoor life, during which my horizon had been practically bounded by the well and the wood-pile, and I enjoyed even the roughness of the track. "It will jolt your bones up a bit," as Jack truly said, and I had to plant my feet firmly on my "grip," lest it should be shot out, and keep an eye on my trunk fastened on behind.

But jolts and bumps were a trifle when one was drinking in the intoxicating air. Summer had come with a rush. The grass was starred with purple and white violets, tiny wallflowers, pansies, and dainty stitchwort; grasshoppers were chirruping loudly, and the frogs ("peepers," Harry called them) were croaking in a jubilant chorus from every pond we passed. The air was full of down from the poplars, a kind of summer snow; small yellow canaries (I heard later on that they came from Florida) flitted about, and there were orioles, blue-birds, and wild-duck.

Everything was so full of life and freedom that I was quite sorry to reach the little prairie station and bid farewell to my driver. He shook hands with me warmly, saying that he hoped all would go well with me, and when I thanked him for having been kind and helpful, he blushed up like a girl, but looked pleased in his rather boorish way. "Don't go to Canadians in your next place, they know too much," was his parting advice, words that showed me that he had not been unobservant of my numerous deficiencies.

I had made my first venture, and though I had been a failure, yet I knew that I had got more or less into Canadian ways, and should probably succeed better in my next situation. My mistress had shown me much kindness, and I saw by the light of later experiences that I had had a very easy place with her, which only my lack of training prevented me from filling properly.

The fine air had made me feel very fit, and capable of doing double the work that I could have accomplished in England, but all the same I had a conviction, that only strengthened as the months went on, that the post of home-help is not a suitable opening for an educated woman, unless in some specially selected district, where she can live in conditions more akin to those of which I had read before I came out to the Dominion.

[From the Winnipeg area, Miss Sykes travelled to Saskatoon, Edmonton, and then Calgary, where for a second time she advertised for work as a home help. While waiting for replies to her ad, she registered at a hostel for women, where conversations with others in search of work prompted reflections on the country and its ways:]

At the hostel we all took a frank interest in one another, and one or two of the lodgers who were of all classes, seemed as anxious for me to get a "position" as they were to get one for themselves.

There was a certain jealousy between the British and the Canadians, which came out now and again in the talk at table, at which both races were represented. An inmate of the hostel related that on one occasion she went to apply for a post at a house in the town. "We don't want any English here," was the rude remark of the mistress, when she presented herself; but it elicited the retort, "If I had known you were a Canadian, I should never have applied for your situation," and Miss Bates flounced out with her head held high. The lady sent after her, saying that she would like to engage a girl who showed so much spirit, but Miss Bates refused, not unnaturally, to go.

Of course there are faults on both sides to account for this attitude, but from what I saw during my tour, I am bound to say that my compatriots are a good deal to blame for it. They will persist in criticising Canada and things Canadian by British standards, and do not bear in mind the precept that you must "do at Rome as Rome does," apparently forgetting that they have come to the Dominion to earn their livelihood. As I was nearly six months in the country, staying in many places, usually in the humble position of a home-help, and was treated throughout with kindness and courtesy, it seems to me that this antagonism would speedily be done away with were every Britisher to divest himself of English prejudices and come out with a perfectly open mind.

Canadians are naturally intensely proud of the Dominion, and have every reason to be so; and if, as yet, they have not the culture that has come to England as a heritage from former generations, they are abundantly endowed with qualities far more valuable to pioneers. I was once asked whether I were not afraid of travelling alone in a strange country, but answered that as I was among my own kith and kin in the Empire, I felt at home; and this I maintain is the right attitude.

Some of the inmates of the hostel had no right to be in Canada at all, and had come out after reading the alluring literature, in which things are, to say the least of it, seen through rose-coloured glasses. One lady, elderly and far from strong, who had had good posts in England, had actually taken her ticket for the Dominion after a talk with an enthusiastic Canadian lady, who had spoken vaguely of the "crowds of openings for women." My poor friend did not find many when she arrived in the country, and when I met her she was worn out with much work and little pay as a matron, and was having a rest before trying her luck afresh. She was skilful with her needle and could dressmake, but, as she could not use a sewing-machine, it would have been impossible for her to get work in a land where "more haste" is *not* always considered "worse speed." It was pathetic for one of her upbringing to have to go as housekeeper to three men on a ranch, and I confess that I saw her off at the station with considerable misgiving. Some months later, in passing through Calgary on my way East, I called at the hostel, and found her back again. Her health had broken down at the ranch, she had also had an accident, and was about to take a post as housemaid in a "rooming" house for a month, at a low wage, after which she hoped to get work again as a home-help.

Another, a particularly charming woman, had been a governess with excellent posts, and was, moreover, an accomplished milliner. Unluckily she refused to turn this talent to account, but was determined to be a home-help. A place was found for her, and off she went, but returned in a couple of days, and amused us all with her account of her experiences with a fussy old lady. As I sat next to her at table, I asked why she would not go round to the shops and see whether she could get taken on as a milliner, but the bare idea of asking for work at a "shop" was abhorrent to her. I offered to accompany her in the quest, but she still clung to her "home-help" idea.

"You are most unfit for the post," I said to her bluntly; and indeed a delicate, highly-strung woman, not in her first youth, cannot do the rough work that is expected of her in Canada. "Why won't you be a milliner or do dressmaking, and take to something that you *can* do, and that will bring you in money?" I asked.

"I hate the idea of it," was her answer. "I want to live in a home and arrange the flowers and help the lady of the house with her correspondence."

"I do not believe that there *is* such a post in all Canada," I retorted, but she was by no means convinced. Her next step was to try work at an hotel in the Rockies, but the high altitude was too much for her nerves, and when I ran across her again she had thrown up the post and was doing nothing.

Another lady said that she had been a governess in England, and could cook, iron, sew, had taken charge of a house, and in her native land was considered most capable. But it was very different when she got to Canada, and because she could not scrub or do heavy washing she was looked down upon as stupid and incompetent, and had, as I had, a feeling of depression and helplessness. Certainly the Canadian women are extraordinarily quick and clever in every kind of housework, and I never ceased admiring the way they could turn their hands to anything. The houses are always spotlessly neat, they are first-class cooks, and, as a rule, are very spick and span in the way they dress, however simple may be their clothes. On the farms they make the soap, cure the ham and bacon, bottle quantities of fruit for winter use, rear poultry, and on occasion can milk the cows, groom, harness and drive the horses, and are most handy with a hammer and nails.

[Miss Sykes's ad in the Calgary paper produced a response from the owners of a ranch to whom, in her published account, she gives the name of "Brown":]

I was with the Browns on Coronation Day, and to mark the event I gave "Coronation" post cards all round at breakfast. Mr. Brown said that he thought he ought to run up a flag to show his loyalty, and of course I applauded the idea warmly, but nothing was done — we were all far too busy. It was washing-day for us women, and directly we had cleared away breakfast and had swept the rooms, we began, Mrs. Brown rocking the "cradle," and I turning the wringer. She did not make nearly as toilsome a business of the whole operation as I found prevailed elsewhere in Canada, and we got the family washing all hung out to dry soon after midday. On the other hand, it was by no means as snowy white as when I saw it done by other housewives, though probably the sand that got into everything may have been the cause of this. Certainly I have never been in a place where so much sweeping was required, every breath of wind seeming to cover the kitchen floor with sand in spite of all our care.

Mrs. Brown had had a hard life since her girlhood, and, though a comparatively young woman, looked far older than her years, worn out with ceaseless work. Like the great majority of Canadian women, she was extraordinarily quick and capable, and, as I told her, would have concocted a cake and put it in the oven, and perhaps baked it, before I had collected the materials to make mine. But the Demon of Work had got her in its clutches, as it seems to get so many Canadian women, and she *could* not rest or take things easily.

She had been for four years on a ranch — completely bare of crops, as it was a cattle-range — and she said that the great expanse got on her nerves, and she hated it, save when in the spring the ground was starred with myriads of tiny flowers. Her husband and the other men were off with the cattle during the greater part of the day, and she told me that without her children she thought that she would have gone mad.

In summer the heat was great, and the mosquitoes were so bad that she hardly ever left the house, but lived behind the wire screens, which were in front of all the doors and windows; and she often watched her husband riding off, looking as if he and his horse were in a mist, so dense was the cloud of these pestilent little insects. The men all wore veils and gloves, and covered their horses as much as possible with sacking. The poor cattle, however hungry they might be, dared not feed when the air was still, but lay in the barns to get refuge from the mosquitoes, waiting there until a breeze sprung up, when they would hurry out to the pasture. Sometimes the winters were terrible, so severe that the cattle died on the ranges, and she was kept indoors for weeks at a time. Mr. Brown, most fortunately, had a great store of hay, and once fed his sheep, over two thousand in number, daily, and he and his partner had a snow-plough that tossed away the snow, and enabled the animals to feed on the grass underneath. They got to understand the purpose of this plough very soon, and the whole flock would follow it in a straggling line, perhaps a mile long, browsing as they went.

Canadian as she was, Mrs. Brown had ever a good word for the English, who, she said, were considered to make the kindest husbands of any, in the way of helping their wives, though the Canadians were supposed to give money more freely for household expenses. Again and again on the prairie an Englishman would give her a hand with the interminable dish-washing, and would sometimes be sneered at by the other men for so doing. The rough old Scotchman, her husband's partner, would never help her in any way, and she quoted to me more than once the remark of a Scotchwoman on the prairie, who said to her, "My countrymen seem to think that there is no limit to a woman's strength."

Day after day she rose to a round of unending toil, and during all the incessant work her three children arrived. The second came before his time, and as a snowstorm was raging, it was impossible to go for the doctor; so she and her husband had to do as best they could. Usually the women go into the nearest town for their confinements, every hospital in Canada having large maternity wards for the purpose; and as all Canadian men are as handy at household "chores" as their wives, they can look after themselves and the children very well for a time.

My employer and her husband were a thoroughly united couple, yet she assured me that had she had a vision of what her early married life would be, she would never have linked her fortunes with his.

"I haven't a single good word for the prairie," she would say, "and I got to hate the very sight of a man when I was there." I was surprised at this, and inquired why.

"Because a man meant preparing a meal. Our ranch was on a main trail, and man after man as he came along would drop in and ask for food, as a matter of course, and very seldom did he give me a word of thanks for it."

"How horrid! I should have felt inclined to refuse to cook for such ungrateful creatures," I remarked.

"Oh, well, I felt like it very often," was her reply; "but if I had done so, we should have got a bad name in the district, and I had to think of my husband. It was a life of slavery. Just imagine it! In shearing-time I had to cook for fifteen men, and they needed five meals a day, and I couldn't get a woman to help me for love or money. I was too busy to go and see my neighbours — the nearest lived four miles off — and I just got into the way of thinking of nothing but how to get through the day's work."

"Don't you think that the men would have helped you if you had asked them?" I said. "I met a girl who told me that her husband had a ranch, and that she rode half the day and 'jollied the boys,' who did her work for her."

"Yes, there were women in our part who went on like that, but," and Mrs. Brown's voice had a tragic note, "they could never get free of the prairie as we have done. They took their freedom while they were there, wasted the time of the hired men, and there they will have to stay all their lives," and she shuddered at the mere thought of it.

"But aren't there some women who love the life? In England we hear so much of the 'call of the prairie.' "

My mistress looked dubious. "There may be some," she conceded, "but I never met them. All my friends hated the loneliness and the lack of amusement and the same dull round day after day. Do you know, if ever I sat down and wrote, or did some sewing, Kitty would come up to me to ask whether it were Sunday, so astonished was she to see me resting, as on the week-days I was on the 'go' all the time. I have heard since from two or three of our neighbours, and they are all suffering from 'nerves,' and I myself am worn out and old before my time with the life."

This was true; but I pointed out to her that now, as they were so well off that Mr. Brown need not work at all, she ought to rest every afternoon, or go out and see some of her neighbours. But this was a counsel of perfection. She saw its wisdom, but said sadly that she was so wound up, as it were, that she positively *had* to keep going all day, and that she had now lost all desire for social inter-course. And this I found to be the case with many Canadian women. The habit of work was so deeply ingrained in them that they went on when there was no necessity for it, and far too often broken health and mental derangement stop this activity. From the Atlantic to the Pacific the women in country districts, as a rule, wore far worse than the men, and the monotonous work, too much tea, little outdoor exercise, and few neighbours or amusements appeared to me to be the causes of this. The men have a far better life, though the extremes of heat and cold must be very trying. They work with other men, and have the animals to look after, and, best of all, are in the open air most of the day. As Mr. Brown remarked to me when talking of their life on the ranch, "The prairie is no 'snap' for a woman."

[By the time of her third "situation," again in the Calgary district, Sykes was feeling herself reasonably competent in routine household tasks. But her week of service with the family she calls the Downtons introduced her to an as-yet-untried responsibility, infant care; and here she met with experiences she did not care to repeat:]

The neighbourhood to which I now betook myself was supposed to be one that afforded great openings for the home-help, and I felt sure that I should speedily find a post.

As usual, I went to insert my advertisement in the newspaper, and when the editor heard my errand he gave me an address to which to write, and pointed out a situation that might suit me in last week's issue. Would I take a place where there were many children? Remembering how tired I had got of the perpetual clamour of the juvenile Browns in my last post, I frankly confessed that I preferred their absence to their presence. With that he looked at me with the most reproachful face, and without a ghost of a smile exclaimed, "And you a woman!"

I should like to have inquired whether he had any of his own!

An English woman whom I shall call Mrs. Downton, appeared to engage my services, and I asked for details of the work. She wished me to do all the cooking and cleaning of the house, and look after her children on two afternoons of the week. Could I have a room to myself, an hour or two off during the afternoon, and should I be treated as one of the family? I asked. She agreed to all these conditions, but her whole manner was that of a superior to one vastly her inferior, and I saw at once that I was "up against" the English "caste" system.

As I had been "one of the family," almost more than I wished, elsewhere, I wondered how it would feel to be treated as a menial, and I prudently offered my services for just a week if she cared to accept them for so short a period. As she was hard up for help at the time she agreed, and offered me wages at the rate of fifteen dollars (£3) a month.

The time of my arrival coincided with the departure of the last "girl," and the leave-taking between mistress and maid was anything but cordial. Mrs. Downton then led me into the kitchen, and, pointing to a paper fastened to the door, said, "Here are my rules for the work of each day," and showed me my room, comfortable save for the lack of a chair or any place to put my things, except a few nails on the door, and told me to prepare supper as soon as I had taken off my hat and jacket.

This was eaten at seven o'clock in the dining-room, and, in my capacity as lady-help, I sat at table with the husband and wife and the "man," a depressed youth, who never opened his lips. As Mr. Downton, kind and pleasant from first to last, was conversationally inclined, I quite forgot my inferior position, and chatted away during the meal, though I had had rather a blow as I entered the room. "Does *she* eat with us?" had been the remark of Master Tom, the elder hope of the family, and he stared at me, greatly surprised, as I took my place!

I cleared away after supper, and during the washing-up Mrs. Downton looked into the kitchen and asked very stiffly whether I would care to sit with them in the drawing-room. I politely declined this honour, and immediately my employer's manner became less glacial, so great was her relief, poor woman, and indeed I could sympathise with her. This was the first and last occasion that I was invited to enter the family circle, save at meal-time.

On Saturday I had to work my hardest, as not only were there special cleaning operations, but I had to cook everything for dinner and supper in order to devote myself to the baby during the afternoon when the Downtons went off to a party.

All instructions as to baby's bottles, his undressing and putting to bed were given to me, and I hoped to have a peaceful time reading and writing in the verandah, with the child sleeping in his "pram."

This programme, however, was by no means carried out. Baby was easily amused as I washed and put away the dinner things, but when the time came for him to take his first bottle, there ensued frantic struggles, yells apparently of fury, and an unmistakable determination not to imbibe his milk and barley-water. Feeling that I was somehow in fault, I warmed the bottle again and again, and only after a weary hour with much rocking of the perambulator did he condescend to take some nourishment. This incident had spoilt his temper, so my ideas of reading or writing were quite dissipated, and I had to soothe his screams as best I could.

With the second bottle there ensued the same scene as the first, and in the middle of it all little Tom came howling to me to say that the two dogs were killing a sweet little kitten that had been a real joy to me in the kitchen. Baby and bottle were deserted, and I rushed after the boy to the spot, to find the "man" already there and driving the dogs off, but, alas, it was too late. Tom had set the dogs again and again on one or other of the cats in spite of all that his parents and I could say, and now I turned upon him and "spoke my mind," only wishing that I could have whipped him soundly for his cruelty. I think, however, that the sight of poor kitty lying dead made a far greater impression than anything I could say, for though a mischievous boy, he was likeable in many ways.

Baby's yells made me hasten back to my charge, who had to be rocked and carried about until it was time to put him and Tom to bed, giving the latter his supper.

It was a great relief when my youngest charge finally dropped off to sleep, and when Mrs. Downton returned she discovered that she had put no sugar into his bottles, this omission amply accounting for his trying conduct. She was full of sympathy for her "poor darling," but had none for the home-help, who had passed a most harassing afternoon in consequence of her mistress's negligence. I wonder if that editor who reproved me had ever been in charge of an enraged baby?

[Following a chapter on work in a town household (all her other situations were on farms of one kind or another), Miss Sykes compiled a chapter of general recommendations for her British readers, "Openings in Canada for Educated Women":]

There is work and to spare for the right type of woman — one who is robust, adaptable, and thoroughly trained in some calling that is needed in a new country. Very few on the wrong side of forty ought to try their fortune across the Atlantic, because they are, as it were, in the British groove, and will find it almost impossible to fit into an entirely new environment. Let me quote the words of a Canadian lady who has done a great work for the English girl in the Dominion. "Canada," she writes, "is essentially a country for the young and strong, both mentally and physically, as the crudeness of many things out here are only sources of amusement and provocative of renewed energy to overcome them to the buoyancy of the young; but to the woman turned forty, they are burdens."

I hear often that British girls are not strong enough for the life in Canada, but I do not hold at all with this opinion. Young women who are experts at tennis, hockey, or golf will do well there, if they will only fit themselves beforehand for the different existence that they will have to lead.

If a girl has a comfortable post in Great Britain and an assured future, perhaps she had better stay in the Old Country; and she who has spent her whole time in playing games will be sadly disillusioned if she thinks that her amateurish efforts will pass muster in a land that has no use for the inefficient. There are hundreds of girls at the present day who are living in country parsonages, or whose fathers are retired officers, professional or business men. What prospect is there for many of these when the head of the family passes away? Far too often a poverty-stricken future awaits them. Some, for lack of anything better, may fill the already over-stocked profession of governess, which reminds me that a few days before I sent this book to press, a friend told me that in answer to her advertisement for a nursery-governess she had between seventy to eighty replies!

Some of the girls that sent her those letters may possibly end their days as pensioners of some charitable society, or even — and the cases are more numerous than is usually believed — in the workhouse.

Surely it would be better to stave off such a fate while a girl is young, and can be trained for some profession that will ensure her a comfortable livelihood and the opportunity of laying by for old age? If she has that dash of pluck and the pioneer spirit in which our race has never been lacking, she will make light of the hardships and discomforts inseparable from life in a new country.

Her reward will be a wider outlook and more opportunities of "making good," than she would probably have found in England, and after a time she will share the legitimate pride of all Canadians in this splendid part of the Empire. As a British woman of this type said to me in Victoria, "I could never go home again for good because everything seems so poverty-stricken in England in comparison with Canada. Out here we can all make our way, and there isn't such a thing as a beggar in the country."

But whatever she undertakes, a girl must not think of coming out to the Dominion without a knowledge of cooking, washing, and so on, this being absolutely necessary in a country where only five per cent of the women have servants. She must also be smart in appearance, as that will tell greatly in her favour when seeking work. An English lady, living in a big Canadian town, told me that she always knew her own country-women by their ill-hung skirts, their badly-cut blouses, with a gap between skirt and waistband, and their general slovenly appearance, in strong contrast to the Canadian working woman in her well-starched "waist," or neat cotton dress. British girls make a great mistake when they think that "anything will do" for an office.

HOME-HELPS

The one calling in which a girl can get immediate employment is that of home-help, but I fear that this occupation has not always been presented in its true light. The mere words "Golden West" teem with allurement, and there is a charm in the idea of helping with the pioneer work of a new country. Before I went to Canada I gathered from the literature treating of this subject, that I should probably have riding or driving in the afternoons and that there would be some social inter-course among the neighbours, many of whom would be of my own class. Nothing, or hardly anything, of this fell to my lot in the five situations that I filled during the summer, and maid-of-all-work as I was, I should have been too tired to have enjoyed such distractions had I had the chance of them. Canada is cer-tainly the paradise of the labouring classes, but the girl who goes by the name of "lady" in the British Isles will find that her culture is little if at all appreciated by her employers. I also found that in the towns the home-help was treated merely as a servant, and was not in any way made one of the family, even in the case of an English clergyman's daughter, who was acting as nurse to some children.

One of my mistresses told me that her former companion, a nice-looking girl, usually played the part of a wall-flower at the winter dances, and I was astonished when she accounted for this by saying that the men looked down upon her because she was a home-help; and later on, a lady confided to me that she had filled this position before her marriage, and begged me not to mention the fact.

Personally, I was treated almost as a guest when on the farms, but in two of my situations I was made to feel that I filled an inferior position, none of the visitors of either sex who came to the house taking any notice of me, and, as a rule, I had to work from morning till night without any time to cultivate my mind, and often without the privacy which is usually so priceless a possession to the educated woman. Of course, owing to my lack of training, I did not get through my work quickly, and it must also be remembered that the life is greatly simplified. Yet I think that my experience would be corroborated by the majority of home-helps throughout the Dominion, but, as exceptions prove the rule, I believe that on Vancouver Island, and in a few other places, a woman may become a home-help without degenerating into a drudge, and will have the opportunity of mixing on equal terms with her own class. In support of this I will quote the words of a lady who worked in that capacity on the Island for over a year. She says: "If real ladies come here, and are young and capable, willing to learn and ready to begin at ten to twelve dollars a month (£2 to £2, 8s.), they will have a really good time, as there is a large Anglo-Indian society here, and the girls are invited to all the dances, picnics, and lawn-tennis. The idea is for everyone to live a happy, healthy, outdoor life, and, as Chinese servants demand exorbitant wages, the residents are delighted to get lady-helps to assist them, but they do not want ill-educated and untrained girls to enter their home-circles."

The following concerns two applicants of the Colonial Intelligence League, who went to Western Canada as home-helps:

June 1912.

We have been very fortunate in getting posts at once. . . .

We are going to do the cooking and the diningroom. There are only three meals a day, and as there is no meat or fish, the establishment being conducted on strict vegetarian principles, there will be no really dirty work.

The house is heated with central heating, and there is electric light everywhere. The cook's salary is $35 a month (£7), and the one who undertakes the dining-room work will get $20 a month (£4).

We think ourselves extremely fortunate in getting posts so quickly, and also to be with gentlefolk. We must and will do our best to keep them. . . .

It is a great pity that more of the upper classes do not come out. There are certainly openings for all.

With the last words of the letter I am in complete agreement, but unless a girl is really fond of domestic work I should advise her to take the post of home-help merely as a stepping-stone to something better, which is certain to turn up if she be competent.

Let us now discuss some of the other openings in Canada that might commend themselves to a capable and energetic woman.

In every case, save that of home-help, the demand for which is never ending, a woman ought to have sufficient money to keep herself until she finds suitable work.

Teaching in the Government Elementary Schools offers a fair prospect to a girl, who is already qualified in England, or who would be ready to go through a training in Canada, and details can be obtained from the office of the Board of Education at Whitehall.

The demand for teachers throughout the whole Dominion far exceeds the supply, and the Deputy Minister of Education for Alberta informed me that he could give posts to some two hundred girls annually in that one province, and had entered into an agreement with our Board of Education, by which certain British certificates held by girls would enable the possessors to start teaching at once in the Dominion, gaining their Canadian certificate later. But they would be wise to go through a six weeks' course, planned by the Minister, this entailing no expense save their board and lodging and a few books.

The minimum salary is £125 per annum, but I have lately read a budget of letters from English girls, all in their first posts, and in each case the salary was £132, and they were paying £3, 4s a month for their keep. Several of the letters said that the prospects for teachers were far better in Canada than at home, and certainly the social position is a good one in the country, all the farms competing for the honour of boarding the teachers.

The following is taken from the letter of one of the girls helped by the Colonial Intelligence League:

> Winter of 1911
>
> The authorities were exceedingly kind, and had I not been in communication with you (the representative of the League in British Columbia), would have interested themselves in me, and found me a post. . . .
>
> Everybody on the island is exceedingly pleasant, and does everything possible to make my life happy. There are eight children in the school, between the ages of six and fourteen years, which makes the teaching a little complicated, but one soon gets used to it. I am very fortunate to have got a post like this. . . . I am boarding in a most comfortable house, and am well looked after. . . .

Of course there are drawbacks. An English girl, accustomed to plenty of friends at home, may find living on a lonely farm rather trying, for in many cases there is no social life whatever. Her pupils may be under a dozen, and of all ages, but, as a rule, she will find that they are very intelligent, and eager to learn, never staying away from school if they can help it. They may also consist of half a dozen nationalities, and she will have the splendid work of turning them into loyal citizens of the Empire.

Behind the neat schoolhouse, over which the Union Jack flies, there will most likely be a stable, for probably some of the children have to ride or drive long distances, the Government, I was told, providing a horse for the teacher if she has to board far from her work. One Canadian ex-teacher told me that she had had to drive five miles to her school in all weathers, only passing two houses on her way;

"but," she added with a laugh, "I had the best social position in the district, and the pick of all the husbands!"

If the British girl "wins her spurs" in the country, she will, in time, be eligible for a town school, with higher pay, or she may find a position in one of the Secondary Schools. In passing, it is well to note that as all classes send their children to be educated at the Government Schools, there is practically no demand for governesses in the Dominion.

Nursing is another good opening for a girl who has the qualifications for this profession. But by this I do not mean that nurses who have received their training in England should come out. Unless these latter possess a three years' General Hospital certificate, they will not be admitted into the Canadian Nursing Association; and as the methods in use in the Dominion are in various instances different from those in vogue in Britain, it is not to be wondered at that Canadian doctors prefer to employ Canadian-trained nurses. This, at least, was the case in Winnipeg, Edmonton, and Calgary during my tour. But there is a great demand for *probationers,* between the ages of twenty-two and thirty-four. The work is hard during the three years' course, but the girls are well looked after, carefully nursed if ill, and their future is assured when the training is over—£4 to £6 a week being given for private cases.

I cannot do better than quote from a letter sent to me by an English girl who has gone through one of the big hospitals in the West, and has lately married a Canadian doctor.

The nurses serve two months as probationers, and then have an entrance exam. If this is satisfactorily passed, and the Lady Superintendent considers the girl likely to make a good nurse, she is received into the training school, signing a paper to the effect that she will stay three years, unless prevented by illness.

. . . Board, lodging, and laundry are all provided. We had a very nice Home, with a large reception-room and library, and each class was allowed to entertain one night a week from eight o'clock to ten o'clock; on special occasions we were given late leave till twelve o'clock. As for other distractions, the day nurses were off duty at 7:30 P.M., and could go where they liked, provided they were in by 10 P.M., when the Home was locked up. But the training is a hard one, and social distractions after twelve hours' hard work do not appeal to you as much as your bed!

The training is an excellent one in every branch. The hospital is very loyal to its graduates, and the Lady Superintendent finds them posts when they first leave the school. . . . I consider that nurses are better treated in Canada than in England, and it is the Land of Opportunity for young people who are willing to work, but it will only spell disaster to those who go expecting to get something for nothing.

These last words ought to be taken to heart by every girl who thinks of trying her fortune in the Dominion.

Stenographers, (i.e. shorthand writers and typists). These are in demand throughout Western Canada, the salaries ranging from £8 to £20 a month; but as Canadian girls go in much for this profession, with the result that it is overstocked with indifferent typists, the British woman must be thoroughly competent in order to succeed. More than one man, however, told me that he would take an English in preference to a Canadian stenographer, as the former was, as a rule, better educated all round, and could write a letter from notes and take an intelligent interest in the details of the business.

This letter from an applicant of the Colonial Intelligence League, who has tried her fate in Western Canada, is full of encouragement to the efficient:

June 1912.

I was only a week here when I started work as stenographer at $55 a month (£11), with the promise of $60 to $65 later on (£12 to £13). . . .

Of course there is a great deal that I have to learn, as Canadian business methods are very different to those at home; but in about a month, I think, I shall have grasped these, and then I have been told by various business men here that I shall have no difficulty in getting $75 a month (£15).

There is a large demand for experienced stenographers here. Any girl of average ability would have no difficulty in getting a situation here within a week of her arrival.

Journalism did not strike me as a very promising opening save for a few who have special gifts for that calling. I met one English girl who had supported herself entirely for six years as a journalist, but she told me that every now and again she had been out of work, and had had a hard time. Another gave me the details of a day's work, which partly consisted in constantly telephoning to hospitals and fire-stations in order to report all accidents and fires, and also running a "Personal and Social" column, reviewing books, music, and the drama. The hours were long, the strain continuous, and the average salary of the rank and file was only about £10 a month, which seems little enough when the printer, who sets up the type, is often paid at the rate of £1 a day!

Dress also is a considerable item, as the journalist is expected to mingle with the guests at social functions, in order to describe the toilettes there displayed; but one acquaintance told me that this part of her work was so distasteful to her that she was accustomed to mount into a gallery and make her observations with the aid of opera-glasses.

Dressmaking and millinery are most profitable professions for the expert, and from Toronto to Vancouver I heard complaints as to the dearth of skilled *couturières.*

A lady, lately come from British Columbia, told me that she had paid between £13 and £14 for a perfectly plain though well-cut coat and skirt in which to travel to England; she could not get a passable "knockabout" hat under £3; and she assured me that £20 was a usual price to pay for an evening dress by no means out of the ordinary run. I noticed that, in the Western towns, really smart hats were priced £5 to £10, and I reluctantly paid over £3 for a headgear that I could have got for 12s. 9d. in any of the Kensington High Street shops, and when I looked at straw shapes with an eye to trimming a hat myself, I found that £1 was a usual price. These figures only apply to Canada west of Winnipeg, and relate to the year 1911.

All the shops give high salaries to dressmakers and milliners, as they fear that they may start business for themselves, thus entering the market as rivals. But I should advise no woman to risk her capital in this way for several months. If she does not care to work in a shop, she can get 8s. to 10s. a day and her meals by going out to make blouses and cotton dresses, or she can advertise saying that she will take in work at home, and, if quick and clever, she will in all probability get far more orders than she can cope with.

Waitresses, at good hotels expect to earn about £8 a month, including their tips, and are lodged and boarded; but as this is a favourite calling for the alert Canadian, the British girl must be particularly brisk and capable if she is to succeed.

I met an Englishwoman who was starting a restaurant in a Western city, and begged her to employ educated British women as waitresses. But this she declined to do, on the ground that they were too slow, and that only a few days before she had been inquiring about some compatriots who had been working in a Canadian café, and the answer was, "Oh, we fired them all out; they were no good, as they couldn't hustle." Certainly a Canadian waitress, when I asked her how she remembered all the orders she had to take, gave me much the same idea. "Sure it's 'hustle' that does it. At first I used to say all my orders over and over — 6 roasts, 4 mashed, 5 corns, and so on — and one had to be pretty quick in picking up the dishes in the kitchen, I can tell you; it was more like a baseball match than anything else with all of us calling out at the same moment. But it is often the men who are tiresome, and Heaven help the man who can't order properly!"

"What do you do then?" I asked.

"Oh, we bring him something to eat, and then there's a row; but one must make up one's mind to that," and she shrugged her shoulders philosophically. On the other hand, I came across British girls who were getting on well in the C.P.R. summer hotels and the Hudson Bay Stores tea-rooms.

Factories, shops, &c. At Toronto the "white-wear" factories (*i.e.* blouses and underlinen), offer £1 a week to start with, rising to £2 or even £4, the surroundings are clean and airy, and the hours eight and a half daily. Shop assistants have shorter hours than in England, but I should only recommend educated women to take up these callings until they found more congenial work.

Manicure, hairdressing, and *face-massage* are certainly profitable when practised in the towns, and several English girls whom I questioned told me how much better they were doing in Canada than they could possibly do at home, and those that had been a year or so in the country said that they could easily start a lucrative business for themselves had they sufficient capital.

"Were you obliged to wait some time before you got employment?" I asked women in different towns, and the answer was invariably the same.

"Oh no, I went to the shop with my references, and they took me on then and there. You see they are always afraid that a girl will set up for herself in opposition to them." But in spite of this I should not recommend a woman to have these professions as the only string to her bow, nor should she depend on playing or singing at the C.P.R. hotels during the season, or at restaurants during the meal-times, though possibly she may find employment for these talents, or even succeed with acting, photography, or painting, after she has learnt the ways of the country.

If two or three capable women with some capital could join and start a *boarding or a "rooming" house,* the venture, if well managed, would be a profitable one, the usual plan being to put down £80 to £100 at first, and pay off the rest by monthly instalments.

Hundreds of men are obliged to live in hotels in Western Canada, and many would much prefer a boarding-house, where they would pay according to accommodation. In a "rooming" house no meals are provided, but hot and cold water and electric light, with steam-heat in winter, are supplied to each room.

Restaurants and tea-shops are also lucrative; but women, I was told, should serve in a smart, up-to-date American café before starting on any venture of their own in the Dominion, in order to get *le dernier cri* in the decoration of their rooms, the arrangement of their wares, and the newest mechanical contrivances to assist them in their work. In all these cases it is imperative that the girls should be able to do the entire work of boarding-house or restaurant themselves, as hired help of any kind is uncertain, and, if efficient, is costly.

Only the other day an Englishwoman discussed with me her idea of starting a boarding-house in Canada, with the aid of servants that she would bring out with her from England. "Could you manage the cooking and cleaning yourself, supposing your maids got married or left you from any cause?" I asked; and, as I expected her astonished answer was in the negative.

There are many openings for the woman fond of an outdoor life, and if she has capital she could start *small fruit, vegetable, or flower-raising* (in 1911 strawberries in the West were 8½d. of lb., cauliflowers 1s., cabbages 5d., tiny bunches of carrots and turnips 5d., while a dozen roses fetched 4s. arum lilies 4s. a bloom and violets 1s. a bunch, all this at the height of the season; while tomatoes or mushrooms raised under glass realised high prices in Vancouver). I was told more than once that the *tending of small town gardens,* or landscape gardening, or bulb- and seed-raising, would be lucrative callings, while *bee-keeping* is not to be despised as a side-industry in a clover district.

Poultry-farming is another pursuit fitted for women, and at Vancouver eggs fetch 2d. when the fowls are laying their best, and 3d. to 4d. during the winter.

Girls, however, must be prepared to do all the work themselves, as the jobbing labourer and the handy-boy are practically non-existent in Canada.

Again and again it was pointed out to me that women ought to take up *dairy-work,* as there is plenty of pasture in British Columbia, and at the present time Canada imports much of her butter from New Zealand.

But I should strongly dissuade a woman from laying out capital in any of the above callings until she has been some time in the country. She might, as I have said before, take a course at the Agricultural College of Pullman, Washington State, America, if she intended to settle in British Columbia, or one at Guelph College, Ontario, should she elect to start in the East. Failing this, she could get employment in some market-garden or chicken ranch in order to gain the practical experience that will be invaluable to her later on. I should certainly not advise anyone to act in the way that one Englishwoman whom I met contemplated doing. She wished to buy a chicken ranch and start working it, having had only one month's training at an English agricultural college and no previous experience. She admitted that her equipment was scanty, but said that she was advertising for some one with the requisite knowledge to enter into partnership with her — by no means a safe proceeding in a new country such as the Dominion. I think, however, that my remark that if she put her trust in strangers she would probably gain experience at the painful cost of losing her capital made her reflect somewhat.

To sum up, though I do not affirm for a moment that women will make their "fortunes" by going in for any of the above openings, yet they will gain their living, and will be able to look forward to old age without apprehension, especially if they invest in the Government Annuity Scheme, by which they can get £120 per annum after fifty-five.

It is also no exaggeration to say that the judicious investment of savings in a country that offers such a large return for capital as does the Dominion, may possibly result in real affluence.

This chapter may not unfittingly be concluded with the words of a distinguished Canadian journalist, words that gave me much food for thought: "In the Dominion," she remarked, "we consider that there is something wrong about a woman if she cannot earn her own livelihood."

[Towards the end of September, as her tour of investigation drew to a close, Miss Sykes applied for one last position as home-help:]

I was about to enter upon my last situation, and had given as an excuse for its temporary nature, that I was now leaving Canada and returning to my own country. I had felt that my experiences would be incomplete unless I were on the prairie during the busy season of harvesting, and that over, I intended to fling aside my working dress and aprons for good. The position of home-help had not appealed to me. Though I had experienced much kindness from some of my employers, and though by this time I was by no means incompetent, yet I felt it would be an awful fate to pass my days in cooking and dish-washing, sweeping and scrubbing, having practically no time to cultivate my mind or to care for my appearance — in fact, to sink to the level of a household drudge.

The Canadian women often evoked my warmest admiration. My fourth mistress, for example, was a perfect miracle of activity. I have seen her do the weekly wash in the morning, have a guest to lunch, after which she might go for a ride or play golf, getting afternoon-tea for herself and any friends, and in the evening have a bridge-party, or sally forth, gaily attired, to some friend's house. She was always neat, and could on occasion look as if she had just come out of a fashion plate, and added singing and playing to her list of accomplishments. But it must be noted that she was quite young; and I remarked that the older women by no means rejoiced in household "chores," and I often heard them lament that they were unable to have many outside interests, so tired did they become with the day's toil.

If Englishwomen come out to the Dominion they most emphatically ought to come *young*. An elderly lady with whom I travelled one day told me that she and her husband and family had all gone out to Canada to live on a ranch, and that though the younger generation loved the life, yet the change from her British ways had nearly killed her. After little over a year she had had a serious nervous collapse, and when I met her she was leaving the ranch for probably six months. "I have heard people in England talk about the 'call of the prairie!'" she said, "but I never could see any charm in it, and I only felt that I was the 'prisoner of the prairie,' caught and helpless and never able to escape. I had always loved music and sketching, and though I could turn my hand to household work, yet it was intolerable to have to do it day after day, and to find no time or opportunity for the things I cared about. I could not play, as we had no piano, and as for trying to sketch the prairie —" and she shivered at the bare idea. This talk confirmed me in my conviction that the middle-aged should not come out to Canada, as they can seldom adapt themselves to an environment so totally different to that to which they were accustomed in the British Isles.

Monday was an extra busy day, as the weekly wash had to be done as soon as the breakfast things were cleared, and the dining-room and kitchen swept out. Mrs. Anderson and I would drag the heavy washing-machine out of the coal-house into the keen air, and the boiler, full of soft water, was already on the stove with a cake of soap sliced into it. My special duty was to work the machine, which I did by pushing a handle to and fro, in order to make the clothes revolve in the soap-suds with which the big tub was filled. I had to do this for ten minutes to each relay of garments, then pass them through the wringer, after which I took them into the kitchen to be put into the boiler on the stove. From here they were soused in a tub of cold water, squeezed through the wringer, and then dipped into blue water and wrung out for the third time. Certainly the linen looked snowy white when we hung it up on the long lines, and I enjoyed working out of doors, though the wind was cold and the sun gave little warmth here at the end of September. When the last consignments, terribly stained overalls, shirts, and socks belonging to the men, had been rocked in the water (they had to be put into the machine twice), and had been wrung and rinsed and wrung again, I felt almost as if my arms had been torn out of their sockets. We used to work from seven o'clock till half-past eleven, and then had a rush to get a midday meal of fried ham and eggs and the inevitable potatoes ready. After dinner the washing-machine was rinsed out and dragged back to the coal-house, there to rest for another week, and the wringer and washing-board went to keep it company. When a very high wind was blowing we were obliged to take down the clothes from the lines lest they should get torn, and I always had to wash over the kitchen floor before I could get upstairs at half-past two or three o'clock for a badly needed rest. At four o'clock I was down again, sprinkling and folding up the clothes in preparation for the morrow's ironing, after which there were scones and buns to be made for the half-past six supper.

I have a theory that one reason for the small amount of crime in Canada is that everyone works so hard. Satan, according to the rhyme of our childhood, occupies himself especially with the idle, and as practically everyone is busy in the Dominion, and there is no drink to be had on the farms, all the world behaves as it should.

The speed and ease with which the average Canadian woman gets through her work, was partly explained to me when I saw Daisy, aged five, sweep out the rooms, iron small articles quite nicely, or try her tiny hand at kneading the bread — in short, beginning at her early age the proverbial "practice that makes perfect."

Unfortunately, all the children were rude and mannerless — such a contrast to their polite parents and aunt. At meals they shouted their loudest for "Meat!" "Cake!" or "Sauce!" (by this latter they meant fruit preserved in syrup which we often had for supper), and no one reproved them for their lack of courtesy. They were also very greedy, and if they considered anything to be "terrible nice" or "terrible good," they would take far more on their plates than they could possibly eat, and little Daisy was munching something or other all day long. As I was brought up on principle of "nothing between meals," it surprised me to observe their frequent visits to the cupboards or cellar to get buns, scones, or fruit, and I was sometimes annoyed, as they would gobble up my choicest efforts in this line, a large cake seldom sufficing for more than one meal owing to their depredations. Indigestion, according to the advertisements, and according to what I heard and saw, appears to be one of the staple complaints of the Dominion, and I should think that this indiscriminate eating must have much to do with it. If the children were not eating they were chewing "gum," and this habit prevails throughout the whole country, young and old being apparently equally addicted to it. At first I imagined that the people were not "through" with their meals, as the jaws of hotel managers, whom you approached on the question of rooms, were working busily, and the habit only added to the impression I gained that there is little repose in Canada. The nation is a "live wire," as a man expressed it to me, and the climate induces a ceaseless energy, though I fancy that it must wear people out by over-stimulating them.

Certainly I could never have done in England half of what I accomplished in Canada; but when I reached the Pacific Coast, my energy partially deserted me for the time, and I felt as though I could have slept all day long.

Tastes certainly differ, but for my part I felt thankful that I was not called upon to spend my life upon a Canadian farm. There would be too little "call of the prairie" and too much "call of the kitchen" for me, too much work and too little relaxation. On Tuesdays, for example, I had to iron three to four hours on end, and my back seemed broken when I had at last smoothed out the extensive family wash. Moreover, every three or four days there was churning to be done, and a heavy barrel of cream had to be made to revolve by means of a foot-treadle and a handle. Once or twice Mrs. Anderson did not trouble to get the cream up to the right temperature before she set me to work, and the result was an hour's hard labour before the little round of glass at one end of the barrel was clear, showing that the butter had formed, and on one occasion a swollen knee, which made me feel extra nervous in negotiating the breakneck cellar steps. To be a home-help on the prairie would, as a rule, have little attraction for an educated Englishwoman, and she would greatly feel the lack of social intercourse, the want of books and congenial companionship, unless she had the good fortune to be with people of her own class, in which case it would be very different.

At last the day of my departure arrived, and I was glad to be leaving, though I was not ungrateful for all the kindness that I had received. As I turned out of bed at half-past four, I felt thankful that it was the last time that I should have to make pancakes in floods of tears! Mrs. Anderson offered me a dollar over and above my wages (I refused it with thanks, though highly gratified at this recognition of the worth of my services), and she said that she had much enjoyed my company and would miss me, while Mrs. Mackenzie, to whom I had bequeathed my "dandy" aprons and various other extremely shabby belongings, presented me with a keepsake of her own handiwork, begging me to write to her, and both united in hoping that I should get home safely to England. At seven o'clock the farmer brought his buggy round, my belongings were hoisted in, and I was driven off amid warm farewells from the women and children. I felt half ashamed of myself for feeling so delighted to be leaving them all, but the life was by now becoming intolerable to me.

[Finally, from the last three pages of *A Home-Help in Canada,* this summary:]

I had been since the end of April in Canada, and had tried never to lose sight of the fact that I was in the country to investigate what it offered to the educated British woman, and now I had come to certain conclusions which I will sum up shortly.

The quality that spells success in Canada is *efficiency,* and if that is allied to an energetic, adaptable nature possessing some business capacity, its possessor will without fail "make good."

Canadians are so capable themselves that there is no room in the country for the amateur, "unskilled labour," save in the kitchen, being even more at a discount here than it is in Great Britain.

The British woman who comes out well equipped with something that the Dominion needs may very likely have to "start in" at the bottom and work her way up, for she is beginning her life across the Atlantic under entirely different conditions to those that prevail in the Old Country. But, to counterbalance this, the girl who is dependent on her earnings is not looked down upon socially, except, perhaps if she be home-help in a town. "We despise people out here if they won't work," were the words of a cultivated English woman in the Far West, and the bracing climate is of marvellous assistance in inducing energy and optimism. In Great Britain there are over a million more women than men; in Canada, west of Winnipeg, I am told that there are about a dozen men to every woman, therefore the field for feminine work is immense. Life in the "Golden West" may be devoid of many of the comforts that we in the United Kingdom have come to look upon as necessaries, but it offers opportunities that are not to be found in the crowded British Isles. In the words of a travelling acquaintance, "In England, whenever there is a good post, there are hundreds after it, but out here there may be only one woman capable of filling it."

One of the heads of the Emigration Department, in speaking about the objects of the League, said of the British woman of to-day, "The stock is all right, but the *training* is all wrong," and his words are well worth considering.

But though efficiency is so important, yet character perhaps counts for more in Canada than in the British Isles; and the most highly trained girl, if devoid of energy and resource, might very possibly go to the wall in a land where all must fend for themselves.

I shall be richly rewarded if this book, in which I have tried to portray things exactly as I saw them, makes some of my sisters realise the importance of becoming experts instead of being amateurs; and though I trust that the unfit, such as I was, may be discouraged from trying their fortune in the Dominion, yet I hope that what I have written may be useful to the right type of woman, who cannot see her way to earning a livelihood and providing for her old age in England. In weighing the "pros" and "cons" of settling in Canada, she ought to take into consideration what kind of a future will probably be hers if she remains at home.

We hear so much talk nowadays about the "superfluous woman," that surely, rather than be included in that depressing category, it would be well worth a girl's while to put up with some discomfort and toil in the Dominion, where she is badly needed, and where, if of the right type, she will in all likeihood succeed beyond her anticipations.

I consider that it is an Imperial work to help girls of a high stamp to seek their fortunes beyond the seas — women who will care for our glorious Flag and what it signifies, who will stand for higher ideals than the worship of the "almighty dollar," and who will do their part in the land that their brothers are developing so splendidly.

It is not too much to say that a British woman, worthy of her great heritage, can, in Mr. Chamberlain's unforgettable words, be in very deed a "missionary of Empire."

The impact of any one book on the actual course of historical events is difficult to gauge at the best of times, and where women are concerned the relative scarcity of documents makes speculation doubly hazardous. How many clients of the Colonial Intelligence League acted on Ella Sykes's guarded recommendation of Western Canada as a home for superfluous women? And of those that did, how many found her advice well-founded? No doubt the records of the CIL contain some clues to these questions, while others lurk in the private letters, diaries, and other repositories of family memorabilia held by the descendants of former genteel home-helps. There should even be a number of first-hand testators still alive and capable of being interviewed, although they would be at least in their eighties now.[1]

In the meantime, some rough estimate of the response to Sykes's book can be formed by noting references to it in contemporary publications. One small example of this kind of evidence appears in a book originally published in 1915 by the London firm of John Murray. Its title is *In Western Canada Before the War; A Study of Communities,* and although copies of the first edition are seldom available, the book has recently been reprinted.[2]

The writer of this book was a Scotswoman named Elizabeth Mitchell. She was born in Edinburgh in 1880, attended Oxford, where she earned first class honours, and then became actively involved in the town and country planning movement in Britain. She spent a year in Canada in 1913-14, most of it in the western provinces. Her book is considerably more analytical than most travel-books of the period, and she has many incisive and prescient things to say about Western Canada's future development. Among several topics of continuing interest to the Canadian social historian, she offers an entire chapter on "The Women of the West." The few pages reprinted here come from that chapter.

1. See note 12 to the introduction (p. xxvii above) concerning current research into British home-helps in Canada by Marilyn Barber of Carleton University.
2. *In Western Canada Before the War: A Study of Communities* was reprinted in 1981 by Western Producer Prairie Books of Saskatoon, which holds Canadian rights to this book. The whole chapter from which selections are made here will be of great interest to students of Canadian women's history, while fuller information on Mitchell's life and work may be obtained from the brief introduction by Susan Jackel.

Elizabeth Mitchell

The Women of the West

Any study of Western women's life would be seriously incomplete if it did not touch on the Servant Problem. In the country it is exceedingly difficult to get a girl; in the towns and smaller cities it is possible, but there are inconveniences. A certain couple of nice English maids arrived at M——— and said they were housemaids. They were greatly taken aback when they found that not even the smartest woman in town had two servants. The "girl" or "help" has to be prepared to try anything, and the mistress generally has to do the skilled work herself. A Galician or other "foreigner" or a little girl of thirteen or fourteen has drawbacks of one kind; a competent "help," Canadian or British, besides being costly, will usually expect to have meals with the family and to share their life. This might be pleasant enough, if it were conventionally correct, with some old retainers at home, but with a constantly shifting succession of strangers it is genuinely uncomfortable, it prevents all ease of talk. The "help" is often free after three o'clock to go her own way (any later service being done of grace by special arrangement); but this is not unreasonable, as she works most energetically from an early hour. Some rule of the kind may have to be made before long in England.

The lack of service has various results in social life in the towns. Teas are commoner as entertainments than dinners; and this accentuates the social separation of the women and the men, so marked in comparison with either England or the prairie. People do not often go to stay in each other's houses except from necessity or with near friends. Visitors, when they *are* received, lend a hand with the work, and consequently a Western visit is a much more intimate thing than at home; one makes acquaintance much quicker in the kitchen over a dish-tub or a cake-tin than sitting on a proper chair in a drawing-room with folded hands wondering what to say next.

Having no servants at all may be exceedingly pleasant. The town-houses are compact and well-arranged and full of labour-saving devices; the furniture has few knobs and crannies; and a woman in good health with an average family seems to find little to grumble at. Two women living together can have good meals and well-dusted rooms and yet get through their work early and have large leisure for hospitality and outside occupations. One's house is one's very own, and there is no one to look glum if a party of hungry travellers do turn up towards evening wanting food and lodging. The whole basis of life cannot be suddenly upset by Jemima's leaving without notice. The great thing is to decide what is most necessary, and concentrate on that. The real proud Canadian housewife does everything at home, but probably any woman unaccustomed to manual labour will be wise to spare herself where she can, to let some of the washing go out, and to have some one in from time to time for heavy scrubbing. It costs money, but it makes a tremendous difference to the housewife's health and spirits; if she is spared this heaviest work and if she is willing to learn Canadian ways, an Old-Country lady may come through the ordeal of life in a prairie town not discreditably, and may even prefer it in time to the lap of luxury. But the housework cannot be shirked on any plea; a saint or a princess with a messy house would have little position or following among Canadian women.

Miss Sykes has dealt in her excellent book, *A Home-Help in Canada,* with the question of openings for English women of education, and I only wish to add a few notes to what she says. Girls were still wanted, even in the bad times since 1913, though so many men were unemployed; but working-girls are the easiest to fit in. It remains to be seen how the War will affect women's employment out there; but certainly no educated girl should go alone to the West without money to keep her for a few months or to buy her ticket home. As Miss Sykes says, there is no room at all for anyone wishing "to do light work," and Canada is a country where the feeble and inefficient find very little mercy. On one point in her account of "home-helping" I have a criticism to make: I think usually a home-help on the prairie has more amusement than Miss Sykes could have, staying as she did only a fortnight in each place, and at the busy season. But I quite agree with her that this is not a position for educated women, except in the houses of friends.

In teaching there was an opening for adaptable girls able to look after themselves and willing to take a short Normal Course for the Canadian qualification. I have heard a Deputy Minister of Education mourning over his lists. "Year by year we rush students through the Normal Colleges, we issue special permits by the dozen and the hundred, and still we are just where we were. Where do our teachers go? They seem to disappear into the sandy soil!" The Minister had his suspicions as to the cause of the leakage, but it was not a cause he could remove. The salary-scale is fairly good, even considering the high cost of living, and women teachers seem to have more leisure and a far better social position than at home; but there are at present practically no "plums," as all the highest posts are held by men. Most teachers have to serve at least a year in a prairie school before reaching a High School post. "Stenographers" (typists with shorthand) were in demand, but I am not certain that this is still true. There were numbers of nurses out of employment towards the end of 1913, not that there was not need for more nursing, but there was no money to pay for it.

Thus the professional openings are very few, and yet women are greatly needed. The young woman is, of course, both the most needed and the most difficult to arrange for, but there are other curious gaps. In the youthful towns old ladies are exceedingly rare and correspondingly valued; on any social occasion the white hair of some visiting mother will prove the strongest attraction, for amidst a certain inevitable harshness and crudity the memories and kindliness of age are very precious. There are perhaps more old people in the country, but even there the grandmothers have the worship which sometimes goes in England to the grandsons. As nearly all the women are young and fully occupied with young families, it follows that there is a lack of women of leisure for the very necessary odd jobs. Who is to look after the girls coming to town, to spend trouble and time in getting them suitable places, to help the foreigners to learn English, to visit the hospital, to help a delicate mother with bustling children, to sit on school-boards, to organize the leisured girls, where there are any, to do some kind and useful work? One constantly sees at home a pair of sisters or friends with a modest independent income, settling down with a touch of regret to grow old quietly in a town where there are dozens or hundreds like them. Many are capable women who never had their opportunity, and some chafe inwardly as they look down the narrowing vista ahead. If any two sisters of spirit would simply go with a stout heart and settle in any prairie town (outside of the large cities) they would be busy enough and important enough before a year was out, far too busy to think about growing old for another twenty years. There is a handsome roomy niche waiting in the West for the Professional Maiden Aunt as well as for the grandmother. As to the assured income necessary, there are fewer "appearances" to be kept up out there, but prices are far higher. An income which in England has to be spent mostly on necessaries would not in the West provide a living at all.

One thing I think more girls from comfortable homes might do, and that is go out to make homes for their brothers. Life out West may be rather a terrible thing for a young wife, but for a girl in good health with her own familiar brother, it is no more than an adventure which will bring out what is in her. The brother has a bad time by himself and is diffident about asking his sister to forsake her comforts for his sake; but women are not really so wedded to luxuries as they are supposed to be, they are all Lady Catherines who "love to be useful," and few regret coming out in this way. Housework, even hard and monotonous housework, is so visibly different according as you are doing it as a hireling for people you do not care about, or zealously and honourably in your own house for your own people. Only let no girl, sister or sweetheart, idealize the prairie, or lay fine schemes that she will do this and she will not do that. She will have to do as things will do with her, and far the best training would be six months as a general servant either in England or Canada. Then she will be prepared for what is hard in the life, and will enjoy the more the many parts of it that are delightful.

9 | *The Woman Canada Needs*
Commentary

The author of the final selection in this volume, "The Woman Canada Needs," was Emily Poynton Weaver. She was born near Manchester, England, in 1865 and emigrated with her family to Ontario at the age of fifteen. She published many historical books on Canadian subjects, both fiction and non-fiction, between the early 1890's and her death in 1943.

In *The Oxford Companion to Canadian History and Literature,* Norah Story describes Weaver's book of 1914 *Canada and the British Immigrant* as "a very simplified descriptive and historical work for the information of prospective British immigrants" (p. 824). Simplified it may be, but it has the merit of containing clear, thoughtful advice from someone who remembered the transplantation of her mid-teen years and who had since observed the fortunes of her countrymen and countrywomen in Canada for over three decades. Looking back on her family's first few years in Canada, Weaver wrote in her prefatory note: "We settled ourselves on a good-sized farm in a fertile district of Ontario, and there we had an experience probably broadly resembling that of many new arrivals — sometimes amusing, sometimes vexatious, or worse. Of course we made some mistakes and had to pay for them; and we took, I am inclined to think, several years really to settle down. But in the end we all 'believe in Canada,' though I dare not say we believe in everything we read about Canada." Both her faith and her caution are reflected in her admittedly general comments on "The Woman Canada Needs," in this chapter from *Canada and the British Immigrant.*

Emily Weaver

The Woman Canada Needs

Judging by statistics, it may be averred that Canada needs women in general, especially in some districts, even more than men. At any rate, according to the census taken in 1911 there was, in a total population of a little over seven millions, an excess of males over females of four hundred and thirty-seven thousand, and as each year the immigration returns show the arrival of more men than women (the figures for 1911 were 211,266 males and 82,922 females), the disproportion between the sexes is growing continually greater; but it cannot be said that at present the Dominion makes the same effort to attract women as men. For instance, the bonus given to booking agents is less on a woman than a man, and the only way in which a woman can acquire a free grant of Dominion crown lands is in the character of a widowed mother of a child, or children, under eighteen years of age.

Possibly this inequality of opportunity has arisen from the notion that a woman is not suited for doing homestead duties — and many women are not — but as a matter of fact the wife of a struggling newcomer is often left alone for weeks at a time on the homestead, while her husband "hires himself out" to a farmer, or works on a new railway. In British Columbia, as already mentioned, a woman may take up a pre-emption, which is practically the same — so far as the obligations of residence and cultivation are concerned — as the Dominion free grants.

It must, I think, be frankly admitted that the isolation of the life in many instances either on a homestead or on a great Western farm is hard for the woman. Some little time since I met a bright young woman, with one small girl of four or five, who was thankfully travelling south to Vancouver from an island in the neighbourhood of Prince Rupert, where for a considerable part of two years she had been living on a pre-emption whilst her husband had been away working on the new railway. She told me that, with the exception of one solitary young man — a neighbouring homesteader — she had had no neighbour nearer than three miles away, and that there had been days during the two years when she had been so ill that she could not leave her bed to give bread to the little one, who, scarcely out of babyhood, had had to be sent herself to the "bread box" to get something to eat. Such a story seems suggestive of possible tragedy, but the woman did not dwell on what might have been, but rejoiced simply in the fact that the hard task was over, and that, largely through her effort, they had the patent for the land, which now they would be able to sell if they could find a purchaser.

I could not help thinking that one quality of the woman that Western Canada needs is courage, and another is resourcefulness; and perhaps if I repeat here the story told me by the wife of a successful pioneer farmer in Saskatchewan, it may help, more than any generalities, to give an idea of a woman's lot on a prairie farm. Mrs. Smith — as I will call her — had gone as a bride to a little house of one lower room (fourteen feet by sixteen) and a half storey upstairs. She, by the way, had spent her girlhood in the West, and perhaps knew from experience how to manage under circumstances which would have sorely tried an Englishwoman of her class.

The tiny dwelling, lined with building paper and thin boards, was not plastered for a year or two and at first the one room was kitchen, dining-room and wash-house. The house was a full mile from the next one, and stood in the centre of a great field of wheat, which sometimes, when the babies (who soon arrived) began to toddle, seemed to the young mother to grow perilously high, for she had heard stories of little ones wandering off into the tall wheat and being lost.

The coming of the little ones to a pioneer woman is often a terrible test of courage and endurance, for it is hard to get either doctor or experienced nurse at the right time. Sometimes the prospective mother goes into town to a hospital or to some friend; but generally she stays at home. The neighbours do the best they can, and often all goes well — and sometimes it does not. In such a case and in many another emergency the rural telephone is a wonderful boon and comfort — and may be even counted a life-saving agency. Incidentally, I may mention that women, competent to take care of mother and infant or to help in case of sickness, who would be willing to take charge also of the domestic arrangements of a little house, while its mistress was incapacitated, would not be likely to lack work in the West. Many people, who could hardly meet the high charges for a regularly trained nurse, would be glad to pay well for such services. Mrs. Smith told me, however, that it was practically impossible to get help, and that a neighbour had driven hither and thither for a week in a vain search for someone to take care of his wife, at last getting an old woman from the immigrant shed in a somewhat distant town. My informant's impression was that there was "a great chance" for "hired girls" in these prairie communities, for on the farms they are treated like "one of the family." Nevertheless they generally prefer to stay in the towns.

Gradually things improve as the neighbourhoods get settled, though the great farms of the exclusively wheat-growing districts "make few neighbours." The more so, because many a Western farmer develops a passion for adding field to field — or "quarter-section to quarter-section." The Smith farm, for instance, grew to be "seven miles" round; and the husband was often working a mile away from home, but after the first few years he managed to get a man and his wife to live on the farm. Despite the isolation, Mrs. Smith did not regard the life as a hard one. She "liked the farm very much," she said, and thought the women in the West had "easier times" than those in the East, for the regular "hired men" lived in the bunk-house, though they came to the house for their meals, and after the first two years she did not have to cook for the harvesters and threshers, whose meals were provided from "a cook car." She was, however, fortunate in having a husband who was both considerate and capable.

As to the social aspects of life, she had been used in her girlhood, though that, too, was spent on a prairie farm — near Regina — to go out a great deal in the evenings "with her musical brothers" to meet other young people, and no doubt she felt the change to the new district, where, of the few women who could be counted neighbours, some were very rough. But soon there were alleviations. From the first there was a church only five miles away, and later there were services in the school-house, which, by the way, in that section at least was very much of a social centre.

Mrs. Smith usually boarded the lady who taught there, and the section had "fine teachers," who brought on the little flocks of from sixteen to twenty-six children most successfully, lent books to the readers of the community and got up the summer picnics in connection with the school — the more enjoyed, perhaps, because other entertainments were so few and far between. These consisted of a Sunday school Christmas tree, an occasional concert, or a public dance to which "nice women" did not go — at least, in that particular district — as it was open to everyone who could pay, and was attended by men of the rougher sort, who thought it impossible to enjoy themselves without much whiskey.

By the help of the neighbours, the mail was usually brought from the post office, ten miles distant, three times a week, and the Smiths subscribed for several magazines and newspapers. The telephone, when it came, was "a great help"; but, when "the children began to want to see people" and to need somewhat better education than could be gained in the little country school, this family moved into one of the gay, bustling little prairie towns. Mrs. Smith's experience, it must be remembered, was that of a pioneer, and there are districts in the provinces where that kind of life is becoming a thing of the past, though pioneers are still plentiful.

In the particular town to which the Smiths moved (and I have reason to believe it not exceptional) there is a high proportion of young people in the population and brides are often numerous, whose trousseaux are, perhaps, accountable for setting the pace in a style of dressing which is costly, and which seems almost incongruously handsome in comparison with the tiny houses in which many of the young couples dwell. But money is easily earned and quickly spent by the eager optimistic Westerner; and, doubtless, if domestic servants were easier to get and to keep, more well-to-do folk would turn their attention to building larger houses.

In the rural districts of the older provinces there are plenty of somewhat isolated farmhouses; but there are also many farming communities where the families are close enough together to enjoy a good deal of social life; and where this is the case the country life is a delightful one, for young folk especially. The boys and girls on the farms learn early to do the work of men and women; but it is work which, if not overdone in amount, is healthful for mind and body; and the informal country merry-makings have a charm of their own.

A sleigh ride of several miles, on a moonlight night, through a lovely snow-covered landscape of hill and woods and valley, does not detract from the enjoyment of an informal carpet dance, especially when the vehicle is a big box sleigh, filled with a dozen lively lads and lasses, whose songs and laughter ring out above the jingling bells. A wedding feast or a barn-raising bee, a church social, or a school concert, a "strawberry festival" or a "Christmas tree" — country folk know how to enjoy all these things; as they enjoy chance meetings in the store or at the church door — and now there are in most provinces Farmers' Clubs and Women's Institutes to aid in the good work of drawing together country neighbours of all the different denominations. Above all, the country is the place for the little ones, where they may spend their first years amongst the animals and birds and flowers, which the normal child loves, leading a simple, outdoor life.

But one of the needs of Canada is more women (she has some already) who shall appreciate the country and know how to make the best of it for themselves, their families and their neighbours. She wants women of any race, British or foreign, who are strong enough and wise enough to discover ways of developing the fine possibilities of country life, and counteracting any tendency towards its degeneration into dulness and stagnation. To-day the trend of the population of this new and supposedly agricultural country citywards is a fact which is at once remarkable and rather disquieting. Perhaps it is due in part to "the earth hunger" that besets many a farmer, and inclines him to sacrifice to it the comfort of his family and the possibilities of congenial society. Whatever its cause, women may, perhaps, do quite as much as men to stem the current and make country life what it ought to be.

The woman Canada asks for, by the official voice of the Dominion Immigration Department, is the domestic servant, and when necessary the government assists the girl with a loan of £4 for her passage money. Now there is no question that from coast to coast there is a demand for the woman who will help with domestic work. A healthy, intelligent, industrious girl, if she has had any experience in general housework, can command wages of from $10 (£2) to $16 (£3 4s.) a month in the East up to $30 in the West, in both cases with room and board included, whilst a housekeeper or a competent cook gets $30 (£6) or $35

(£7) or even more. For domestic servants the demand is practically unlimited both in town and country. The wages are not quite so high in the rural districts, but in many cases the girl in farm and country houses is treated like a member of the family, so far at least as having her meals with her employers; and not infrequently a good girl is actually treated like a daughter of the house, taking her share in whatever little festivities there may be.

Perhaps, however, an "Old-Country" girl, brought up amongst the servant-keeping instead of the service-giving class, and coming to Canada to act as "home-help" or "lady-help," is sometimes deceived into expecting too much by the phrase of "being treated like one of the family." In the first place, if, as sometimes happens, the mistress, who unreservedly treats her domestic help as "one of the family," is herself not a highly-educated woman, the "lady-help" too frequently assumes a condescending attitude towards her employer, and the connection naturally proves unsatisfactory. In the second place, a "young lady" from England often hardly understands what hard work really means, and she is too apt to feel that she ought — in virtue of her education — to be excused from various necessary household duties. But if a girl intends to take a "home-help's" position in Canada she should make up her mind not to think any task beneath her dignity which some woman of the house must do. No one really wants a "lady-help" for an ornament, though a lonely woman here and there may desire to have one partly for the sake of companionship. When, indeed, the "help" really makes it her business to "help," the relationship may be very satisfactory; and when she has proved both her usefulness and her refinement she will usually be able to get a situation which ought to satisfy her. Often, however, this will be where the mistress is elderly, or invalided or widowed, for there is not much demand for this kind of assistance in families consisting largely of lively young people. If a lady desires a position as "home-help," I believe it would be well for her to obtain introductions, if possible, to ladies in the province where she is going, as friends often know of each other's needs in such a case, and will gladly assist in bringing the would-be "help" and prospective employer together.

There is a generally good though rather intermittent demand for charwomen and occasional helpers in towns, cities, and the settled rural districts; and the wife of a man who has obtained employment on a farm may often add considerably to the family resources by washing and doing other work for the farmer's wife or neighbours. The wages in the East range from about $1 (4s.) a day in the country, to $1.25 (5s.), always with meals, in the cities. Some little time ago an enterprising party of young Scotch women, who had come to Toronto to be ordinary servants, clubbed together, took a room or two, and went out working by the day, with the result that they earned more money and had their evenings and Sundays to themselves. They had no difficulty in obtaining as much work as they desired; and their experiment points towards one probable solution of the domestic help problem; but, of course, there are great risks for unprotected girls in every city; and in most Canadian cities the rent of rooms and the cost of living is very high.

Apart from housework, in any form, immense numbers of immigrant girls find employment in shops and factories, and not a few as typists. In Toronto, a typist coming out through the colonization department gets an initial wage of $10 (£2) a week, and one who is also a stenographer gets from $11 (£2 4s.) to $15 (£3) the week. In Winnipeg (where there are said to be "ten thousand lady stenographers and book-keepers") "the wages run from $35 (£7) to $75 (£15), or even $100 (£20) per month." The saleswomen in shops do not receive nearly so much, and good wages are very necessary in the towns if a girl is to live under proper and healthful conditions. Women's work is not as yet much organized in Canada, though in Montreal and other cities there are a few women's labour unions.

There is perhaps nearly as much demand for competent dressmakers as for domestic servants, either to make dresses at home or to go out by the day. This demand comes not only from the cities, such as Toronto, where, for example, good dressmakers can earn, in addition to their meals, from $1.50 to $2 (6s. to 8s.) the day, or Winnipeg, where their charge is $2 or $2.50 (8s. to 10s.) the day; but from country towns and rural districts. In the latter they can earn $1 or $1.25 (4s. to 5s.), with board and lodging, for the time of their engagement; and I think it would be well worth while for girls who understand dressmaking to try their fortune in some village in a good farming country. I know that there is a large demand for their services in such places, and though they would not receive city prices for their work, neither would they have to pay city prices for the rooms which they would need as headquarters. In a good village two sisters or friends might very well make the experiment together; or a girl understanding dress-making, whose parents were coming to the country, might easily work up a good business connection. I should not forget to say that the farmers' wives are quite willing to send a "buggy" or carriage a considerable distance for the dressmaker.

There is a great demand in Canada for teachers, and a father who comes out with a family of young people might well endeavour to get some of them (if they show any aptitude for the work) trained for teachers. It is desirable that the students should finish their preparation and pass the necessary examinations in the province where they intend to teach, as professional teachers' certificates only hold good in the province where they are granted, though temporary "permits" to teach may be given in other provinces.

The rate of salaries varies somewhat in different parts of the Dominion, the salaries given in the West being generally higher than those in the East. There are not many openings for private governesses, though a few find employment in ladies' schools, and there is a small demand in the households of the rich for nursery governesses for very little children.

Girls coming out with the intention of entering any occupation (except that of domestic servants) should have a little money in hand to support them whilst looking for employment; but for women, as for men, there are numerous oppor-tunities in Canada for the alert, intelligent girl — "on the spot" — who knows how to work.

With regard to the acquirement of land, opportunities in Canada are by no means as favourable for women as for men. In a general way women can only obtain land by purchase, and are shut out from the advantage of homesteading; but, as already mentioned, they are permitted in British Columbia to take up pre-emptions on practically the same terms as men. The laws, by the way, concerning the civil rights of women vary in different provinces; but from the women's point of view Canada lags behind some of the States of the Union, in the fact that not one of the nine provinces of the Dominion has, as yet, accorded parliamentary representation to women. Even the people most strongly averse from the change are, however, beginning to prophesy dolefully that "it has got to come."

In educational facilities, the women of Canada are treated liberally. In the public and high schools co-education is general, and usually the universities admit women on the same terms as men. The medical profession is open to women; and in some provinces that of the law also. There are many women journalists and writers who are banded together into an organization for the Dominion — "The Canadian Women's Press Club."

A very active and comprehensive organization in Canada is the "National Council of Women," with which many other women's associations are affiliated. Among these may be named the Women's Institutes (which, in Ontario alone, have over twenty thousand members), the Women's Art Association, the Girls' Friendly Society, the Victorian Order of Nurses, the Canadian Suffrage Association, the National Historical Society, the Peace and Arbitrations Society, etc., etc. There are many other extremely important women's organizations, such as the Missionary Societies (called by different names) of the several churches, which, besides supporting foreign missions, make an especial effort to aid religious work in the newer sections of the Dominion. There is also the Women's Christian Temperance Union, which has for long been engaged in effective work against the liquor traffic.

It may be asked what has all this to do with "the woman Canada needs," and with opportunities for women? My answer is that such a list (which might be much lengthened) shows what the women of Canada are thinking about and working for; that what has been done, may be done again; what is being done now, may be multiplied enormously with the advent of more workers. That these organizations are flourishing suggests the need and the opportunity there is for the work of public-spirited, true-hearted women in Canada — in helping to refine the rough, to smooth down the rugged, to hold up the higher ideals of life in this new land; to fill its towns with pleasant, beautiful homes, and to make its solitary places blossom like the rose.

Canada has scope for the employment of the energies of all of the best types of women, and we have got beyond the notion that there is only one noble type of woman; but if one goes back to that severely practical document, the Census Report, it really looks as if the woman which Canada needs above all is the wife and mother, who is awaiting in the Old Land the chance to rejoin her immigrant husband; and the "marriageable girl." "The Imperial Home Reunion Associations" already mentioned are doing good work in bringing out the former, with her children; but it is a more delicate matter to settle the latter in regions where her best opportunity lies. In the early French times, the authorities managed this matter with business-like frankness, shipping out consignments of girls and marrying them in haste on their arrival in the colony. Such a method is distinctly out-of-date, but more might be done to encourage the immigration of families and of young women (under proper conditions and safeguards), for in the West especially, behind the opportunities for girls as workers in household service and shops and factories and offices, many of them find the opportunity of taking up the *role* of the wife, the mother and the "home-maker."

Unfortunately it is a common assertion, that a considerable proportion of girls "in business" are so occupied with the probabilities of "having homes" of their own, that they regard their work at the typewriter or in the office as a mere stop-gap, to be performed perfunctorily. Let us hope this is a slander; and at any rate some business men testify that the girl clerk is, as a rule, quite as conscientious, steady-going and dependable as the boy clerk, if not more so. However that may be, the fact remains that there is a need for the coming out to Canada of a good type of girls, more in proportion than at present to the numbers of the male immigrants, if the Dominion is to be, in accord with the best Anglo-Saxon ideals, a nation of homes.